# Frank del Olmo

## Commentaries on His Times

A Los Angeles Times Book
Editors: Frank O. Sotomayor and Magdalena Beltrán-del Olmo
Designer: Tom Trapnell
Copy Editor: Bobbi Olson
Cover Photo: Los Angeles Times
ISBN: 1-883792-26-6
Copyright 2004, Los Angeles Times
202 W. 1st St., Los Angeles, CA 90012

First printing August 2004
Printed in U.S.A.

Los Angeles Times
Publisher: John P. Puerner
Editor: John S. Carroll
Vice President, Planning & Community Initiatives: Kim McCleary-La France
Vice President, Public Affairs: Gisselle Acevedo-Franco
Book Development Project Manager: L.C. Strudwick-Turner

*To Valentina and Frankie,*
*Frank's proudest achievements — his children*

# TRIBUTES

## GABRIEL GARCÍA MÁRQUEZ

*(Winner of the 1982 Nobel Prize for Literature)*

I wish I hadn't read the news of Thursday, Feb. 19, of this dreadful leap year: Frank del Olmo was dead and no disclaimer or correction was possible. We met in Mexico City in the late 1980s, with an *abrazo* that felt like a premonition we would become old compadres. We continued to see each other, sometimes just the two of us, other times in the company of friends.

Our conversations invariably centered on the news of the day. Those of us who are born journalists discover early in our lives, and often against our will, that our craft is not just a calling, a fate, a need or a job. It's something we can't avoid: It is a vice among friends.

Frank del Olmo knew this better than anyone else. And he embraced it as a prize awarded to him by life. He did journalism without pause, enslaved by the certainty that the world would be better as long as we faced it as he did. He was a giant at his craft because he felt an inexhaustible thrill enjoying and enduring reality and because he had the fortune of being loved by his friends around the world.

That morning, on the 19th of a month that lasts an extra day, Frank del Olmo hardly had time to stand up from his desk when he was stricken, betrayed by his own noble heart. That morning he became the news, the sad and irreparable piece of news of that ill-fated Thursday.

*—Translation by Sergio Muñoz*

## CARLOS FUENTES

*(Novelist, critic and professor)*

Outwardly serene, internally intense, forever in search of the truth, Frank del Olmo was my student at Harvard while enjoying a Nieman Fellowship for excellence in journalism. Frank believed in information not only as a duty but as a right. He was a bridge between Mexico, Mexican Americans and the larger U.S. public. The bridge was made of paper. We now realize it was really made, like Frank's heart, of gold.

## LISA SALAZAR JOHNSON

*(Daughter of the late Los Angeles Times journalist Ruben Salazar)*

I thought [the memorial service for Frank] was the most beautiful, sincere tribute to a man respected and loved by so many of us. I will miss him very much.

Now, two powerful voices, two dedicated journalists, two great men are gone, but we can be sure they have met up again to continue their friendship.


## JOHN S. CARROLL

*(Editor, Los Angeles Times)*

American journalism was dealt a cruel blow on February 19, 2004, when Frank del Olmo died in the newsroom of the Los Angeles Times. For many journalists, particularly those of Latino background, Frank was a symbol of what is possible. Rising from humble origins, he distinguished himself with Pulitzer Prize-level work, and he lifted countless of his colleagues with his principled advocacy and wise counsel.

Nationally, he was known as both a crusader and a gentleman. Upon his death, countless admirers from all social stations came forward to express their gratitude. Because of Frank's work, innumerable journalists hold meaningful jobs today on U.S. news staffs. Equally important, he was instrumental in opening the eyes of major newspapers, including the Los Angeles Times, to the importance of covering the nation's Latino communities. In Los Angeles, Frank was well known for his column, which appeared on the op-ed page of The Times, a paper he served for more than 33 years.

Frank's death at the age of 55 left his colleagues with a formidable burden: To continue his important work in securing a place at the table for people from all ethnic backgrounds. Columns in this collection serve as reminders of Frank's beliefs and of his deep commitment to family, community and social justice.


## OTIS CHANDLER

*(Former publisher, Los Angeles Times)*

It was a terrible shock to me when I heard of Frank's passing. He was a great reporter and, later on, one of the best editors that we had on the paper. He had a great career at The Times, and I will always remember my many years with him.

## Dr. Félix Gutiérrez

*(Professor of journalism, University of Southern California)*

As a journalist and advocate, Frank del Olmo made an impact *in* the newsroom and *on* the newsroom. As his own career reached unprecedented heights, he elevated journalism by advocating better newsroom opportunities for all and analyzing tough issues with a depth that fostered understanding of people that media long ignored or misrepresented.

## Joel Simon

*(Deputy director, Committee to Protect Journalists)*

Frank made an enormous difference as an advocate for press freedom, particularly in Latin America. In his quiet, understated way, Frank made a compelling case that the fractious Mexican press had an interest in putting aside differences to confront government pressure. I believe it was this authority and resolve that eventually broke down the resistance.

## Arturo S. Rodriguez

*(President, United Farm Workers of America)*

We knew Frank over the more than three decades he covered and wrote about Cesar Chavez and the farmworkers as a journalist and columnist. During that time he never wavered from the first duty he owed to his profession. But Frank also worked tirelessly to ensure the farmworkers received a fair shake inside the newspaper.

## Zvi Vapni

*(Deputy consul general of Israel in Los Angeles)*

Frank knew how important it was to bring people from different backgrounds together. He would give me an open, honest assessment of every issue with the combination of his sensitivity and his vigorously intellectual mind. In the Jewish tradition, we have a saying that the memory of a good person is a source of blessing. Frank's memory is certainly a blessing, and he will not be forgotten.

# TABLE OF CONTENTS

# ACKNOWLEDGMENTS

After sundown on a cool winter evening, my husband's boss, Los Angeles Times Editor John Carroll, knocked on my front door.

On the previous day, Feb. 19, 2004, his colleague, Times Associate Editor Frank del Olmo, suffered a heart attack while working in the newsroom. Immediately after he was stricken, Frank's assistant called to gently tell me my husband was being taken to a hospital.

As I maneuvered through the thick L.A. traffic, I nervously envisioned myself arriving at the emergency room to find my beloved resting. I was prepared to remain strong, ready to absorb the medical information. I wanted so much to tell Frank we would do whatever was necessary to return him to good health. Tragically, that vision never came to life.

It's why John was at the del Olmo home that evening; he came to pay his respects. We talked about the profound shock he and the newsroom staff were feeling and about Frank's contributions to journalism. John's words were compassionate. His respectful Southern manner comforted my broken heart. He asked me if there was anything he or The Times could do. That question made me stop crying, as I instantly recalled myriad conversations with my husband over the 14 years we were together.

I would often say to Frank: "You need to publish a book of your best columns." I would list the merits: He had written for three decades at The Times, often affecting policy changes or contributing thoughtful public discussion about city, state, national and international topics. Certainly, there was abundant content for this book, I argued.

Frank's answer was always the same and reflected his tendency to focus not on himself or his work but rather on strategies to improve Times news coverage and to enhance the field of journalism. "The book can wait until later," Frank would quietly say. "There are more important battles to wage right now."

Quickly I told John about the book idea. John smiled and, with a determined look in his eye, said to me: "I think we can do the book." And so was born "Frank del Olmo: Commentaries on His Times."

Which brings me to acknowledging the following individuals who were vital to this book's creation and helping my stepdaughter, Valentina, my son, Francisco, and me cope through the saddest period of our lives.

First, I give my loving thanks to Times newsroom staff members who valiantly attempted to save my husband's life, comforted him in his final moments and never left his side so that he did not die alone.

For his leadership, I thank John Carroll, who continues to pay tribute to Frank's courage. To John Puerner, the Times' publisher, I acknowledge his compassion, candor and pledge to help keep Frank's legacy alive.

To this book's co-editor, the Times' Frank Sotomayor, friend and colleague to my husband for 30 years, thank you for your elegant prose, insightful editing and partnering with me to sort through hundreds of columns to select the best ones, all the while demonstrating sensitivity to my grief. Thanks also to Meri Sotomayor for her wonderful suggestions.

I thank the Times' Gisselle Acevedo-Franco, who was with me at the hospital, along with Frank Sotomayor and KCBS' Stephanie Medina-Rodriguez, the day Frank died. Gisselle is the force behind the book's business plan. Her vision to position it beyond journalism audiences has been energizing. To her husband, Victor Franco, I thank him for making Frank laugh so much during the last few years of his life and for the kindness he and daughter Noelle have shown to our family as Gisselle has spent countless hours working with me.

I also thank:

Two engaging artists, for their fine drawings of Frank that appear in this book, Pulitzer Prize-winning editorial cartoonist Paul Conrad, with whom Frank shared a decades-long friendship, and Lalo Alcaraz, whose "La Cucaracha" comic strip Frank had a hand in featuring at The Times;

Former Times photographer José Galvez for his touching image of Frank and Valentina;

Janet Clayton, Frank's longtime colleague, for her help with the Politics chapter and for sharing triumphs and struggles during the years they worked in Metro, Editorial, Opinion and, ultimately, as newsroom executives;

Sergio Muñoz, for his friendship with Frank and the time they spent with Carlos Fuentes and Gabriel García Márquez, Frank's friends and fellow lovers of *palabras bellas* (beautiful words);

Chris Strudwick-Turner, Bobbi Olson, Steve Padilla, Carla Lazzareschi and Tom Trapnell, for excellent editing, design work and advice on production of this book.

Colin Crawford, Susan Denley, John R. Hernandez, Ruben Macareno and Susan Okita for their generous assistance with this project;

Frank's dedicated assistant, Ingrid Farmer, for her work with me in managing 600 condolence messages that arrived following his death;

The Times' Lynne Jewell and consultants Patricia Perez and Martha Tapias-Mansfield, for believing in this book and promoting it;

Julio Moran and Sylvia Wells, of the California Chicano News Media Assn., for tapping CCNMA's archives for rare images of Frank early in his career and to longtime CCNMA members Dr. Félix Gutiérrez, Frank Cruz and George Ramos, for their counsel and historical context about Frank's career;

Dr. Jorge Garcia and Everto Ruíz, professors at California State University, Northridge, and Frank's *compadres,* for their richly detailed background on Frank's early days and their moving tributes at his memorial, and the university's Urban Archives Center, where the Frank del Olmo papers are preserved;

The board and staff of my employer, The California Wellness Foundation, and its CEO, Gary Yates, who has helped me more than words can express, and the communications team and consultant Rob Ritter;

My fellow Cal State Northridge alums — Stephanie Medina-Rodriguez, Linda Romero, Maryhelen Campa-Mena, Rosie Leal-Cepeda and Josie Aguilar — for checking on me as I have grieved;

My sister-in-law Elisa Garcia for being wonderful to Frankie as I have labored long hours on this book; Valentina, for helping with her Pop's columns and her insight on key moments in his career; and to Theresa Previtire and Margie Maldonado, for their moving remembrances of their brother;

My sisters, Rhossío Gutiérrez, Beatriz Gutiérrez and Alicia Castañeda, for their unconditional love, and to my brother Fernando Beltrán and brother-in-law, Hugo Gutiérrez, for their emotional support of my son;

To my son, Frankie, for comforting me when I could not stop the tears; and my mother, Beatriz Hernandez Beltrán, who told me on the eve of Frank's memorial to never forget that the strength of her blood flows in my veins. Without you, I would be lost today, Mamá. Thank you for your spiritual guidance. *Te quiero mucho.*

—*Magdalena Beltrán-del Olmo*

# FOREWORD

*"My hope [has been] for a career that would allow me to make a difference in the world, however small."* — Frank del Olmo

A decade after beginning his Los Angeles Times career as a young intern, Frank del Olmo tapped out his first column in 1980 on a battered Underwood typewriter. Over the next 23 years, he produced almost 450 additional columns, forging a connection with readers — informing them, challenging them and touching their hearts.

"We all have friends that we never actually meet and Frank del Olmo was one of mine," a reader commented in a letter to The Times. "Your newspaper and my mornings will both be emptier now."

Frank's life was tragically cut short, at age 55, by a heart attack on Feb. 19, 2004. This volume preserves some of his best columns, providing a historical sweep of hot-button issues of the last quarter century — and a lot more.

Some obituaries called Frank a "Latino columnist" or a "voice for Latinos." Those characterizations are accurate enough — he was proud to be a journalist of Mexican American heritage — but they don't convey the whole picture. While many of his commentaries deal with Latino-oriented subjects, the underlying themes he explored — the search for truth, advocacy for justice, a loving attachment to family — are all-American and universal.

In an interview a month before his death, Frank told Arlene Morgan, an associate dean of journalism at Columbia University, about wanting "to make a difference in the world, however small." He *did* make a difference — as an incisive columnist and as a leader for inclusive news coverage — and his impact was in no way small.

For much of his career, Frank was known for his clear-headed analysis of hardball issues: politics, education, labor, immigration, as demonstrated in this book. Then, in the final decade of his life, a new dimension emerged: the compassionate father of a young son dealing with autism. In eloquent prose, Frank described how he and his wife, Magdalena, first felt heartache — and later hope — about Frankie's condition.

In many ways, Frank was a trailblazer during this 33 years at The Times: reporter, columnist, deputy editorial page editor (making him the first Latino to be promoted to the newspaper's masthead), associate editor, chairman of a newsroom initiative to improve Latino coverage.

I was fortunate, as a Times editor, to have known and worked with Frank for 30 years. We were also good friends. We would often lunch together, share a laugh and map strategy for resolving some newsroom issue. On Feb. 19, I was expecting to meet with him and colleague Steve Padilla to discuss Latino story ideas when Frank was stricken.

Frank Phillip del Olmo never forgot his roots, and his early life experiences — as with all of us — influenced his perspectives. Raised in a Pacoima housing project at the northeastern edge of the San Fernando Valley, Frank acquired a love of reading and writing and respect for his heritage from his mother, Margaret, a single parent.

Blessed with a sharp mind and focused work ethic, Frank was named outstanding graduate in 1970 at California State University, Northridge. He began work immediately as a Times reporter intern in June of that year. As he later recounted in a column, he got a chance to meet Ruben Salazar, the pioneering Mexican American reporter and columnist. Salazar had just moved from The Times to Spanish-language television but continued to write a column for the newspaper that resonated strongly with Latino readers.

On Aug. 29, 1970, during a day of Chicano antiwar protests in East Los Angeles, Salazar was killed by a sheriff deputy's tear-gas projectile. Without a single full-time reporter who was fluent in Spanish, The Times offered Frank, then only 23, a staff position in 1971. He accepted, resolute to continue the work Salazar had started.

Soon, Frank was shouldering the responsibility of covering nearly everything that involved Mexican Americans, including the vigorous Chicano civil rights movement. In addition, he covered stories about farm labor, politics and Watergate. Reporting assignments took him to the capitals and back roads of Mexico and Central America. During the Nicaragua revolution in 1978, he had to dodge bullets as he jotted down notes to phone in his stories. All of these reporting experiences would later prove invaluable to Frank as a columnist.

Former Times reporter Laurie Becklund assesses Frank's impact this way: "Until Frank came along, U.S.-based reporters rarely covered Mexico and Central America, and when they did they defined those areas by the problems they caused the United States. Frank saw a region of people with interlocking human strengths and needs, and you could see that in his reporting and, later, his columns."

In August of 1980, Frank left the Metro reporting staff and became a columnist, but — as was true for his entire time producing a column — he also had other staff responsibilities, initially as an editorial writer.

Frank's first column, about bilingual education, came almost exactly 10 years after Salazar's death. He followed with a column analyzing the so-called Decade of the Hispanic — he thought the catchy phrase a bunch of hype. And, in any case, he wasn't crazy about the term "Hispanics." (See "Latino *Sí*, Hispanic *No*.") In later commentaries, Frank put into historical and social context a variety of topics, such as the popularity of Los Lobos, the military tradition of Latinos and the impact of Cesar Chavez.

Frank never stopped advocating for better coverage of all the underserved communities of Los Angeles. As two of only a handful of Latinos on staff in the late 1970s, Frank and I urged Times editors to hire more journalists who were fluent in Spanish and who had expertise in covering the rapidly expanding Latino community.

One by one, a number of reporters on our "hire list" joined the staff. In fact, by the early 1980s, we had enough journalists to field an office softball team — the Chicano Cubs. That same team conceived, wrote, edited and photographed a 1983 series of 27 stories, "Latinos in Southern California," that won the 1984 Pulitzer Prize for Public Service. (George Ramos, then a Times editor, and I were project co-editors.) Frank wrote authoritatively about Latino politics in two articles and also contributed a column. The Pulitzer Prize board called the series a landmark in demystifying the Latino population to mainstream America.

Outside The Times, Frank was instrumental in founding the California Chicano News Media Assn. in 1972. CCNMA scholarships and conferences over the years have helped launch hundreds of careers and encouraged a more accurate portrayal of Latino life. The Frank del Olmo Memorial Scholarship Fund, established by The Times and CCNMA, will continue to assist upcoming journalists.

In 1982, Frank chaired the first national meeting of Latino journalists, a gathering that led to the establishment of the National Assn. of Hispanic

Journalists, which in turn has opened newsroom doors to hundreds. Frank served on the boards of numerous journalism groups, including the Committee to Protect Journalists, and he studied at Harvard in 1987 under a Nieman fellowship for journalists.

After winning a promotion to deputy editorial page editor in 1989, Frank was influential in Times editorials demanding that LAPD Chief Daryl Gates be relieved of his position following the Rodney King beating in 1991. Later, he faced a dilemma in 1994 when The Times' publisher — reversing a 20-year policy of not supporting a gubernatorial candidate — decided to endorse California Gov. Pete Wilson for reelection over the objections of Frank and The Times Editorial Board.

Frank had argued that neither candidate deserved endorsement. He opposed giving the nod to Wilson because the governor was using an ethnically divisive state measure, the anti-illegal immigrant Proposition 187, as a cornerstone of his reelection campaign. As a matter of conscience, Frank considered resigning from the newspaper. But after taking some time off at the urging of then-Times Editor Shelby Coffey, he decided instead to write a column as a "dissenting opinion" to the endorsement. His forceful commentary and related pieces about Wilson are included in this volume's Immigration chapter.

A year later, right before Christmas, Frank described the emotional trauma of learning that his son suffered from the disabling condition known as autism: "My son Francisco Manuel — or Frankie, as everyone calls him — is 3 years old, so writing his 'total autobiography' shouldn't be as hard for me as it is. What makes it difficult is trying to write with a leaden pain in my heart."

Over the next decade, Frank gave an annual Christmas report of how Magdalena and he had been able to secure appropriate therapies for Frankie. They painstakingly researched the condition and shared their findings in Frank's columns.

The growing Internet-connected autism community embraced those columns. Jonathan Shestack, founder of the Cure Autism Now Foundation, wrote: "Every year these columns were so eagerly awaited by us. We read them twice, we passed them around and faxed them to friends. We lived their fears and applauded Frankie's progress as if he were our own."

In 2002, Frank was in a reflective mood as he was inducted into the Hall of Fame of the National Assn. of Hispanic Journalists. He spoke of four inspirations in his life:

He praised his mother, Margaret, for maintaining reading materials and a loving environment in the home at a time when the family got by only through welfare payments.

He described the accomplishments of his daughter, Valentina, a gifted young woman who earned both bachelor's and master's degrees at Stanford University, adding, "She's made me very proud."

Of Magdalena, a former reporter who works in the nonprofit foundation field, he remarked: "She's my inspiration, my strength and my very best editor."

Frank — his voice nearly breaking — said their "painful, sad journey" with their son had also been remarkable because Frankie had taught him "a lot about the strength of the human spirit [and] the wonders of the human mind."

Summing up his remarks, Frank said: "It's been a great life, a wonderful career."

After the news of Frank's untimely death was spread worldwide, tributes poured in from the powerful and celebrated, including praise from two giants of Latin America literature who were his friends: Gabriel García Márquez and Carlos Fuentes.

Times Editor John Carroll, in eulogizing Frank, told of a tribute from a more humble source. Without indicating his name, a man had come to The Times' main entrance and left a candle bearing the image of St. Anthony of Padua, a patron saint of the poor. In blue marker, the man had written: *Te recordaremos siempre, Sr. Frank del Olmo.*

Yes, Frank, we will remember you always. You made a difference.

—*Frank O. Sotomayor*
May 27, 2004

# CHAPTER ONE

# Politics

*Beyond the 'Decade of the Hispanic' and other slogans*

FRANK DEL OLMO BEGAN WRITING political commentaries in 1980, the advent of the so-called Decade of the Hispanic. That slogan, he noted, proved to be hype — more suitable as an advertising gimmick. It was too early to mark the coming of age for Latinos in politics. But the times were a-changin'; the Latino political punch was slowly building up muscle. In 1996, after Latino voters turned out in record numbers in California, del Olmo laid to rest the offensive political cliché of Latinos as the "sleeping giant."

In August of 2003, del Olmo exposed an abusive vehicle-impounding policy in Maywood, a small city southeast of Los Angeles. One working-class family was assessed a $1,100 impounding fee because Flor Cervantes did not have a driver's license. Cervantes ended up losing her minivan. But, attesting to the influence of del Olmo's column, the city quickly revised its harsh impounding policies.

# 'Hispanic Decade' Stumbles at the Start

T HE SO-CALLED "Decade of the Hispanic" is not getting off to an auspicious start.

For those who don't know, the 1980s were declared the "Decade of the Hispanic" as part of an advertising campaign launched recently by a major brewery, which merely wants more Latinos to drink its beer. Unfortunately, the phrase has been picked up by a lot of Latino activists, who should know better, and has become one of the first political clichés of the '80s.

The activists who jumped on the Hispanic Decade bandwagon earlier this year pointed eagerly to the fact that 1980 was both a census year and a presidential election year. They expected the census to show the continued growth of the country's Latino population, and they were confidently predicting that the election would give Latino voters a chance to display their newfound clout on a national level.

We don't know yet what the census will prove, but the election is showing signs of being a disaster for Latino voters. The upcoming choice between Jimmy Carter and Ronald Reagan, with John Anderson and several others thrown in for good measure, has not been any more inspiring for Latinos than it has for any other group of voters in the country. The result is expected to be a dismal turnout on Election Day.

One Chicano who has long been active in grass-roots efforts in Los Angeles, Rosalio Muñoz, has been getting laughs lately dismissing the Reagan-or-Carter choice with a joke heard often this year — "the evil of two lessers."

Last week, two different events served to illustrate the rampant apathy to be found among Latinos two weeks before the election.

At a nonpartisan fundraising dinner sponsored by the National Assn. of Latino Elected Officials in Los Angeles, the biggest reaction received by any of the political figures there was negative — Reagan's representative was loudly booed.

Al Zapanta, the Los Angeles businessman who heads the California

FRANK DEL OLMO

Viva Reagan Bush Committee, was so surprised at the negative response that his only reply was a lame joke: "I hope those boos are for me and not for Gov. Reagan."

His hasty retreat was rivaled by that of Chip Carter. The president's son preceded Zapanta to the podium and received a cool and distinctly uninterested reception. He seemed ill at ease, and his perfunctory remarks could barely be heard above the murmur of a crowd of about 2,000 people.

The coup de grace came last Saturday, however, when another nonpartisan group, Hispanos Unidos, held its third annual unity rally in Pico Rivera.

The previous unity events had attracted a few thousand people, and the rally's organizers were boldly proclaiming that they represented 25 organizations with a combined membership of 1 million Latinos.

About 200 of those Latinos showed up.

After a turnout like that, the most charitable assessment one could make of Hispanos Unidos' clout was that it could use a little shoring up at the grass roots.

Nevertheless, the organizers of the rally went on with their charade, telling the press they had decided to make no endorsement in the presidential campaign. Some billed this as a repudiation of Carter, and some Reagan backers, including the peripatetic Mr. Zapanta, called it a victory for their man.

The reality, of course, is that there were no winners as a result of the Hispanos Unidos debacle, only losers.

And the biggest losers of all in this lackluster campaign will probably be the thousands of Latinos who are (barely) starting to feel that they are welcome on the national political scene but find themselves coming into it at a time when national campaigns are becoming so homogenized that even Anglo voters are turned off.

The campaigns have become one big media event, with the candidates telling whatever audience they meet whatever it wants to hear. And none of them has said anything new or challenging about the issues that interest Latinos.

Whether it's Carter, Reagan or Anderson, they are for the right things — bilingual education, more jobs, more investment for Latinos in business, amnesty for "undocumented workers." (No politician trying to win Latino support calls them "illegal aliens," at least not in public.)

And, of course, they all make the standard promises about appointing Latinos to top government positions.

It's all very routine, and very boring.

Even on the issue of illegal immigration from Latin America, the most complicated and far-reaching issue facing Latinos this year, and probably for the balance of the decade, the candidates have been woefully short of specifics and imagination.

President Carter two years ago sent to Congress his proposals for dealing with illegal immigration, the Alien Employment and Adjustment Act. It was a mixed bag of several oft-suggested "solutions" to the "illegal alien problem." It included a seven-year cutoff date for amnesty; more Border Patrol officers; sanctions against employers who hire illegal workers and liberalized rules for the importation of foreign workers.

Like several of Carter's other grand designs, it was shot to pieces by special-interest groups and died, unmourned and barely remembered, when Congress adjourned.

When Reagan spoke about immigration recently in Texas, he got himself into another one of his did-he-say-it-or-not routines. He endorsed a plan proposed by that state's Republican Gov. William Clements to provide work permits for Mexican laborers coming into the country for three months to a year. Reagan, however, said the visas should allow those workers to remain here "for whatever length of time they want to stay."

When reporters asked Reagan about his variation on Clements' plan, the candidate denied saying anything different. When a tape-recording was produced, Reagan said it was a faulty recording and insisted he meant the workers could stay "within the time of the visa."

Even Anderson — who made his early reputation by going into lions'-den situations where he told voters things they did not necessarily want to hear — was as bland as white bread when he talked to a Latino audience about illegal immigration.

He also suggested a guest worker-type program, providing "temporary work permits" for Mexicans, as one way of dealing with the dilemma but added that he had no specifics on how it would work. He asked his audience for "any ideas you might have along those lines."

But they never got around to discussing ideas. Anderson left the meeting within a half-hour, television camera crews in tow, heading for his next media event.

When a campaign has been as vapid and uninspiring as this one, it should come as no surprise on Election Day to find most Latinos sitting at home, watching old movies on TV and sipping some of that "Decade of the Hispanic" beer.


NOVEMBER 11, 1982

# Will Gloria Molina Lead Us Into Decade of the Hispanic?

ALL THE MEDIA HYPE about how the 1980s would be the "Decade of the Hispanic" just may prove true if Latinos do as well in elections over the next eight years as they did in 1982.

Last week's voting increased the number of Latinos in Congress from six to nine. California and Texas, which had two Latino congressmen each, now have three. New Mexico has two Latino congressmen, up from one, and also elected its second Latino governor, Democrat Toney Anaya. Californians also confirmed the appointment of Justice Cruz Reynoso as the first Mexican American on the state Supreme Court, although only by a slim majority.

Latinos gained no seats in the California Legislature, but they didn't lose any, either. That is no small feat, considering some of the infighting and jockeying for position that took place among the state's Latino politicos before the election.

That internal maneuvering almost prevented the single most significant achievement of the 1982 election for California Latinos from taking place — the election of Gloria Molina, an East Los Angeles Democrat, to the state Assembly. She is the first Latina ever to serve in that body and, as far as anyone can determine, only the fourth Latina in a state legislature anywhere in the country. (The others are in New York, Texas and Colorado.)

By almost anyone's reckoning, a candidate like Molina should have had no problem getting elected to office. While only 34, she is a veteran political activist who has worked on the staffs and in the campaigns of several prominent Democratic politicians, including former President Jimmy Carter, state

Assembly Speaker Willie Brown, Los Angeles Mayor Tom Bradley and state Sen. Art Torres, who preceded her as East Los Angeles' Assembly member.

Molina is a Democrat born and brought up in one of the most reliably Democratic districts in California. East Los Angeles is a sprawling barrio in which voting for the party of Franklin D. Roosevelt and the Kennedy brothers is almost traditional, which is not always the case in the more affluent Latino suburbs farther from the central city. It is not unusual for Democrats in East Los Angeles to get 80% of the vote or more.

Molina is also a campaign manager's dream — a bright, articulate and strikingly attractive woman. But being a woman was also her main problem. Many Latino political activists, most of them men, had serious doubts that a woman could be elected to office in a Latino district.

What makes Molina's election so significant is that she proved that kind of thinking wrong. The idea that Latinos cannot accept women in leadership roles should have been laid to rest long ago.

I was one of the optimists who thought that the myth about macho-oriented Latino voters was already dead. We learned how wrong we were early this year when Molina had the audacity to challenge the political leadership in East Los Angeles by launching her candidacy.

Last February, several of the city's Latino political leaders gathered at an Eastside restaurant to try to agree on who would run in the new legislative districts created there through reapportionment.

While some people saw that meeting as an attempt by a clique of political insiders to become kingmakers, it was a rational strategy. In the past, Latinos had hurt themselves by running several Latino candidates in the same district, thereby allowing non-Latino candidates to win. This year they were determined not to make the same mistake.

Among those attending the meeting were the veteran Los Angeles congressman, Edward Roybal; Esteban Torres, a former Carter White House assistant who had returned to Los Angeles to run for Congress, and several Latino legislators, including Assemblymen Art Torres, Richard Alatorre and Matthew "Marty" Martinez.

Pointedly excluded from that meeting was Gloria Molina. She was not the only political aspirant who was not invited, of course. Many would-be candidates and self-styled political honchos were left out in the cold that day. What made Molina's exclusion so surprising, and so galling to many of her supporters (both male and female), was the fact that she had tried so carefully to play by the political rules beforehand. She had paid her dues in many lower-level jobs and had even approached most of the same politicos who organized the meeting to seek their blessings and support for her campaign.

Despite the criticism that was leveled at them for holding that private meeting, the politicos made some good choices that day. Both Esteban Torres and Martinez wound up being elected to Congress, after Torres agreed to move out of Martinez's district. Art Torres was elected to the state Senate. The only candidate to emerge from that meeting who did not ultimately succeed was Richard Polanco, the young man designated to run for the Assembly seat that Molina will fill.

Polanco is another well-known political activist in East Los Angeles. After he was tapped as the favored candidate, some politicos advised Molina not to challenge him in the primary. She was told to run in another district. Much to her credit, she refused. And much to their credit, at least two of the leading politicos on the East Side, Roybal and Art Torres, later endorsed Molina over Polanco. She defeated him with 52% of the vote after a hard-fought primary election campaign.

Polanco is a respected activist whose political views differ little from Molina's. One can make a good argument that he would have represented the area as effectively as Molina. But the election of another Latino male would not have had the symbolic impact that Molina's did. Because if the 1980s are really going to be the Decade of the Hispanic, men alone are not going to make it so.

NOVEMBER 1, 1984

# Do We All Chug-a-Lug Now for Social Justice?

THE LOS ANGELES OLYMPICS had everything from an official automobile to official junk food, so I suppose that there's nothing wrong with a handful of Latino organizations deciding that Coors should be the Official Hispanic Beer.

Under the plan announced Monday by Adolph Coors Co. and six

Latino advocacy groups, the brewing company agreed to put 8% of its sales, estimated to be $1.1 billion in 1983, into Latino-owned banks, investment firms, insurance companies and Spanish-language advertising across the country. It also agreed to hire more Latino workers, name a Latino vice president and increase the number of Latino distributors who handle its beer.

Finally, the company said that it will donate $500,000 per year to non-profit Latino groups like the six organizations whose leaders signed the Coors agreement: The National Council of La Raza, National IMAGE Inc., the American GI Forum, the Hispanic Chamber of Commerce, the National Puerto Rican Coalition and the Cuban National Planning Council.

It sounds like an agreement with something for everyone — investments for Latino business, private-sector support for Latino activists and more potential beer sales for Coors in the growing Latino market. But wait. There's a catch.

The plan includes what Coors officials call an "incentive commitment," a clause saying that when the agreement lapses in 1990 all future benefits will be pegged to how much Coors beer Latinos have consumed in the meantime. Company officials estimate that Latino consumers currently represent about 5% of their sales. That must rise to 8% by 1990 if Coors is to increase the benefits.

In other words, the more Coors that we Latinos drink, the more money that Coors will put back into our community.

It follows that the community activists who made this deal are not expected to make it a success by pushing the "official" Latino brew.

The agreement announced Monday is similar to one that the company reached two months ago with the Los Angeles chapter of the NAACP, including the "incentive commitment."

Coors has been doing poorly in minority markets lately. Latinos and black leaders, alleging discriminatory hiring practices by Coors, have called for consumer boycotts. So has the AFL-CIO, charging the family-controlled Colorado brewery with anti-union activities. The company's chairman, William K. Coors, has long been identified with conservative political causes and recently was quoted as saying that blacks are intellectually inferior in a speech to a minority-business conference in Denver. Company spokesmen say that the quotes were taken out of context.

With Coors sales concentrated in the Western states, where the Latino market is strong — and strongly pro-union — I suppose that the trade-off between the brewery and the six Latino organizations makes coldhearted business sense. But what about other groups concerned with the well-being of the Latino community?

I wonder what the reaction was in the Alcoholism Council of Greater East Los Angeles, which has been campaigning for years to focus public attention on the problems caused by alcohol abuse in the Latino community. A state-sponsored survey in the late 1970s found that among Latino males the incidence of death from alcohol-related causes was 10% higher than for other ethnic groups.

And I wonder what the reaction was in corporations that have generously donated to Latino causes over the years but never insisted on "incentive commitments."

Will Atlantic-Richfield, a leader in constructive corporate involvement in the Los Angeles area, now insist that Latinos buy more ARCO gasoline before it supports projects in East Los Angeles?

Will the Bank of America refuse to donate money to Latino groups unless they bring in more Spanish-surnamed depositors?

And how about The Times? For years editors and business executive here have explored ways of gaining more readership in the Latino community. They have talked about more news coverage of Latino issues, or special Spanish-language editions. Instead, maybe they should hold hostage the Latino community groups that this newspaper helps support, like the Plaza de la Raza arts center in Lincoln Heights or the nearby Los Angeles Boys and Girls Club.

Of course, I don't expect any of these corporations to take such a cynical view. They see corporate giving as philanthropy, not a marketing tool. And, considering the wretched record of Latino hiring that Coors had before the boycotts of the late 1960s, one could make a case that the brewery owes Latinos more than just philanthropy, but redress for past injustices.

The Latino leaders who signed the Coors agreement Monday hailed it as a precedent, which it is. A bad one.

# *Se Habla Inglés*: **Prop. 63, a Cruel Joke, Could Cost Us Dearly**

POSTED NEAR MY DESK at The Times is a gag sign that reads *"Se Habla Inglés"* (English Spoken Here). A Latino friend gave it to me because so many of the assignments that I have covered for this newspaper, from farm-labor strikes in the San Joaquin Valley to revolutions in Central America, have involved the use of Spanish.

I have come to treasure that silly sign more than ever in recent years as public concern has grown over the widespread use of Spanish and other foreign languages in this country and the presumed threat that this trend represents to the dominance of English. That sign summarizes my feelings about the bilingual controversy: It's a joke.

I know that sounds flip, but I'm serious. With the growing dominance of English as the language of technology and finance all over the world, and the overwhelming influence that English-language media — from movies to music videos — have on young people in every culture, I find it amazing that anyone is worried about the language's future in this country.

By the same token, I can't understand why people get themselves so worked up about the fact that some people in cities like Los Angeles still use foreign languages, especially Spanish. That has always been the case with new immigrants. Wait a few years and their children will be listening to rock 'n' roll like their peers. Every time I hear someone carrying on about them not speaking English like the rest of us, I stifle a yawn. It's not only a joke, it's also a bore.

Which brings me to Proposition 63, the initiative on next November's state ballot to make English the "official" language of California. Many Latino and Asian American activists are criticizing it as mean-spirited and anti-immigrant. They are right, and I admire their honorable stand. But they're wasting their time in fighting the measure. It is likely to be approved by a wide margin. A recent California poll found that 65% of the state's voters are aware of the initiative and support it by more than 3 to 1.

The state's balloting on Proposition 63 will be just the latest in a series of political moves across the country in which voters and public officials vent their resentment against people who don't speak English.

Probably no city in the nation has benefited more from an influx of new Spanish-speaking residents than Miami. The Cuban refugees who migrated to that city beginning in 1960 helped diversify the economy of a sleepy resort town and turned it into a major shopping and banking center for all of Latin America. Yet the first overt sign of the growing antipathy toward Spanish in this country occurred there in 1980 when Dade County voters rescinded a resolution that declared the county to be officially bilingual.

A few months later, voters in San Francisco, long regarded as the most tolerant city in California, approved a ballot proposition that urged the federal government to stop requiring the city to print voter-information material in languages other than English. The vote stemmed from a controversy over ballots printed in Cantonese, Mandarin and other languages used by elderly Chinese residents of the city — the very people whose visibility helped give San Francisco a reputation for cultural diversity.

When people in Miami and San Francisco vote in such a small-minded way, what hope is there?

Personally, my hope lies in the fact that Proposition 63 is the first of the English-only measures that would have more than a symbolic effect. It would amend the California Constitution to require the Legislature to establish and enforce English as the official language. And that would create some messy political and legal challenges.

The backers of Proposition 63 get lots of mileage out of the mistaken public perception that recent immigrants don't want to learn English or assimilate into U.S. society. In fact they do, which is why thousands of new arrivals to this country are crowding into English classes at adult schools all over the state. What happens to them if Proposition 63 passes? Will the state have to provide even more money for English classes? Or will the English-first forces try to do away with such classes?

Nobody can say for sure, because while some Proposition 63 supporters are sincere people who genuinely want to promote wider use of English, others are just ignorant nativists and racists who don't want government doing anything for anybody who's different. And it is sheer hypocrisy for Proposition 63 backers like former Sen. S.I. Hayakawa to pretend that this is not the case.

In fact, Proposition 63, like so many other well-intentioned but poorly drafted initiatives that show up on the California ballot, would create as many problems as it would solve. And those problems would cost state government time, trouble and money.

Like other English-first proposals, Proposition 63 is a cruel joke — not just on the immigrants whose labor is helping keep this state prosperous and growing, but also on the California taxpayers who will pay the consequences if it passes.

SEPTEMBER 22, 1986

# Prison Issue Inspires Eastside to Do Battle

THE LATEST POLITICAL BATTLE CRY energizing Latinos in Los Angeles and the rest of California is "No Prison in East L.A." The funny thing about it, though, is that the prison site in question is not on the Eastside.

The 30 acres where Gov. George Deukmejian, Assembly Speaker Willie Brown and other state officials want to put a new prison is west of the Los Angeles River, the boundary that separates the Eastside from the rest of Los Angeles. But that doesn't matter, because the technicalities of the prison project long ago became less important than its symbolism. California Latinos are so opposed to Deukmejian's prison that he couldn't make them any madder if he suggested building it in the Vatican.

For a long time it looked as if Deukmejian would get his Los Angeles prison with relative ease. After all, there is merit in the Department of Corrections' arguments for a prison somewhere in this city. State officials point out that Los Angeles County sends 38% of the state's male inmates to prison yet is home to no state lockups. And a site near the Los Angeles Civic Center would be convenient not just for attorneys and law enforcement personnel but also for the families of prison inmates who live in the inner city.

The trouble started when state prison officials began insisting that the only acceptable site was at 12th and Santa Fe streets, an industrial area just across the river from predominantly Latino Boyle Heights. Deukmejian and his underlings badly underestimated the resentment that many Mexican Americans feel toward public works projects — especially on the Eastside, which already has more than its share of unattractive government facilities, including maintenance and storage yards and three large county jails.

If California has a Chicano capital, it's the vaguely defined place called "East L.A." But, as a Chicano activist once told me, "East L.A. is as much a state of mind as a place." When Chicanos think of "East L.A.," they mean more than the six square miles of unincorporated county territory officially designated as East Los Angeles; the term also refers to adjacent city neighborhoods like Boyle Heights.

The sprawling Mexican barrios there grew with the rest of Los Angeles, starting slowly at the turn of the century and speeding up after World War II. The resentment over urban renewal stems largely from the postwar era, when no fewer than five freeways were gouged through the Eastside. That also is when old Mexican neighborhoods were bulldozed on Bunker Hill to make way for high-rise buildings and in Chavez Ravine to make way for Dodger Stadium.

There was community resistance in all those cases, but stronger political and economic forces prevailed. The resentment remains to this day, however. When Chicano activists rail against the evils of urban renewal, they always cite the freeways, Bunker Hill and Chavez Ravine. They are political symbols, and now so is the downtown prison because the Eastside has more political clout today than in the 1950s.

It was a local member of the California Assembly, Democrat Gloria Molina, who last year began rallying residents of neighborhoods near the proposed prison site against the project. She now is supported by a broad coalition that ranges from local chambers of commerce to churches and activist groups.

It was the local state senator, Democrat Art Torres, who made the prison a statewide issue. For several years, Torres has been quietly planning a campaign for statewide office and in the process has developed political contacts with Latinos throughout California.

When Torres held a Sacramento press conference on Sept. 2 to denounce the prison, he was joined by Latino leaders from as far away as San Diego and Santa Rosa. Even Latino activists that far afield know the sad experience that their Los Angeles *hermanos* have had with urban renewal.

The Deukmejian administration didn't catch on, however. A spokesman for the governor even told reporters that opponents of the prison were a vocal minority with no significant support. The next day hundreds of Eastside residents staged a protest against the prison and were joined by Archbishop Roger Mahony and several politicians — including California Senate President Pro Tem David A. Roberti (D-Los Angeles), who now leads the anti-prison forces in Sacramento.

I wonder if Deukmejian finally has realized his mistake, now that opinion polls are starting to show a decline in his support among Latinos just six weeks before the November election. The Times Poll, for example, has recorded a 31-point drop in Latino support for Deukmejian since March. The prison controversy is probably not the only reason for that dramatic decline, but it certainly can't help.

And it won't help backers of the prison that the perception is growing among Latinos that Molina, Torres and their allies have fought state government to a standstill. The Legislature has yet to give final approval to the Los Angeles prison plan, despite being called into special session by the governor two weeks ago.

The "East L.A." prison has taken on a life if its own, beyond the merits of the project itself, and the issue will carry heavy symbolic overtones long after it is settled. Whatever the final outcome, the battle cry "No Prison in East L.A." will inspire Latino activists in the future and make it even harder for government to put unpopular public works projects anywhere near the Eastside.

FEBRUARY 6, 1987

# Two Eastside Machines?
# Let's Hope Not

**E**LECTION NIGHT PARTIES can be very revealing. In the euphoria and relief that mark the end of a victorious campaign, candidates and their most ardent supporters often say, or do, things that they wouldn't under normal circumstances.

That happened Tuesday night at the victory celebration for Gloria Molina, the Democratic assemblywoman from East Los Angeles who scored a surprisingly easy win over Board of Education member Larry Gonzalez for the right to represent the newly created 1st District, just north and west of the downtown area. It was an emotional night for Molina's backers, who had a tough challenge in Gonzalez. Not only was he well funded, he also had the support of two of the most powerful Latino political leaders in the city, Councilman Richard Alatorre and state Sen. Art Torres.

Amid the din of joyous celebration I was approached by a prominent Molina supporter who shouted into my ear, "Now there are two machines!"

Two machines? *Dios mio!* I hope not.

I suppose that heady reaction was to be expected from someone who worked hard to put Molina onto the City Council, where she will be the first Latina ever to sit in that 15-member body. Because Molina has successfully bucked Alatorre and his political allies several times before, her campaign seemed to attract every Latino activist who ever felt wronged or slighted by the "Eastside machine." So maybe there's an element of gleeful vengeance in talk of a "second machine."

But in the clear light of day that always follows election night revelry, Molina and her backers must realize that there's no need for a second Latino political machine in Los Angeles. First, as I have pointed out before, the political clique that Alatorre and Torres lead is not really a "machine" in the sense that the word is understood in American politics. Alatorre and Torres can't deliver elections the way the late Mayor Richard J. Daley used to in Chicago, or the way Tammany Hall's operatives did in New York City at the turn of the century. Now, *those* were machines. Torres and Alatorre have an organization effective at fundraising and campaigning, but it is not unbeatable — as Molina proved.

Even if one accepts the idea that Alatorre and Torres control a machine, does that justify creating a second one? That implies to me that Latino activists and voters in this city will henceforth have to march in lock-step behind the leaders of one or the other. Thankfully, that is not feasible in a community as diverse as the 4 million Latinos in the Los Angeles area are. In fact, one thing that I find encouraging about Molina's victory is that it may finally convince outsiders that Latinos are diverse and speak with different voices even on issues that they all agree on — not unlike Anglos, blacks and other ethnic groups. The idea that Latinos must rally behind one candidate in an election is out of date, unrealistic and downright condescending.

But the most important reason for not even thinking about a second machine is that it would make internecine political battles like the one between Molina and Gonzalez routine.

That may happen anyway, unfortunately. Molina is sure to support another Latino to take her Assembly seat in Sacramento, and Torres and Alatorre will probably back a candidate of their own. A similar face-off is likely in the election to fill the Board of Education seat that Gonzalez gave up.

Now, I can accept the fact that some political infighting is inevitable on the Eastside and in other large Latino communities. But lately this has started costing lots of money, a scarce resource too valuable for Latinos to waste. Molina and Gonzalez each spent more than $200,000 in a campaign that drew fewer than 12,000 voters to the polls. Why should Latinos, even well-heeled Latinos, be asked to ante up again and again in round after round of what is basically a contest for power?

Contests between candidates are the essence of democracy. Contests between machines for the glorification of the boss are something else. Of course, there may be rich Latinos who don't mind paying for these intramural squabbles. But it would be a major step toward political maturity for Latinos if the successful and prosperous leaders of their community (attorneys, doctors, businessmen and the like) were to take some of the money that they donate to individual politicos and put it into an independent political-action committee.

There is no Chicano PAC in California, partly because most of the money that Latinos put into politics is given to politicians like Alatorre and Molina. And if they sometimes use it to play kingmaker, who can blame them?

But a Chicano PAC with money to spend on candidates (both Latino and non-Latino) or issues important to the community would add a whole new facet to the growing political clout that Latinos have in this country. And have no doubt that a Chicano PAC based in Los Angeles, where so much Latino wealth and talent is concentrated, would be a major force in the politics of not just California but also the Southwest and the entire nation.

Why, people might even start calling it a machine.

# The Political *Veterano*
# of Melrose Avenue

**T**HE TRIBUTES ARE POURING IN, as well they should, for Frank Casado, who died last week at the age of 66. He was well known — and not only in Los Angeles — as the co-owner, maitre d' and resident philosopher at Lucy's El Adobe, a popular Mexican restaurant on a rather seedy stretch of trendy Melrose Avenue.

Because Lucy's is a hangout for folks from Paramount Studios, right across the street, and several nearby TV stations and recording studios, the tributes are playing up the Hollywood angle, focusing on the movie stars who ate there and especially the young rock musicians that Frank and his wife, Lucy, helped and encouraged with many a free meal and margarita.

That's fine, and I must admit that even a jaded, native Angeleno like me sometimes enjoyed stopping by Lucy's to stargaze. But the Frank Casado I want to remember had a harder edge to him — an edge that pushed him and his wife to become political leaders in the Mexican American community long before it was fashionable, or easy.

I'm referring to that almost-forgotten period between 1945 and 1960. Back then the Casados (because you really can't talk about Frank without including Lucy, the two were that close) were among a handful of Eastside activists who circulated petitions and got out the vote to help elect a young social worker named Edward R. Roybal to the City Council in 1949, making him the first Latino on that body in this century. In the 1950s, the Casados helped found the statewide Mexican-American Political Assn. to promote the candidacy of other Latino politicians. They remained active in MAPA until it began to fade in the 1970s, when Chicano politics got too sophisticated for any one organization to speak for a growing and complex community.

Late into many an evening, I enjoyed listening to Casado reminisce about the early days. He gave a young political reporter many insights into what Latino politics was like before TV, radio, specialized mailers and high-paid consultants turned it into a vaguely picante version of modern mass-media politics everywhere.

I learned from those conversations that the successful restaurateur never completely forgot the resentment he felt as a Latino growing up in Boyle Heights, being regularly harassed by the cops for no particular reason. In current terms, Frank would be referred to as a wannabe *pachuco*. But before he could become a genuine gang member, World War II broke out, and he joined the Navy to fight in the Pacific. The Eastside, indeed the entire city, are better places for that happenstance. Like many Chicano veterans, he returned from the war matured and eager to exercise his rights as an American.

As noted, Lucy Casado had a great deal of influence on her husband. She grew up in Texas, where anti-Mexican prejudice has historically been more overt (if not more pervasive) than in California. Frank, whose father had immigrated to the United States from Spain, often spoke angrily of the discrimination Lucy had experienced. That also influenced them both to become active in politics on a national scale.

Their close friendship with former California Gov. Edmund G. Brown Jr. brought them some notoriety in the 1970s. But long before they adopted Jerry Brown, they worked for various nationally known politicians, like Robert F. Kennedy, who was a special favorite. But for all the big-name Democratic and Republican politicians who dined at their restaurant — making it as much a journalistic and political hangout as a Hollywood one — they never lost touch with their roots in the politics of the Eastside.

One of the Casados' proudest memories, one I find especially illustrative, is of the intense 1968 presidential campaign. The soon-to-be-assassinated Bobby Kennedy was trying to win the Democratic nomination with a strong showing in the California primary. Yet Frank and Lucy persuaded him to take time off from a hectic schedule to meet privately at El Adobe with a group of Chicano college students.

The young people who met Kennedy included some of the student leaders who, earlier that same year, had gotten into lots of legal and personal trouble for helping organize walkouts at several local high schools that are still remembered as the "East L.A. Blowouts." Historians now consider those 1968 protests as a turning point in the political development of the nation's Mexican American community. If they were, there must have been a symbolic passing of the torch that day from old *veterano* Frank Casado to the young Blowout leaders, many of whom still play important roles in local Chicano politics.

Kennedy's taking time to pay attention to those young Chicanos — most of whom could not yet vote and who probably didn't tell the senator anything he couldn't already figure out about the shortcomings of public education in the nation's barrios — is just one more vignette that explains why Kennedy is still revered by many Chicano activists.

The Casados, going to the trouble of helping set that session up — in the hopes of enlightening a powerful politician to the needs of their community and to convince some angry young activists that they would be listened to even by a quintessentially establishment figure — illustrates why Frank Casado will be missed by many more people than the denizens of the wonderful restaurant he ran.

JULY 14, 1996

# Secession Flap Gives Valley an Edge

IT LOOKS AS IF the San Fernando Valley — the much misunderstood and oft-maligned part of Los Angeles where I grew up — will lose a battle in the Legislature that would have made it possible for the Valley to secede from the rest of the city. But no matter. We Valleyites have already won this war.

I am exaggerating a bit, of course. The struggle in Sacramento between Assemblywoman Paula Boland (R-Granada Hills) and legislators from other parts of Los Angeles over AB 2403 was really little more than a skirmish. Boland's bill only made the secession process easier to start; it didn't make it happen.

AB 2403 would revoke a law enacted in 1978. Back then, in response to an earlier threat by Valley residents to bolt, the Legislature gave the City Council veto power over any secession effort — be it based in Sylmar, San Pedro or the dozens of other communities in between that periodically get annoyed with the powers-that-be in City Hall.

After getting through the Assembly with relative ease, Boland's bill has bogged down in the state Senate. There, Democratic Sen. Richard Polanco, who represents the city's Eastside and has made no secret of his desire to kill AB 2403, persuaded the Democratic Senate president, Bill Lockyer, to trap Boland's bill in committee. If AB 2403 is still in committee when the

Legislature adjourns, which could be in the next few days, it dies.

Boland is crying foul but has little to complain about. She got loads of publicity with her bill, and that will make it easier for her to run for the state Senate in November now that her Assembly term is ending. And even if Boland never returns to Sacramento, someone will revive AB 2403, because the Valley's discontent with the rest of Los Angeles won't go away now, any more than it did in 1978.

The irony of this, as hinted above, is that while the Valley can legitimately grouse about being taken for granted at times by City Hall, it long ago won its cultural war with the rest of the metropolis that sprawls south of the Santa Monica Mountains.

Because the Valley is L.A.

For all the bad-mouthing the Valley's suburban sprawl gets from folks who wish L.A. were more New York-with-sunshine, all those tract houses built in the postwar years symbolize Los Angeles to outsiders. And most like what they see. Beverly Hills, after all, is too glitzy to seem attainable to folks in Chicago or Caracas. But they can aspire to live in nice places like Canoga Park, where even working-class families can own comfortable homes with big back yards.

Other parts of greater Los Angeles that grew after the Valley, from Camarillo to Costa Mesa, reflect the same dream of a cozy suburban life. In the ethnic enclaves of L.A.'s inner city, hard-working families strive for that dream closer to home, pursuing it to mostly black suburbs like Inglewood, mostly Asian suburbs like Monterey Park and mostly Latino suburbs like Montebello.

As banal as sophisticates might find such middle-class aspirations, they undergird the hopes of thousands of families who built Los Angeles and keep it prosperous — like the one I was raised in. I grew up in Pacoima, where our family patriarch retired in the 1920s. All of my relatives still live nearby, in places like Sylmar and Mission Hills. I moved only as far as Glendale.

As a lifelong "Valley guy," I am amused at the simplistic notions some folks have about my home. The conventional wisdom would have it, for example, that Boland's bill reflects the desire of a middle-class enclave to break away from L.A.'s big-city problems. In truth, the Valley has urban problems of its own, including poverty and crime. The talk of breaking away from L.A. only represents the desire of people in the Valley to have a bit more control over the public issues that affect their lives. That's an attitude people in the Valley share with virtually everyone else in town.

For the record, I'm not convinced that breaking up L.A. is going to get any of us that much further along toward solving our problems. I'd even argue that what keeps L.A. going despite riots, earthquakes, fires and floods is the fact that most people here have not yet given up on the middle-class suburban dream that the Valley epitomizes.

I am so confident that the Valley will continue to represent the best hope of L.A.'s future that I'll venture a prediction that should give Boland some satisfaction as she fumes over how Polanco apparently trumped her:

When Los Angeles again gets around to electing a Latino mayor — which will be sooner rather than later, given our rapidly changing demographics — it won't be Polanco or anyone else from the Eastside, like City Councilman Richard Alatorre or County Supervisor Gloria Molina.

It will be Richard Alarcon, who grew up in the East Valley and now represents it on the City Council. And if it's not Alarcon, it will be someone very much like him: a Latino leader bred to the Valley's lifestyle. This will be the kind of Latino leader all L.A. likes, because he or she will understand the real Los Angeles and its quintessentially middle-class dreams.

APRIL 1, 1996

# The Machines' Days Are Numbered

I MUST CONFESS. Some years ago, for a few weeks, I was a Republican.

For most of my career as a journalist, I've been registered as an independent. I figure that is most appropriate for someone who reports on public affairs and tries to write about them in a fair, balanced manner. Like other journalists, I take pride in routinely being accused by Democrats of being a Republican and by Republicans of being a Democrat.

But I must confess my brief affiliation with the GOP because it will help explain why the most important outcome of last Tuesday's primary election was the enactment of Proposition 198, the Open Primary Initiative.

Starting in 1998, all voters — Democrats, Republicans and 1.5 million political independents like me — will receive primary ballots listing the names of every candidate in every party, major or minor. And we can cast our ballots for whomever we like best, regardless of political affiliation.

Not surprisingly, leaders of the two major parties are threatening to take Proposition 198 to court. But I can't envision too many judges in California deciding that political parties have more rights than individual voters — although I know plenty of people in both major parties who act that way.

I "became" Republican, in fact, because of an especially egregious act of arrogance by one of the two Democratic factions that dominate politics on Los Angeles' Eastside.

The factions revolve around the two senior Latino officials in town, County Supervisor Gloria Molina and City Councilman Richard Alatorre. Their loyalists constantly maneuver against each other to recruit and groom candidates for seats in the Legislature, City Council and Board of Education.

Apparently, casting your lot with one side is akin to taking a blood oath against the other. But loyalty I can understand. Grooming candidates-in-waiting is forgivable too. What irritates me is how they hand-pick candidates.

Well before any election where a seat is open on the Eastside, word goes out from one faction, then the other, designating their favored candidates. That's a signal to fundraisers and activists to swing into action on behalf of the man or woman who has Richard's or Gloria's blessing. (Last names are never necessary.)

What galls me is the unspoken assumption that thousands of Eastside Latino voters should have no say in the matter. Once the two factions fight it out in the Democratic primary, the Eastside residents' vote in November is a mere formality.

That's because most Eastside districts are gerrymandered to heavily favor Democrats. Which means that even when those Democrats are political hacks — which has been the case more than a few times — they still manage to win public office.

That was the situation a few years ago, when a particularly dense but slavishly loyal operative in one of the Eastside factions narrowly defeated a smart, young businessman for a seat in the Legislature.

I was venting my frustration over that turn of events late one evening at Lucy's El Adobe, the Mexican restaurant in Hollywood that has long been a hangout for political junkies. I'd had too many margaritas and was boasting to the late Frank Casado, the Latino activist who ran the restaurant with his wife, Lucy, that even I could beat the clod the Eastside machines had come up with this time.

"I oughta register as a Republican and run against him," I shouted.

Frank, always up for making political mischief, reached under the bar and came up with a voter registration card. And with a somewhat shaky stroke of the pen, I became a Republican.

I didn't remember what I'd done until a few weeks passed and I started getting lots of junk mail addressed to "My Fellow Republican." I quickly reregistered as an independent, swearing never again to join a political party or let Casado ply me with his margaritas.

As for the Eastside hack, he's won reelection regularly ever since, despite his lackluster record. But his days are numbered. In a few years, he'll fall victim to another political reform that California voters enacted by initiative: term limits.

Political party leaders predicted the onset of anarchy in state government when term limits passed in 1990, but it hasn't happened. (Or if it has, nobody has noticed.) We may yet find that open primaries also work out better than naysayers claim. Open voting can cripple the machines' control by giving all primary voters choices outside the anointed favorites. This may not screen out all the hacks and political extremists who've made California politics so unproductive of late. But it does set up one more hurdle for them to overcome before getting elected: the many independent-minded Californians who often don't vote nowadays because we don't like the choices major parties give us.

# Time at Last to Slay a Giant Cliché

**L**OS ANGELES' MAYORAL ELECTION this month confirmed something first noted in last year's presidential vote: The so-called sleeping giant is finally awake. (And this giant is a good deal more pragmatic and less partisan than people had assumed.)

For the better part of a generation, the "sleeping giant" cliché has been used by journalists and academics alike to describe the large but often politically impotent Latino population in California and a handful of other key states.

Like most clichés, it came into such wide use because it seemed to be based on fact: Latinos simply did not turn out to vote in large numbers. As a result, their political clout did not match their numbers in cities like Los Angeles and San Jose, or states like Colorado and Arizona.

That clearly began to change last November when Latinos turned out in record numbers. One postelection survey put Latino turnout in California at 70% of eligible voters, for instance, compared with a 65.5% statewide turnout. And roughly 70% of those cast their ballots for Democrats, helping President Clinton win reelection and 20 Latinos win seats in the state Legislature.

But while the April 8 balloting in Los Angeles also featured a big Latino turnout, the results offer the Republican Party more hope than did the 1996 election. For here, according to a Times exit poll, an estimated 60% of Latino voters chose (albeit in a nominally nonpartisan contest) Mayor Richard Riordan, a Republican.

That means the newly awakened giant is not necessarily angry at the Republican Party — although it is obvious, in retrospect, that it was the GOP that stirred him from a long slumber.

The process began in 1994, when Gov. Pete Wilson decided to use immigration as a "wedge" issue to help him win support among older, mostly Anglo state voters who were concerned about social problems posed by California's changing demographics.

As often happens in the heat of a political campaign, a legitimate but complex issue wound up being distorted into its most simplistic, and scariest, terms. Thus Wilson's immigration wedge was symbolized by Proposition 187, the initiative to bar illegal immigrants from public schools and social services.

And while 187 did get Wilson the support of thousands of worried Anglos, it also frightened thousands of older Latinos who had postponed becoming citizens for many years into finally doing so. And it angered their children into becoming politically active with an eye toward getting back at Wilson and other anti-immigrant candidates in future elections.

That payback process began in the 1996 election, when GOP presidential candidate Bob Dole unwisely took Wilson's advice and also tried to play the anti-immigrant card, this time with a notable lack of success.

But Riordan's victory suggests that the simmering anger that new Latino voters have against the GOP can be overcome.

Riordan did it by being a centrist mayor who worked not just with Latino business people, his natural constituency. He also reached out to the many poor and working-class Latinos who, while more inclined to support Democrats, are far less interested in a candidate's party or ideology than whether he or she has practical solutions to their problems.

Riordan's pragmatism was symbolized during the Los Angeles campaign by his vocal and enthusiastic support for Proposition BB, the $2.4-billion school bond initiative on the ballot. The overwhelming majority of students in the city's schools are now Latinos, so BB was a gut-level issue to their newly enfranchised parents.

That's why 80% of Latinos voted for BB, according to The Times' exit poll, providing the votes that helped the bond measure exceed the difficult constitutional requirement that any tax increase must be approved by a two-thirds margin.

Riordan has shown his fellow Republicans that they can get along quite well with the giant they have awakened. But first, GOP leaders must rethink strategies that can anger or alienate Latinos — immigrant-bashing or issues that can be perceived as immigrant-bashing, like trying to make English the official language or cutting government benefits to legal immigrants.

Having had to write about the "sleeping giant" more times than I care to remember during a long career in journalism, it's nice to finally put that cliché to rest. But while doing so, I would advise the Republican Party to look past another time-worn cliché, this from the realm of children's fairy tales:

Giants aren't always threatening.

# Exaggerating an 'Ethnic' Rift

**M**UCH IS BEING MADE of the ethnic difference that may have played a part in a recent hard-fought election in the San Fernando Valley. Too much, in fact.

So much that an otherwise routine rivalry between ambitious politicians — one of whom happens to be Latino and one of whom happens to be Jewish — is being blown out of proportion. The two pols, of course, are former state Assemblyman Richard Katz and City Councilman Richard Alarcon.

Both badly wanted the Democratic Party's nomination for the 20th state Senate District seat, representing the eastern end of the Valley. They spent roughly $750,000 apiece trying to win it in last month's primary election. Alarcon came out ahead by a mere 29 votes out of 77,127 cast.

In any election, such a narrow margin brings the news media arunning to remind an increasingly apathetic electorate how important even one vote can be. But another more volatile element has been injected into postmortems on the Katz-Alarcon contest: ethnic politics.

Katz is Jewish. Alarcon is Mexican American. Large numbers of both groups live in the 20th District. Both candidates sought votes all over the district but obviously looked to their own communities for a foundation of support to build a winning campaign. It is the tactics Katz and Alarcon used to solidify their respective foundations that have stirred controversy.

Katz sent out campaign literature that questioned Alarcon's financial dealings as a councilman, suggesting he had "dirty hands." Alarcon claims this was an effort to link him with a controversial Latino council member with whom non-Latinos often confuse him — Richard Alatorre, whose finances are currently under investigation by the FBI.

For his part, Alarcon's campaign sent out a last-minute mailer that linked Katz with past Republican Party efforts to intimidate newly registered Latino voters. Because there are so many new Latino voters in the Valley, Katz claims this tactic amounted to "race baiting," and respected Jewish community organizations agreed with him.

In both instances the tactics were dishonest, if also sadly in keeping with the rough-and-tumble of modern campaigns. They have diminished the reputations of two men that I previously considered among the best and the brightest of local political representatives. That's disappointing. But if the Katz-Alarcon rivalry degenerates into a permanent political estrangement between Latinos and Jews, that would compound disappointment with tragedy.

For there are far more simple, and benign, explanations for what happened in last June's voting than a Latino-Jewish rift.

In my view, Alarcon just ran a better campaign. And I write that not just as a journalist who covered many such campaigns. I also happen to have grown up in the 20th District and still have friends and family living there, from Reseda to Sylmar, who provide as good a source of grass-roots information as any political reporter could ask for.

The assessment of neutral political activists in the 20th District, like members of local labor unions and leaders of such church-based groups as Valley Organized in Community Efforts, is that Alarcon's get-out-the-vote effort was much bigger than Katz's.

One VOICE leader told me she recruited 50 volunteers, "which is a lot for us," to telephone registered voters and remind them to go to the polls. Alarcon had almost 800 volunteers.

"Maybe Katz was complacent," the VOICE leader wondered aloud.

Speaking of complacency, I spoke with several well-to-do political activists who regularly donate to campaigns in the area and who have given money to both Katz and Alarcon in the past. All were pestered by Alarcon this time, and some contributed. Not one heard from Katz, including two who were prepared to help him.

"Alarcon called me 12, 15 times before I spoke with him," said a top executive of a major employer in the district. "He even called my friends and asked why I wasn't returning his calls. I gave him a check just to get rid of him. But Katz never called, which is weird."

Maybe not so weird. I suspect that Katz and his campaign manager, Harvey Englander, were operating from an old paradigm that can hobble Democrats as well as Republicans, although the GOP gets bashed for it more. They assumed that Latinos don't vote in numbers equal to the size of their population.

Consider: As longtime incumbent officeholders in the Valley, both Katz and Alarcon had name identification in the district. Katz's chief advantage was $130,000 left over from his last Assembly campaign. Alarcon's advantage was harder to measure: thousands of freshly minted Latino citizens who had recently registered to vote for the first time.

Under the old paradigm, it was safe for Katz to assume those new citizens would not vote, especially in a primary election where voter turnout is traditionally low. So Katz not only underestimated the eagerness of those new Latino voters, he also underestimated the hunger of his opponent, who pulled out all the stops to get as many of those Latinos to the polls as possible.

So if there is a future trend for Los Angeles elections in the 20th District, it is not a Latino-Jewish rift. It is the willingness of thousands of new Latino voters to turn out at the polls, if they are motivated. And that is no threat to any politician — Jewish, Latino or otherwise — but an opportunity.

JANUARY 12, 2001

# Don't Shed Any Tears Over Linda Chavez

T HE QUESTION WAS NEVER if Linda Chavez would actually become secretary of Labor in President-elect George W. Bush's Cabinet but how long it would be before something she had written, said or done in the past would bring her nomination down in flames.

Two days was faster than even I had expected. But that only proves what a bad idea Chavez's nomination was from the moment the right-wing commentator was suggested for a serious job in the new administration.

Chavez withdrew her name from consideration after it was revealed that in the early 1990s she had allowed an illegal immigrant from Guatemala to live in her home and that, during the vetting process for her nomination, she had not been forthcoming with the FBI about the details. In the political shorthand of Washington, she had a "Zoe Baird problem," so-called after the woman President Clinton failed to get as his first attorney general after her employment of illegal immigrant domestics generated a similar controversy.

Chavez said she didn't want to be a "distraction" to Bush as he moves into the White House. But it's not like she really had all that much to offer beyond being a Spanish-surnamed female who added a bit more gloss to the incoming administration's veneer of ethnic diversity. Truth be told, other women Bush has nominated, like New Jersey Gov. Christie Whitman for the Environmental Protection Agency and former California Agriculture Secretary Ann M. Veneman for the Agriculture Department, are much more qualified and accomplished than Chavez.

Except for stints in government service as a congressional staffer and, later, as head of the U.S. Commission on Civil Rights under President Reagan, Chavez's career has been spent as a member of the so-called chattering class. She writes books and columns out of a series of right-leaning ivory towers inside the Beltway, venturing out long enough to provide a reliably conservative talking head for cable TV talk shows. Her fame is as the professional "anti-Latino" for a variety of right-wing lobbying groups and think tanks.

In contrast, the Mexican American friend Bush named his White House counsel, Texas Supreme Court Justice Alberto R. Gonzales, and the Florida Cuban American he nominated to be his Housing and Urban Development secretary, Mel Martinez, have far more legitimate claims to being genuine Latino leaders. For one thing, both won elections to public office before Bush singled them out for top jobs on his team.

Chavez lost the only election she ever ran in, despite an all-out Republican Party effort in 1986 to elect her to a U.S. Senate seat in Maryland, where she lived at the time. The 53-year-old New Mexico native now lives on the other side of the Potomac River, in Virginia. Which only reinforces my view that Chavez epitomizes a breed of professional "Hispanics" — I call them Beltway Bandidos.

There aren't that many of them, but like Chavez, who first moved to Washington in the 1970s, they find the heady atmosphere of the nation's capital more edifying (not to mention profitable) than working in the trenches of this nation's far-flung barrios and *colonias*.

Most of the Beltway Bandidos are political liberals. But even that worked to the advantage of someone as patently ambitious as Chavez, who spurned her roots in the Democratic Party to become one of the political right's most reliable mouthpieces. She lent her Spanish surname to groups that oppose bilingual education, affirmative action, minimum wage laws and other issues promoted by mainstream Latino civil rights groups.

Being a knee-jerk contrarian is simple when you spend most of your career in the unreal hot-house that is official Washington. It is easier to dismiss the minimum wage as a "Marxist" idea, as Chavez once did, when you don't come into daily contact with the millions of Latinos and other working poor for whom a minimum wage increase can mean the difference between sleeping on a bed or the floor.

Which is not to say that it's wrong to challenge the sometimes rigid and uncreative agendas of some mainstream Latino groups. Some very thoughtful Latinos do. Essayist Richard Rodriguez and the late Dallas Morning News columnist Richard Estrada come to mind. But Rodriguez is an independent thinker — as Estrada was in his time — capable of staking out positions on any given issue that are as unpredictable as they are provocative. The political right does not like unpredictability, and that has never been a problem with Chavez.

Which is why her conservative sponsors will surely find a cozy place for her to land now that her career arc toward Washington's center of power has been so rudely interrupted. Chavez will land on her feet — leaning, no doubt, to the right.

As for Bush, in the future he needs to look for his Latino appointees as far outside the incestuous little world of Washington as he can. There are plenty of Latino leaders in business, education, law enforcement and other fields who are capable, conservative and far better equipped than Chavez was. Whether they come from his home state of Texas, from California or another state, they're sure to be more pragmatic — and need I add, more effective — than another Beltway Bandido.

# Maywood's Mean
# Money Machine

**A**NY WORKING MOTHER can envision herself in the stressful situation Flor Cervantes faced recently. She finished her shift at a fast-food restaurant and picked up her two children at a day-care center in Montebello. As she hurried home to South Gate, it was hot and the kids were restless. To avoid congestion on the Long Beach Freeway, Cervantes took Slauson Avenue through the city of Maywood. There, she literally came to a roadblock and fell victim to Maywood's draconian policy of holding cars hostage.

Cervantes, a former preschool teacher in Mexico, is an illegal immigrant with no California driver's license. Like many other cities, Maywood not only cites such drivers but impounds their cars. But Maywood police officers take an aggressive approach in looking for cars to impound. They routinely set up roadblocks to catch unlicensed drivers. The vehicles are held the maximum time allowed by state law, 30 days, so the fines and fees add up to hundreds, even thousands, of dollars.

That's what happened to the 12-year-old Dodge minivan that Cervantes was driving in May when she was stopped at one of Maywood's "routine" Friday afternoon traffic checkpoints.

The roadblock created a sizable traffic jam, even by L.A. standards. Cars, trucks and MTA buses were backed up two blocks in one direction and half a mile in the other, into the City of Commerce. A Maywood police officer blocked each of the four traffic lanes, stopping every motorist and asking to see a driver's license. Those who didn't have one were waved to a side street, where a dozen more police officers were waiting.

Also stationed there were six tow trucks to haul cars away. The trucks belong to Maywood Club Tow, which has the contract to handle Maywood's lucrative impound business. Maywood Club Tow executives have not returned phone calls requesting an interview to discuss how much they make off the impounds, but Maywood officials told me their town (just over one square mile, population 28,000) has earned about $1 million over the last 3½ years from its share of the fees and fines.

Cervantes did not realize why traffic was slow ahead of her, although a large electronic sign between traffic lanes was flashing an alert, in English, that a traffic safety checkpoint lay ahead. A few drivers who understood the sign turned back only to be intercepted by Maywood motorcycle cops, who cited them for making illegal U-turns.

When Cervantes got to the head of her lane, she admitted she did not have a license. She was pulled over to a side street, where she asked another officer if he could just cite her for not having a license and not impound the vehicle. Her husband needed the minivan to get to his uphol-stering job in Gardena. She also pointed to her children in the back seat, but the officer refused.

"I was already so ashamed," she said later, "and he made me feel as if I had committed some terrible crime."

Cervantes stepped out of the minivan and unloaded everything she could from the vehicle onto two baby strollers. She used one for 2-year-old Benjie and had 4-year-old Brian push the other as they made their way to a nearby bus stop. Brian began to cry, asking why the police had taken his father's "new" car.

Maywood Police Chief Bruce Leflar wasn't there that hot afternoon, as I was. But he probably would have told Brian his officers were only trying to keep the streets of Maywood safe.

Each month, more than 800,000 vehicles use the city's two main thor-oughfares, Slauson Avenue and Atlantic Boulevard, according to a letter the chief recently wrote to a state legislator who questioned the use of road-blocks at rush hour.

Last year, Maywood police impounded more than 1,800 cars at such roadblocks, intercepted seven drunk drivers and arrested eight other sus-pects, Leflar wrote, making the traffic checkpoints "a success."

Financially speaking, yes, Maywood is a poor city with an annual bud-get of between $8 million and $9 million, so the roughly $250,000 a year it gets from the release, or resale, of impounded cars is not chump change.

But politically, the roadblocks are a public-relations disaster. For every immigrant, such as Cervantes, who assumes the stops are another bur-den that comes with living in the U.S. illegally, there is an angry citizen in Maywood or a nearby city who finds them not only an inconvenience but insulting to the majority of licensed drivers.

Two grass-roots organizations in the area have begun campaigns to abolish the roadblocks, and I'll discuss the statewide ramifications of their efforts in my next column.

But any change in Maywood's policy will be too late for Cervantes. Her husband wanted to reclaim the minivan he bought for $2,000, even though it would cost $1,100 in fines and impound fees. But by the time he scraped the money together by postponing a rent payment, the car had been sold at auction.

"Maybe it's for the best," Cervantes sadly told me. "I really didn't want to miss our rent payment."

----

Soon after this column appeared, Maywood modified its "traffic enforcement" policies, including the impounding of vehicles.

# CHAPTER TWO

# Mexico and Central America

*Immersed in lands brought
to the boiling point*

AS A REPORTER, Frank del Olmo traveled to Central America during the late 1970s to cover revolution and civil conflict. As a columnist, he continued to trek through the highlands of Guatemala, the dirt roads of El Salvador and the mountain hinterlands along the Honduran-Nicaraguan border in the search for truth. Yet, he acknowledged, those who "expect reporters to write about the region as if there were never any confusion ... are asking the impossible — omniscience from human beings who are covering an imprecise and ever-shifting situation."

Based on his reporting, one thing was very clear for del Olmo. After the assassination of Archbishop Oscar Arnulfo Romero of San Salvador, he opposed U.S. aid to the Salvadoran government. Romero, he wrote, had been a critic of the "landed elite that has ruled El Salvador for generations" (2% of the population controlled 60% of the land) and had assailed the "brutality of the ruling military regime."

# The 'Vietnamization' of El Salvador

*"...the contribution of your government, rather than bringing about greater justice and peace in El Salvador, will without a doubt sharpen the repression."*

THOSE WORDS OF WARNING were contained in a letter sent last February by Archbishop Oscar Arnulfo Romero of San Salvador to President Carter.

Romero, at that time the leading voice in El Salvador for moderate social reform, sent his letter to the White House shortly after the administration announced plans to provide $5.7 million in "security assistance" to the Salvadoran government. The assistance was in the form of defensive materiel — flak jackets, tear gas and communications equipment — to be used in dealing with both rightist and leftist violence.

Within a month of sending his letter to Carter, Romero was dead, assassinated by right-wing terrorists as he celebrated Mass. But despite his warning, and his murder, the Carter administration went ahead with its plans to send military aid to El Salvador for the first time in two years.

Why Carter did not heed Romero's warning remains a troubling question. The archbishop had, after all, been regarded around the world as a champion of human rights long before Jimmy Carter was.

Romero was a critic not only of the landed elite that has ruled El Salvador for generations (only 2% of the population controls 60% of the land in that country), but he also criticized the brutality of the military regime of Gen. Carlos Humberto Romero.

When the general was toppled last year in a coup led by "moderate" military men and replaced by a military-civilian junta, the archbishop did not let up in his activism. He continued to argue for land distribution to peasants and for other progressive reforms, and to criticize both terrorists and government security forces for their violence.

When they argued for military aid to El Salvador before Congress,

State Department officials claimed that the five-man junta that replaced Gen. Romero was the best hope for a "moderate" alternative to a leftist takeover in that country. They have since continued to press for more economic and military aid — $5.2 million is the proposed figure for fiscal 1981 — despite increasing evidence that Archbishop Romero's warning was sadly prophetic.

A series of troubling dispatches has come out of El Salvador this month. Most have been lost in the shuffle of election news and speculation about Iran, but they add up to a worrisome picture that some critics of U.S. policy in Central America are calling the "Vietnamization" of El Salvador.

• Oct. 7 — The Washington Post revealed that 300 Salvadoran military officers are being trained at U.S. bases in the Panama Canal Zone on how to deal with guerrillas "while observing human rights."

• Oct. 8 — Maria Magdalena Henriques, 30, official spokeswoman for the country's Human Rights Commission, was found shot to death and buried in a shallow grave alongside a road near the capital city of San Salvador. She had been kidnapped two days earlier on a busy downtown street. Witnesses, including her young son, said her abductors included men in uniform, possibly police.

• Oct. 24 — Ramon Valladares, the executive director of the Human Rights Commission, was killed by automatic-weapons fire while driving along a main avenue in San Salvador. Like the death of his colleague Henriques, his murder was blamed on right-wing terrorists.

Although there are several leftist organizations in El Salvador, experts agree that they are not as well organized or equipped as right-wing groups, which get financial support from wealthy conservative landowners. Which makes the latest dispatch especially ironic:

• Oct. 25 — The New York Times reported that the Salvadoran government recently launched a major offensive against leftist guerrillas in the country's northeast provinces, along the border with Honduras. Heavy artillery and helicopter gunships were being used to clear out suspected encampments. The newspaper's Mexico City correspondent, Alan Riding, quoted guerrilla leaders who claimed that U.S. military advisors were taking part in the fighting.

These final allegations could not be verified by Riding, one of the best reporters in Latin America, or any other foreign journalists because government forces have blocked all access to the besieged provinces since the offensive began. Many news agencies will not even send reporters into the capital because of the danger. Three reporters have been killed in El Salvador this year, and several others, including Riding, have been threatened with death by right-wing terrorists.

So despite all the evidence that most of the violence is being perpetrated by the right wing, the "moderate" junta is working harder to crush leftists organizing among poverty-stricken peasants than to stop rightists who kidnap and murder people on the streets of the nation's capital.

The attacks on the Human Rights Commission are as ominous as Archbishop Romero's murder. Even the late Anastasio Somoza, at the height of his bloody struggle against the Sandinista guerrillas who overthrew him, never turned against the Human Rights Commission in Nicaragua.

The Carter administration and the State Department have not figured it out yet, but the archbishop's murder may well have marked the end to any hope for a "moderate" solution to El Salvador's desperate problems. Almost 8,000 people have died in political violence there so far this year.

Last Sunday, in a homily delivered from the pulpit of the capital's Metropolitan Cathedral, the Rev. Fabian Amaya, who has become one of the Catholic Church's official spokesmen in El Salvador since Archbishop Romero was killed, charged that government forces are carrying out a campaign of genocide against the peasant population of the northeast provinces. (The Red Cross estimates that 40,000 refugees have been displaced by the fighting.)

Amaya said the military's anti-guerrilla campaign was "exterminating a defenseless civilian population … . Women, children and old people are assassinated."

The priest warned that the repression being perpetrated by the Salvadoran junta "is worse in sadism and bloody cruelty than that of the worst days of [Gen.] Romero."

Observers said it was the strongest language heard from that pulpit since Archbishop Romero was murdered. Isn't it time the United States listened?

# Should U.S. Throw Support to Rebels?

ONE IMPORTANT REASON the U.S. policy in El Salvador and the rest of Central America is so controversial these days is the growing apprehension of many Americans that our government is getting involved on the wrong side. It is not the side of the masses of poor peasants who want to feed their children but the side of landed oligarchs who profit from a nearly feudal economic system and of often brutal military men who guard this old order.

Why, the letters to the editor ask constantly, are we aiding a government whose troops kill nuns? Why do we always leave the oppressed and frustrated outside the purview of our foreign policy until Cubans, Soviets or other cynical outsiders step in to manipulate them for their own, usually anti-American, purposes?

The unstated assumption in these concerns is that it doesn't have to be that way, that the United States belongs on the side of the "good guys" or should at least rethink who the "good guys" are in Latin America these days.

What would happen, one is led to speculate, if the United States did offer assistance to the other side in El Salvador and elsewhere in Central America?

Just think of it: Green Berets helping not the old, corrupt dictatorships of the past but the young rebels who just might represent the wave of the future in Latin America — North Americans outdoing the Cubans and Soviets at their own game.

This admittedly provocative idea first occurred to me during a trip to El Salvador, shortly after the Reagan administration first sent U.S. advisors to help train the Salvadoran army. During a visit to the U.S. Embassy, I caught glimpses of a personnel roster lying on the desk of an official who was conducting a briefing session on the military assistance group. I was not surprised to note that, of the 50 or so U.S. officers and noncoms in El Salvador at the time, the majority had Spanish surnames — Cruz, Carmona, Ruiz, Garcia and the like.

It made perfect sense. To train Spanish-speaking soldiers you need Spanish-speaking advisors. And the large Latino community in the United States has contributed more than its share of young men to the armed services who could easily and ably fill that role.

It occurred to me that those professional soldiers could just as easily help the rebel side in the Salvadoran civil war as they could help the security forces, who are in their own way as ragtag and ill-prepared as the guerrillas.

In fact, U.S. fighting men could do the same in any of several Latin American countries that may face serious insurgencies in the near future — Guatemala, Honduras, Colombia, Peru and Bolivia, for example.

I admit that the idea is mind-boggling. One veteran and respected diplomat responded to my "what if" by first snapping that it was "un-American." But this diplomat is one of the more able men whom the United Sates has sent to Latin America in recent years, so his reaction was more thoughtful than that. He correctly pointed out that it would take a remarkable change in U.S. public opinion in general, and the conservative thinking of the Reagan administration in particular, to even consider changing sides in the current Latin American crisis.

There are difficult political questions, and profound moral ones, raised by the idea. Even assuming that the United States wanted to help leftist insurgents in Latin America, could our specialists even identify and locate them, much less co-opt them? And is it right to undermine another government? Right or wrong, plausible or impossible, the fact remains that there are historic precedents for this strategy. The classic example, to my mind, occurred during World War I when some farsighted diplomats in the British Foreign Office anticipated the collapse of the Ottoman Empire in the Middle East.

In an effort to weaken Germany's main ally in the region, Turkey, and to lay the groundwork for future British influence there, an obscure young archeologist serving as an officer with British Army Intelligence in Cairo was dispatch to the Arabian Peninsula. There Maj. T.E. Lawrence organized a ragtag army of Bedouin tribesmen into a remarkably effective fighting force. His exploits were the stuff of legend, and today the world remembers him simply as "Lawrence of Arabia."

But Lawrence's influence extended beyond the battlefield. He was an advisor to the British delegation at the postwar peace conference at

Versailles, where he is credited with helping bring some degree of Arab self-government to the Middle East. He remained for several years afterward as advisor on Arab affairs to the British Foreign Service.

It is not too unreasonable to suggest that any U.S. citizens who fight alongside insurgents in Latin America might be able to render similar services to their country if, someday, their comrades-in-arms came to power.

These days, U.S. policy in Latin America is following a less dramatic course than what I am speculating on. U.S. diplomats now look to middle-class professionals and businessmen, Christian Democrats and Social Democrats, to replace the repressive governments of the past.

The only problem with this sincere and idealistic strategy is that it may be too little, too late. To the Neanderthal right in Latin America, even moderate conservatives are a threat to the established order. Until recently in places like Guatemala and El Salvador, centrist politicians were murdered as quickly and brutally as rebels — along with labor leaders, teachers, journalists, priests, nuns and anyone else who questions things as they are.

That may be changing, but the results of the recent elections in El Salvador, in which several discredited right-wingers were returned to power, do not give one much cause for hope.

The "Lawrence of Arabia" scenario looks better all the time.


JUNE 30, 1983

# Hard Work in an Area of Shadows

IT'S NOT UNUSUAL to hear words of praise for war correspondents killed in the line of duty. It's also not uncommon to hear criticism of their work while they are still alive and working in the line of fire.

That seems contradictory. But then contradictions are a fact of life for journalists working in Central America, like my two friends who died there last week.

Dial Torgerson, The Times' Mexico City bureau chief, and freelance photographer Richard Cross were only the latest casualties of an undeclared border war that has been going on for a year between Honduras and Nicaragua. Although the number of deaths is disputed by the two governments, neutral observers believe that the conflict has claimed 600 lives.

The Nicaraguans contend that Honduras is helping the Reagan administration give aid and comfort to rebels who are trying to overthrow their Sandinista government. The Hondurans deny this, and charge that the Nicaraguans have been firing into their territory constantly without provocation.

Given these circumstances, it is not surprising that the Honduran government at first blamed the deaths of Torgerson and Cross on Sandinista troops' firing from the Nicaraguan side of the border.

The Nicaraguans denied any responsibility, suggesting that the two men were killed either by Honduran troops or by the anti-Sandinista rebels operating inside Honduras. The most recent reports indicate that the two were killed when their small car hit a land mine.

Anyone who has been in the mountainous hinterlands along the Honduran-Nicaraguan border knows how hard it will be ever to find out what really happened. Ironically, Torgerson and Cross were in that backward region of dirt roads, small villages and heavy jungle to try to determine the truth about what is going on there.

The area is only 70 miles from the Honduran capital of Tegucigalpa, but the distance is closer to 160 miles when measured along the narrow, winding, rutted roads that one often must travel in that country. If isolation were measured like distance, it would seem even farther.

The sheer, physical isolation of so many parts of Central America is one thing that even the most well-informed North Americans often fail to comprehend as they try to make sense of the political turmoil that is taking place there. It contributes to the difficulty of trying to piece together some semblance of the truth about a terribly complex situation.

I last traveled the back roads of Honduras two years ago, visiting refugee camps on that country's border with El Salvador. It took two days to cover fewer than 100 miles by Jeep, traversing five mountain ranges. I interviewed dozens of Salvadoran refugees in those camps, who told stories of brutality perpetrated against them by El Salvador's security forces fighting anti-government guerrillas. Their accounts were later disputed by Salvadoran government spokesmen. I had expected that, for during my long trip there was plenty of time to reflect on how horrible things could happen in such an isolated region and never be fully known to the outside world.

Earlier this year I visited the highlands of Guatemala to try to determine the accuracy of reports of brutal fighting there between the Guatemalan army and guerrillas. At one point I traveled over the *Altiplano*, as it to known, in a helicopter, flying down steep jungle canyons and darting between fog-shrouded mountains more than 7,000 feet high. It was remarkable to see small thatched huts clinging to the sides of those steep peaks and hidden amid the green river valleys. And it was eerie to see so many of them devoid of life — no smoky fire, no waving children, no pets or farm animals.

Who drove away the Indian peasants who once lived on those farms? The government blamed it on the guerrillas. Guerrilla spokesmen in Mexico City said that government troops were responsible. And, as much as I want to determine who was telling me the truth, I still cannot say for certain.

The wars now going on in these isolated places understandably have stirred some heated emotions. The journalists who report them are not only in great physical danger — 12 foreign correspondents have been killed in Central America since 1978, along with scores of local reporters and editors — but their accuracy and even their sincerity also are constantly being questioned.

Within days of Torgerson's and Cross' deaths, the news media were criticized by a group of conservative congressmen who met with President Reagan to warn him that his Central American policies were losing public support, Instead of attributing this development to the many shortcomings of Reagan's policies, they blamed it on "the degree to which the news media, both because of bias and because of style, make it very difficult to communicate the problem," according to Rep. Newt Gingrich (R-Ga.).

Political activists on the left make the same complaint about the reporting from Central America. They claim that not enough publicity has been given to human rights abuses by the security forces in El Salvador and Guatemala, or to the CIA's not-so-secret war against Nicaragua.

Few of these critics on either side have any idea what it is like to try to gather information in Central America. Yet both sides expect reporters to write about the region as if there were never any confusion, never any doubts — as if everything always fell into place neatly, confirming the critics' preconceived notions. They are asking the impossible — omniscience from human beings who are covering an imprecise and ever-shifting situation.

Others have already eulogized Torgerson and Cross, so that is not my intent here. I want more understanding of the difficult task confronting their surviving colleagues in Central America — and some appreciation of the work that they are trying to do.

FEBRUARY 28, 1985

# Trying to Get Mexicans to Be Like Us Is Foolish

SOMEHOW I CAN'T GET very worked up about the latest problem in U.S.-Mexico relations resulting from the kidnapping of an American drug agent in that country and the slowness with which Mexican authorities moved to do anything about it.

It is not that the abduction wasn't shocking. When Drug Enforcement Administration agent Enrique S. Camarena was seized by gunmen on Feb. 7, he became the first American lawman to fall victim to drug traffickers abroad in two years. I hope that he can be rescued alive, but, given the brutality of drug traffickers, the odds of that happening don't look good.

Certainly the Reagan administration's reaction to the corruption and slowness of the Mexican legal system was understandable and effective, at least in getting Mexico's attention. U.S. border agents from San Ysidro to Brownsville brought incoming traffic to a standstill by thoroughly checking every vehicle. A few days after the start of the slowdown, dubbed Operation Intercept, Mexican authorities detained three men for questioning. They have since been released.

What troubles me is a frustrating sense of deja vu, the feeling that we've seen this all before. That feeling is especially strong now because I recently finished a new book about Mexico, Alan Riding's "Distant Neighbors" (Knopf), which reminded me of how often similar flare-ups have happened in the past.

Riding was the New York Times correspondent in Mexico from 1971 to 1983 and was a most astute observer of that country. In his book he argues that one of the most profound issues that Mexico will face in the coming years is not an obvious problem such as widespread poverty, overpopulation or the lack of sufficient water resources. The crucial question, as Riding puts it, is whether Mexico can develop and modernize "in harmony with the majority of its population."

Like other Mexico specialists, Riding argues that many of the problems that the country is having today date from the 1940s, when a series of governments began trying to meet the needs and expectations of the country's urbanized upper and middle classes rather than its many rural poor. In trying to satisfy the desires of a small group that was materialistic and increasingly Americanized, political leaders began to lose touch with the vast majority of "ordinary Mexicans," according to Riding.

It is a provocative thesis that is sure to stir emotional debate on both sides of the border. But Riding is onto something. Mexican political leaders and intellectuals won't say it publicly, but many of them admit privately that their country is indeed profoundly torn between remaining genuinely Mexican and becoming a Spanish-speaking version of the United States.

How does this fit into the dispute over the Camarena case and Operation Intercept? Because U.S. officials are once again expecting the Mexican system to react as ours would, when it is not the same thing. And this has been a persistent cause of the often rocky relations between our two countries.

Does anyone remember the first Operation Intercept in 1969? It was carried out by the Nixon administration to stop drug smuggling across the border, lasted three weeks and also forced the Mexicans to cooperate with U.S. drug agents. They did so aggressively, and within a few years 600 U.S. citizens were languishing in Mexican prisons on drug-related charges.

And then Mexico faced a new problem with the United States: the alleged mistreatment of U.S. citizens in Mexican jails. The hue and cry over that issue forced the State Department to negotiate a prisoner-exchange treaty with Mexico that is in effect to this day.

When the first prisoners who were exchanged under the treaty flew to San Diego from Mexico City in 1976, they were met by a large contingent of the news media and cheering relatives. A Mexican federal agent commented bitterly to me that it looked more like a welcome for returning heroes than for convicted felons. He reminded me why the anti-drug crackdown happened in the first place and asked ruefully, "What do we have to do to please you people?"

I didn't know quite what to tell him. But I know what many other U.S. citizens would have said: We want you to be like us. We want Mexico's political system to be "democratic," we want Mexican business to be efficient and we want Mexicans to disapprove of the things that we disapprove of — from drug abuse to communist influence in Central America.

The problem with this point of view is that it overlooks the fact that Mexico is not the United States and that most Mexicans are not like us. And as long as we try to force them to adopt our view of the world, flare-ups such as this most recent one are inevitable.

So commonplace and pervasive is the view in this country that something is "wrong" with Mexico that I am not sure that things would change even if many people read Riding's book. But if he makes more of us appreciate how different we "distant neighbors" really are, it might make our periodic disputes easier to understand — if not easier to live with.

MARCH 14, 1985

# Washington Is Hypocritical and Naive on El Salvador

IN THE STEADY STREAM of tragic news coming out of Central America, it is easy to forget pivotal events that took place there not so long ago — even shocking occurrences like the assassination of El Salvador's Archbishop Oscar Arnulfo Romero five years ago this month.

A forthright spokesman for peace and justice in a troubled nation, Romero was gunned down in cold blood while celebrating Mass. His murder not only traumatized El Salvador, it also focused international attention on the civil war just starting.

Romero's murder is still unsolved. Not even the government of President Jose Napoleon Duarte, so admired by the Reagan administration and others in Washington for bringing reform and moderation to El Salvador's political system, has made any progress on the case.

It's not that there have been no leads. Within a few days, investigators came up with circumstantial evidence pointing to a conspiracy of right-wing vigilantes — including an obscure army intelligence officer, Roberto D'Aubuisson.

What was lacking was the will to pursue prosecution. The government consisted of an unstable coalition of moderate civilians and mid-level military officers that did not have the leverage or authority to face down El Salvador's powerful military establishment, an old-boy network that protected officers like D'Aubuisson.

These days the Reagan administration would have us believe that things have changed in El Salvador. Duarte was freely elected to be the country's chief executive last year and now claims to have the military under control. The enlisted men arrested on suspicion of killing four American churchwomen were convicted, the first time that Salvadoran soldiers accused of harming civilians were brought to justice.

But no army officer has yet been convicted of a major crime in El Salvador. Even the young lieutenant identified by witnesses as having been involved with the murder of two U.S. labor advisors in 1981 was merely drummed out of the corps.

The most egregious example of how entrenched El Salvador's military caste remains is D'Aubuisson. He is a downright respectable political leader these days. And, in one of the saddest ironies of the civil war, his ARENA party is on the verge of winning more political power in elections to be held March 31, one week after the anniversary of Romero's death.

Lately D'Aubuisson has been talking seriously about becoming president of El Salvador someday, which could happen more easily than U.S. officials might care to admit. Ever since Duarte beat D'Aubuisson in last year's presidential election, ARENA and the other right-wing parties that control the National Assembly have made life miserable for Duarte's Christian Democrats. They have methodically dismantled the reforms that U.S. officials boast about. And, by drafting election laws advantageous to ARENA, the rightists have laid the groundwork for eliminating Duarte — constitutionally.

Some of those new laws, enacted despite Duarte's vetoes, will be tested when Salvadorans go to the polls March 31 to elect new assembly members. The most important allows political coalitions, like the one formed by the right-wing parties, to run the same list of candidates under the different party symbols. Those are important in a country with so many illiterate voters, and analysts expect the tactic to help ARENA and other rightist parties maintain control of the assembly, and possibly even gain some seats.

Christian Democrats are trying to discredit ARENA by making a campaign issue of an incident that was big news in El Salvador but got little attention in this country: the arrest of a D'Aubuisson associate, Francisco Guirola, in Texas last month.

Guirola, one of the original financiers of ARENA when it was founded three years ago, was arrested Feb. 6 by U.S. Customs agents on suspicion of trying to smuggle $5.8 million in cash out of the United States. U.S. officials have been tight-lipped about the case since then. Guirola's links to D'Aubuisson were not mentioned at all until they were revealed by my Times colleague Laurie Becklund and Craig Pyes of the Center for Investigative Reporting.

When seized, Guirola was preparing to fly to El Salvador in an executive jet with eight suitcases filled with 58,000 well-worn $100 bills. That is not the kind of money raised at bake sales, and within days of the arrest a State Department official told National Public Radio that he was "90% certain" that Guirola was carrying drug money. Guirola is now being held in lieu of $2 million bail and is due to appear in federal court in Corpus Christi on April 1.

Modern political campaigns are expensive, and El Salvador is poor. So we should not be surprised if some Salvadoran politicians, like officials in underdeveloped nations all over the world, try to make money any way they can — possibly even through drugs. To assume anything else is naive.

But the Reagan administration compounds naivete with hypocrisy. For at a time when it is trying to persuade Americans that El Salvador's government is moderate and reformist, D'Aubuisson and his ilk are living proof that the Salvadoran political system has a long way to go before we can forget the corrupt, right-wing dictatorships of the recent past. And their brutish reputation won't fade away as long as the memory of Archbishop Romero is alive.

# Nicaragua Myths: As Fuzzy as Our Alamo Impressions

I FIND IT FITTING that President Reagan put his new propaganda campaign against Nicaragua into high gear in the same week in which Texas began its official commemoration of 150 years of independence from Mexico. Both events coincide with the anniversary of one of the most famous and widely misunderstood battles in American history — the siege of the Alamo.

In 1836 in San Antonio, 188 rebels held off Gen. Antonio Lopez de Santa Anna's army for 13 days during the war for Texas' independence. Although the Alamo was eventually overrun, the defenders' stand spawned a famous battle cry and has been immortalized in American myth as a magnificent fight against hopeless odds.

And therein lies the problem, because the popular stories of that battle have been badly distorted by the American media — from dime novels to television.

The romanticized stories of the Alamo are based largely on anti-Mexican propaganda that grew out of the Texas rebellion. Not surprisingly, they portray Davy Crockett and other fighters inside the Alamo as good guys and Santa Anna and his troops as bad guys. These versions omit some significant facts, such as the presence of Mexicans among the Alamo's defenders. There was, after all, significant pro-independence sentiment among Mexican settlers in Texas at the time.

Also, while the Alamo's defenders were outnumbered, they had better firepower and other important advantages over Santa Anna. They had 21 cannons to the Mexicans' 10, their long rifles were far more accurate and deadly than the Mexicans' muskets, and they were holed up in what in those days was considered the strongest fort west of the Mississippi River.

This is not to downplay the significance of the Alamo, only to describe the battle more realistically. It was not the hopeless but idealistic fight of Hollywood sagas. The point is relevant today because it is not just dishonest to portray historic events as simplistic struggles of good-against-evil, it can also be dangerous. Look at what Reagan is doing with Nicaragua.

In his new campaign against the Sandinistas, Reagan wants Congress to give $100 million in military aid to anti-government rebels, the so-called Contras. But the Contras are a losing proposition. Even their boosters in the Reagan administration admit privately that they do not have enough popular support in Nicaragua to defeat the Sandinistas. While they get some aid from peasants in the rural areas where they operate and from groups such as the Miskito Indians that have clearly been mistreated by the Sandinista regime, they have not developed the widespread popular support that a guerrilla movement needs to survive.

Congress suspects this and is resisting Reagan's aid request. So the president is trying to sway public opinion by describing the Nicaraguan crisis in dramatic but distorted terms. Nicaragua is a struggle between "freedom fighters" and communist tyrants, he says. In fairness, some of Reagan's critics are just as bad. They describe the Sandinistas as secular saints, while the Contras are dismissed as hateful remnants of former Nicaraguan dictator Anastasio Somoza's army. Both views are terribly simplistic or cynically dishonest.

Earlier this week Reagan showed his support for the Contras by meeting with several of their leaders. One was Alfonso Robelo, a former member of Nicaragua's revolutionary government who has since fled the country and joined the opposition forces. Robelo is a living example of how complex the reality of Nicaragua is.

When I first met Robelo in 1978, during the early days of the rebellion that overthrew Somoza and brought the Sandinistas to power, he was accompanied by an activist priest, Miguel D'Escoto. Today D'Escoto is the foreign minister of Nicaragua and a harsh critic of Reagan's policy. That day, however, both men attacked Somoza and said that Nicaraguans supported the Sandinistas.

Although they are on opposite sides now, Robelo and D'Escoto are decent, compassionate men in a complex struggle that will not end quickly or easily. But as long as someone like Robelo is with the Contras, they are more than the Somocista brutes that their critics claim. And with men like D'Escoto on their side, the Sandinistas will be more than the atheist thugs that Reagan insists they are.

This uncomfortable reality does not make for neat, simple answers to Nicaragua's problems. Unlike the movies, the good guys don't always wear white and the bad guys black. And things are not resolved in a few hours.

That's why the only thing that giving the Contras $100 million will guarantee is more bloodshed.

These subtleties may be lost on Reagan, who apparently spent too much time in Hollywood before shifting to the complexities of foreign policy. So it would help if, the next time the president describes Nicaragua in simple and dramatic terms, we remember the Alamo. The real Alamo, not the Hollywood myth.

MAY 15, 1986

# Guatemala's New President: Democrat, Survivor, Optimist

GUATEMALA CITY — When I first interviewed Vinicio Cerezo Arevalo in 1983, a contingent of bodyguards picked me up in an armored van and made me put on a bulletproof vest before driving to his home. When I asked about the security measures, Cerezo replied, "Actually, things are better in Guatemala than they used to be. I sleep in my own home every night nowadays, instead of moving around all the time."

I suspected then that Cerezo, the head of Guatemala's Christian Democratic Party, was a remarkably optimistic man. Now I know for sure. Last December, Cerezo was elected his country's first civilian president in 16 years. And, despite a host of internal and international problems, Cerezo is still an optimist. He talks as if he needs only a single five-year term to turn things around.

It's easy to be optimistic, I suppose, when you survive three assassination attempts, as Cerezo has. Characteristically, he considers the attempts on his life to have been "no big thing," just part of political life in Guatemala, where 40,000 persons have died in political violence in the last 20 years.

It is clear in retrospect that Cerezo was right in 1983 when he said that things were improving in Guatemala. The year before, the last in a long line of corrupt, brutal military rulers had been overthrown by younger, more progressive military officers who named the fervently religious Gen. Efrain Rios Montt president.

Rios Montt gave the young officers permission to combat a growing guerrilla movement with a counter-insurgency campaign called *fusiles y frijoles* — bullets and beans — that mixed military force with social programs designed to win the support of Guatemala's desperately poor rural population. Repression was lessened (at least by Guatemalan standards), and the insurgency was reduced to a mere nuisance. Rios Montt also began the political process that led to the presidential election and Cerezo's inauguration in January.

Cerezo has cultivated the support of the same young officers who put Rios Montt in power. At least publicly, they claim to now support Cerezo's effort to move Guatemala toward more democracy. But while the army may be content, the rest of Guatemalan society is not. The economy is in recession; there are shortages of staples like sugar and rice; joblessness and underemployment are estimated at 50%; inflation is approaching 60%.

The nation's private sector, one of the most rigidly conservative in Latin America, is unhappy with Cerezo's plan to use government funds to buy land for distribution to peasants. Cerezo won't call this process "land reform," a term that Guatemala's right wing equates with communism, but that doesn't make it any more palatable to the 3% of landowners who control 80% of the farmland.

Cerezo's old friends on the Guatemalan left are also upset with him. On May Day, some labor unions paraded with banners claiming that Cerezo's economic policies were anti-worker.

International and Guatemalan human-rights groups fault Cerezo for not arresting former military leaders suspected of corruption and brutality. Instead, he promises to appoint a commission to investigate human-rights abuses, including disappearances of thousands of political activists.

Asked about all of these criticisms, Cerezo reminds the questioner that he has been in office five months, while Guatemala's political problems have festered for more than 30 years — since 1954, when a CIA-inspired coup overthrew a leftist government and brought Guatemala under rightist and military control for a generation. A brutal system in place that long can only be changed "very carefully," he says.

Cerezo, who is 44, was a student in 1954. To explain his patient approach to politics, Cerezo likes to tell the story of a friend he had in college. Like Cerezo, the young man was active in politics, but he often criticized Cerezo for aligning himself with the Christian Democrats.

"My friend was Marxist and insisted that he would come to political power faster and more decisively through guerrilla warfare," Cerezo recalled. "He went his way; I went mine. It took a while, but today I'm in the National Palace and he's still in the mountains."

Such faith in peaceful political reform is so desperately needed in Central America these days that one might expect prompt and eager U.S. support for Cerezo. But he does not get on well with the Reagan administration.

Like the military leaders that preceded him, Cerezo will not support President Reagan's covert war against Nicaragua. Cerezo believes that the Sandinistas should be bargained with rather than overthrown. He points out, with some annoyance, that the administration has asked Congress for only $40 million in aid for Guatemala while seeking $100 million for Nicaragua's Contra rebels.

Cerezo is a vocal supporter of the Contadora Group's efforts to write a peace treaty for Nicaragua and its neighbors. He is also promoting the idea of a Central American parliament, to include elected representatives from every country in the region, to be used as a permanent forum where border incidents and other regional problems can be discussed. It will be on the agenda when Cerezo hosts a summit meeting of Central American presidents later this month.

Given the harsh reality of Central America these days — Nicaragua gearing up for war with the United States, El Salvador's government beset by guerrillas, Honduras and Costa Rica letting anti-Sandinista rebels use their territory for attacks against Nicaragua — Cerezo's talk about a regional parliament may sound like a foolish dream. But it used to sound foolish when he talked about being president someday.

# Is Negroponte Clean Enough for the U.N.?

W E'RE EYEBALL TO EYEBALL with the Chinese, talking tough to the Russians and not talking to North Korea at all. It's back to the Cold War.

Call me parochial, but what has me shivering after a brief but chilly visit to Washington is how the Bush administration is reviving the old U.S.-Soviet standoff in a part of the world where I spent my crazy youth as a correspondent: Central America. And if you loved how the Bushies tossed those alleged Russian spies out of the country, wait until you see what's for dessert. Warmed over Contras!

Or, to be more precise, a warmed-over Contra paymaster, John D. Negroponte, who has been nominated to be ambassador to the United Nations.

You remember the Contras — the CIA-funded guerrillas who waged a futile war to overthrow the revolutionary Sandinista government in Nicaragua, until the Nicaraguan people simply voted the Sandinistas out of power. Even those poor Central Americans, it turned out, know how democracy works. But more on the Contras later.

It is no longer news that most of the men (doesn't national security advisor Condoleezza Rice know any women she can suggest for some of these jobs?) President Bush wants to put in key positions on his foreign policy team are Cold Warriors from the days of Presidents Reagan and Bush the First. But some of the guys being hauled out of cold storage have worrisome histories that Congress needs to revisit before punching their tickets. We can start with Negroponte.

During his 37-year career with the State Department, Negroponte has held several sensitive embassy jobs in Asia (Vietnam, during the war, and the Philippines in the 1990s) and Latin America (Mexico, in the years leading up to the North American Free Trade Agreement, and Honduras, during the start of the Contra war against neighboring Nicaragua). It is Negroponte's tenure in Honduras, from 1981 to 1985, that the Senate needs to consider.

I traveled all over Central America in those days, knew Negroponte and members of his staff and have no illusions about anyone who was involved in those brush-fire wars. Some ugly things were done on both sides in the name of national security — from assassinations to wholesale massacres. It was quite literally a bloody mess, and Negroponte was in it up to his elbows.

Just how deep we don't know because Negroponte's involvement in covert U.S. activities in Honduras has never been fully investigated by Congress, even when the Mexican government protested Negroponte's 1989 appointment to run the U.S. Embassy there. Former Mexican President Carlos Salinas de Gortari wanted NAFTA so badly that he probably would have accepted any U.S. ambassador. Knowing that, Congress stamped Negroponte's passport after some token questions about Honduras.

Since then, however, much more has become public, largely because of an excellent, but insufficiently recognized, series of articles published by the Baltimore Sun in 1995. Through interviews with former Honduran soldiers and some of the people they kidnapped and tortured, the articles laid out in gruesome detail the activities of a CIA-funded death squad run by the Honduran military during the Contra war.

Those articles also made a credible case that Negroponte knew about the Honduran death squad, officially known as Battalion 316, and other covert operations taking place under his nose, and he ignored them. Worse, he may have lied to Congress about what he knew.

The Sun documents the fact that embassy staffers knew about human rights violations and duly reported them to their superiors in the embassy (including Negroponte) and Washington. Yet their annual human-rights reports to Congress did not reflect what they knew was going on all around them. In just one of the less egregious cases (no one was killed), the 1982 year-end report to Congress asserted there had been "no incident of official interference with the media" that year. Yet in June 1982, Negroponte had personally intervened with the Hondurans to free a prominent journalist, Oscar Reyes, who had been arrested and tortured by Battalion 316 for a week. The ambassador did so at the behest of his embassy's press spokesman, who warned Negroponte: "We cannot let this guy get hurt. ... It would be a disaster for our policy."

The Sun series should be reread by every member of the Senate before Negroponte comes before them for confirmation later this spring. Better yet, the Foreign Affairs Committee should move beyond what one gutsy newspaper did and thoroughly review any and all still-classified documents that might shed light on just what Negroponte knew about Battalion 316 and the wider Contra war, and when he knew it.

Negroponte is, after all, the guy Bush wants in New York to lecture the Chinese and Cubans about human rights. We ought to be sure they won't have reason to laugh in his face when he does.

# CHAPTER THREE

# Latino California

## A Golden State that can give or take our American Dreams

FRANK DEL OLMO LOVED CALIFORNIA and he felt pride about its multiethnic heritage, including his own Chicano background. He also saw its dark side and wrote to illuminate the implications of misguided policies and attitudes that attempted to demonize Latinos, such as English-only laws.

A lover of history, he had a keen eye for seeing developments that, at first glance, were seemingly small but could prove to be pivotal. One such column was on Latino youth rekindling "the spark of activism" after the passage of a controversial California ballot measure, Proposition 187.

Del Olmo had a way of telling California stories that were compelling, candid or just plain fun. One such gem described the East Los Angeles rock band Los Lobos, then enjoying its first national crossover success. In these columns, readers could better understand, or be introduced to, del Olmo's vision of California, its possibilities, promises and challenges.

# They Are a People Living on the Bridge Between Two Worlds

**N**OW THAT THE TIMES is concluding its three-week series of articles on Latinos in Southern California, about as detailed and thorough a look at that community as any newspaper has ever attempted, there can't be too many questions about Latinos left unanswered for either Latino or non-Latino readers — except one.

Why bother?

It may seem unusual in a city founded by Mexicans, in a state where thousands of place names are Spanish and where 4.5 million people — 20% of the population — are of Latin American extraction, but the question does get asked. And not just by Anglo newcomers. Many longtime residents, even a few with Spanish surnames, wonder why Latinos should be seen any differently than the dozens of other ethnic groups that preceded them into the proverbial American melting pot.

What sets Latinos apart from the other ethnic groups that have contributed to the United States, each in their own unique way and often despite discriminatory treatment, is the fact that for Latinos the language and culture of their Latin American homeland has not faded away with the passage of time. And it will not fade away in the foreseeable future. The homeland is so close that migration to the United States continues virtually unabated to the present day.

Because of this unique situation, Latinos face a choice that no other ethnic group in this nation has had to deal with. How much of their home language and culture should they give up to blend into the Anglo-American mainstream? Or should they give up any at all?

By now it is well known that a Latino can be born, live a long life and die in parts of this country — East Los Angeles, for example, or South Texas — and never speak a word of English or have any significant intercourse with non-Latinos. It is doubtful that this ever really happens, of course, but that doesn't make it any less possible.

To one degree or another, this cultural and linguistic duality is at the root of many of the problems Latinos face in this society — the lack of economic opportunities, limited political representation, the high dropout rates among Latino students in school and colleges.

But as troublesome as it might be in social terms, the Latino's cultural duality is also logical. It is an outgrowth of the fact that the U.S.-Mexican borderlands are the meeting ground of two great cultures — the Anglo-American tradition of the United States and Canada to the north, and the lbero-Indian tradition of Latin America to the south. And any people who have lived in such a region as long as Latinos have will serve as a bridge between two cultures and languages, wittingly or unwittingly.

Once this historic reality is accepted, some of the more controversial goals Latino activists are striving for can be better understood.

Almost everyone wants to reduce the high dropout rates among Latino students, for example. And few people would object to efforts aimed at getting more Latinos to become citizens and vote. But when Latinos push bilingual education or bilingual ballots as answers to these problems, they are also asking for something more profound: acceptance of the fact that the Spanish language is a common means of communication in this country.

Few people would seriously argue that farmworkers don't deserve better pay and working conditions for harvesting this nation's agricultural bounty. And any humane person wants the exploitation of undocumented aliens in our urban industries to be prevented. But when Latinos suggest that these migrant workers could defend themselves more readily if they belonged to unions, and if those who are not citizens had their immigration status legalized, they are also asking for an acceptance of the fact that Latino labor has been important to this country in the past, and still is.

I will concede that both of the previous paragraphs oversimplify some extremely complicated issues, but the key word in them is "acceptance." That summarizes what Latinos want of this society — acceptance not only as individuals but of their cultural heritage. And by heritage I do not mean just food and music, but language and the cultural perspectives that come with it.

In the meantime, it will be difficult for Latinos to be fully accepted in any field of endeavor without limiting to a certain extent their role as Latino spokesmen. Politics is the one area where that is not necessarily all bad. For it is in the give-and-take of public life, and in debating public-policy issues, that Latinos will most clearly define their differences from other Americans yet still find areas of agreement where compromise can be hammered out.

The diversity of the local Latino community was an important underlying theme in The Times series. But it would have been surprising if that community were not diverse, including as it does 3 million people living from Santa Barbara to San Diego, of different social classes, and with varied attitudes toward politics, the arts, religion, morality and even relations between the sexes.

Yet while conceding that this diversity makes generalizations difficult, I have concluded my work on this series convinced that there are notions and issues that unify most Latinos, even across class and political lines.

One is that cliché-burdened but still viable concept Latinos call *el Sueno Americano.* As the headline on one article in The Times series proclaimed, the American Dream is still very much alive in the barrios. And Latinos define that dream of success the same way most other Americans do: a productive career or job with decent pay, a nice home in a pleasant neighborhood, an enjoyable family life and a secure future for their children.

Latinos also want to retain whatever Spanish they know and pass it along to their children. But they are also fully aware that English is the key to success in this country, and so they want to speak both languages.

Finally, we all revere our Latin American heritage. And we took forward to a time when it gets the respect and understanding — the acceptance — it has always deserved from a nation whose rich past it helped build and whose future it can make even richer.

---

This column was part of The Times' 1983 series, "Latinos in Southern California," which won the 1984 Pulitzer Prize for Meritorious Public Service.

# Cross-Over Band:
# Music to Our Ears

**B**ACK IN THE 1950s, in Pacoima's barrio, one of my many childhood fantasies involved starting up a rock 'n' roll band. My aggregation had no name, but in my imagination it had everything else needed to duplicate the hits of those days: electric and acoustic guitars, a set of drums and plenty of saxophones. Of course, my group would have the taste, and skills, eclectic enough to also play jazz, rhythm and blues, country-western music and even the romantic Latin American ballads that my mother loved.

That long-forgotten fantasy came back to me last Saturday night as I sat in the audience at the Greek Theatre, listening to a group from East Los Angeles do exactly what I had once daydreamed about.

Los Lobos, as they are known, are rising stars of the national music scene who play in a wide variety of styles with remarkable ease. Their focus is rock, but they also play blues, country music and even Mexican *norteños* — those wonderfully upbeat polkas often referred to in this country as Tex-Mex music. Four of Los Lobos — guitarists David Hidalgo, Cesar Rosas and Conrad Lozano and drummer Louie Perez — have been together more than 10 years, since they came together as students to play traditional Latin American music. Since expanding into rock three years ago, they have been augmented by saxophonist Steve Berlin.

The concert at the Greek was Los Lobos' hometown stop on a tour that began on the East Coast and will wind up in Japan. Not bad for a bunch of guys who billed themselves, on one of their first albums, as "just another band from East L.A."

The tunes that touched me the most on Saturday night were not only "golden oldies" from the '50s; they were also songs from *my* '50s, in Pacoima: "Come On, Let's Go" and the rock version of the traditional Mexican folk song "La Bamba." Both were made famous by a young rock singer known to the world at large as Ritchie Valens. In Pacoima, his hometown, he was Richard Valenzuela.

Valens was never a major star in rock music, although some students of the field argue that he might have become one had he not died prematurely in 1959, at age 17, in an airplane crash while on tour. Also killed in that accident was Buddy Holly, who at 20 had already set the rock 'n' roll world on its ear. It was Holly's death that made national headlines. They even made a movie about Holly's life, while Valens' name faded into relative obscurity.

But he was not forgotten in Pacoima and other Latino barrios. He certainly helped inspire my youthful fantasy. Valens' success still fuels the more substantial dreams of the many young Chicano musicians who hope to make it big someday but bide their time playing neighborhood parties and dance clubs — just as Los Lobos did until a couple of years ago.

Los Lobos say that they include "oldies" in their act as a tribute to the inspirational role that Valens and other Chicano rock musicians of the '50s played for them. The resounding audience response indicates that the feeling is widely shared. But there is more to Los Lobos' success than that.

Like Valens before them, Los Lobos play up their ethnic background and draw white, mainstream rock fans into it. When they sing a popular Mexican ballad like "Volver, Volver," or a *norteño* polka, they toss in shouts — *gritos*, as Mexican music fans call them — of passionate enthusiasm. They make the fun infectious even for the non-Latinos in the audience (on Saturday night, young Anglos appeared to be the majority).

While there have been many Latino cross-over stars in popular music, Valens was one of the first to do what Mexican Americans in many other fields of endeavor, well beyond music, are trying to do today. He successfully melded the traditional culture of his forebears with the American culture of his own time. Rather than moving from one into another, he tried to bridge the gap, and created something new in the process.

That's what Los Lobos were doing Saturday night. The near-capacity crowd roared its approval and danced in the aisles on every number. And when the set was over, there were, appropriately enough, two encores.

One for Los Lobos and one for Ritchie Valens.

# Latino, *Sí* — Hispanic, *No*

OR SEVERAL YEARS NOW I have waged a personal campaign against the growing use of the ugly and imprecise word "Hispanic" as the term to describe all United States residents of Latin American extraction. It seems to be a losing battle because the U.S. government and corporate America, including my colleagues in the news media, persist in using the word.

But I have not changed my mind. In fact, I am rapidly coming to the conclusion that we must not only do away with the word "Hispanic," but the whole artificial concept behind its use. For, contrary to what some self-serving Latino activists would have us believe, there is no ethnic group, or voting bloc, in this country that can accurately be called "Hispanic."

To explain why, I must restate my objections to the word itself:

First, it is not what Latinos normally call themselves. Walk into a Latin American barrio, from East L.A. to Miami's Calle Ocho, and ask people what they are. You'll get all kinds of answers, including Latino, Chicano, Boricua, Cubano, Mexicano. But unless you wander into the offices of some government-funded poverty program, you won't hear people call themselves "Hispanic." The closest you'll come — in New Mexico, where some residents trace their ancestry to the state's Spanish settlers — is Hispano. But note that they use the original Spanish word, not a translation.

Second, the word has become bureaucratized. Census officials, under pressure to get a more accurate count in 1980 of persons of Latin American extraction living in this country, needed one word that would cover Mexican Americans, Puerto Ricans and Cuban Americans, as well as immigrants from every place south of the Rio Grande. They picked "Hispanic" out of the dictionary, where it is defined as an adjective referring to Spanish, or Spanish and Portuguese. A better choice would have been Latino, which the dictionary defines as a noun referring to a Latin American. The word is widely used by Latinos already, as noted above.

This pressure for a categorical word to define an ethnic grouping was put on the Census Bureau by Latino activists who argued, with some merit, that the consistent undercount of Latinos in this country was depriving them, and the states and cities where they lived, of their fair share of government funds and services. But once it was used by government, the word "Hispanic" began to be applied far too loosely.

Corporations and the media picked it up. When the Census Bureau announced that it had, indeed, undercounted the number of Latinos in this country and that they were, in fact, one of the fastest-growing segments of the national population, every political interest group that could claim even tenuous ties to the Latino community organized a "Hispanic caucus."

True, the various Latin American groups in this country share ties of commonality. Most are members of the Roman Catholic Church or other Christian religions, so they work together quite effectively on religious issues. Most speak some Spanish, so Cuban Americans from Florida work with Chicanos from California to fight laws that limit the use of Spanish in this country and to promote bilingual education programs for Spanish-speaking youngsters.

But beyond language and religion — and especially in politics — there is little commonality among U.S. Latinos. When they vote as a bloc, it is in local elections as a Chicano bloc, a Cuban bloc or a Puerto Rican bloc. They have never done it as a "Hispanic" bloc in a national vote. My views on this were reinforced last week at a University of Texas conference on "Ignored Voices: Public Opinion Polls and the Latino Community."

Representatives of several polling organizations, including the Gallup Poll, the New York Times-CBS Poll and the Los Angeles Times Poll, attended. And all of them explained how hard it is for them to get a precise fix on what the Latinos think about national issues and even how they may have voted in a national election.

In the 1984 presidential vote, for example, the three major broadcast networks varied — from 32% to 46% — in their estimates of President Reagan's Latino support. The best explanation for this uncomfortably wide margin was offered by a polling specialist for the Southwest Voter Registration and Education Project, which has run hundreds of voter registration drives in Latino communities across the nation and keeps a careful tab on Latino voting tendencies. Their breakdown of Reagan's Latino support focused on national-origin groups in different parts of the country. Project analysts found that Reagan's support ranged from 93% among Miami's Cubans to 18% among Mexican Americans in the Midwest. What political professional in his right mind would lump two such disparate groups into a single voting bloc?

Even Rep. Bill Richardson (D-N.M.), the chairman of the Congressional Hispanic Caucus, admitted in his keynote speech that this year the caucus (which is made up of 17 congressmen of Mexican, Puerto Rican and Portuguese descent) has not voted as a bloc on such "Hispanic" issues as immigration reform and aid to the Contras in Nicaragua.

These realities should dispel the myth that all Latinos in this country fit into a single-interest group. At the very least, they should force all the "Hispanic" promoters to be precise about which people they are referring to.

JULY 30, 1987

# Homeboys and Heroes

THIS IS MY LAST COLUMN for a while. My plan was to go back to my old neighborhood in Pacoima and write about the place. It's a run-down part of town, but it's getting more positive attention these days than it usually does, because it was also home to Ritchie Valens, a Chicano rock 'n' roll idol whose brief stardom is the subject of a new movie.

That film, "La Bamba," named after a hit record that Valens made by adapting a Mexican folk tune to a '50s rock beat, appears to be a mainstream success. Even if it isn't, it will be eagerly devoured by Latino audiences, ever hungry for entertainment that positively portrays their community or features Latino heroes and role-models.

Valens, whose real name was Richard Valenzuela, was only 17 when he died in 1959 in an airplane crash that also killed Buddy Holly, another rising young rock star. As with many public figures who die young, the lingering interest in Valens' life stems not just from what he achieved; we wonder what might have been had he lived.

So, after seeing the movie, I thought that I'd return to the old barrio and write something about the homeboy who made good and maybe even some upbeat things about Pacoima itself.

But then they killed Alejandro Salazar.

Alejandro was only 10 when he died last week, hit by a stray bullet fired by a gang member. As I read news accounts of the incident, I could see it precisely.

Alejandro was walking home from Pacoima Recreation Center, the city park where I played every day as a child. It's right across the street from San Fernando Gardens, the housing project where I grew up and where Alejandro lived with his parents, a sister and a brother.

He was standing just outside the park fence, a few yards down from Pacoima Elementary School, where he was in fourth grade. Across the street is Guardian Angel, the Roman Catholic parish school. I attended both as a youngster.

Alejandro's friends said that he was trying to come up with enough change to buy an ice cream from a street vendor when a scuffle broke out between a local Latino punk who deals drugs and some would-be customers, who were black. Also nearby were members of a street gang that have claimed the housing project as their turf. Seeing a homeboy hassled by blacks, one of the gang members pulled a gun and started spraying shots about wildly. Alejandro fell to the ground, blood spurting from his head. He died in a hospital a few hours later.

Alejandro Salazar was the seventh child to be killed or wounded by stray gang bullets this month in the Los Angeles area.

The homeboys are being quiet about it. "They're going around with their heads low right now," according to Manuel Velasquez, a local gang worker. "But I wonder how long it will last."

Velasquez has good reason to be dubious. For six years he has been a street worker for the Community Youth Gang Services Project, the county agency that tries to intervene to stop gang violence before it happens. He's a courageous, caring young man, but he knows the gang mentality all too well.

Chilling as it sounds, the cretins who contributed to Alejandro's death are trying to rationalize what happened.

"Now that one of their friends has been arrested," Velasquez told me, "some of them are saying it wasn't his fault, but the blacks' [fault] for buying drugs, or the guy who was dealing."

Right, fellas. You were just defending the barrio against interlopers. What asinine, macho stupidity!

I remember … .

Growing up in Pacoima 30 years ago, I was supposed to hate guys from San Fernando just because they were from San Fer and I was from Pacas. It makes no more sense now than it did then. And I don't know what makes me angrier about it — the fact that such a backward mentality is still there after all these years, or the fact that Chicanos like me who grew up in places like Pacoima, but moved away, haven't done more to help snuff it out.

Oh, I know all the reasons youth gangs exist — poverty and unemployment, fed by racism and discrimination. I try to struggle against those problems whenever I can, and maybe someday we'll have them licked. But, damn it, in the meantime we must do more to protect innocents like Alejandro Salazar.

More gang workers like Velasquez would sure help. Right now he and the important program that he works for don't get nearly enough money. The gang project's budget is so tight that Velasquez and one other street worker must cover the entire San Fernando Valley, keeping track of more than 80 gangs — a dozen in Pacoima alone. And you can multiply his problems by the hundreds in South-Central Los Angeles and East L.A., in Santa Ana and Riverside.

I'm grateful that people like Velasquez are out there trying to keep a lid on the insanity that lurks on some of our meaner streets. If we need either role models or unsung heroes, there they are, right under our noses. But we don't do nearly enough to help them control the punks like the one who killed Alejandro. As long as there are losers like that around, the many winners that the Latino barrios produce will never get the attention that they deserve.

Alejandro Salazar was just an average student, according to the staff at Pacoima Elementary School — but he was also a popular kid who "had everything going for him," in the words of Principal Robert Owens. He might not have been another Albert Einstein, but maybe he could have been another Ritchie Valens. And until those of us who presume to lead, or speak for, the Latino community do more to abolish gangs, the achievements of Chicanos like Valens will seem shallow in the eyes of society at large.

# It's Hard to Read the Message of Olvera Street in Laker T-Shirts and Tourist Gimcracks

**W**ERE IT NOT for a children's book that I first read as a small boy, it would be awfully hard for this somewhat jaded adult to work up any affection for the worn alley, known as Olvera Street, that marks the birthplace of the city of Los Angeles.

There, 40-odd Mexican settlers founded a pueblo in 1781. It did not take long for Los Angeles to sprawl beyond the community that those settlers laid out, in Latin American fashion, around a plaza and a church. By the 19th century, the area was known as Sonora Town, the city's first barrio. Olvera Street was a slum when civic leaders first restored it as a Mexican-style marketplace in the 1930s.

Many Latinos still remember when Olvera Street and the adjacent plaza were the heart of the Mexican American community — a place where people gathered for social and civic events. But to a kid from the faraway San Fernando Valley, Olvera Street was a place visited only infrequently. And I remember being taken aback when I first saw it in the early 1950s.

Before that my only exposure to La Calle Olvera was through a small book titled "Pedro, the Angel of Olvera Street" by children's author Leo Politi. It is a delightful story, one that I later enjoyed reading to my own daughter. It explains the Mexican Christmas pageant known as Las Posadas, which reenacts the search of Joseph and Mary for lodging in Bethlehem, through the eyes of a boy who portrays an angel in the celebration held on Olvera Street.

The picture that Politi drew of the street was simple and idyllic, far from the gritty reality of the place. And the more I know about Olvera Street as an adult, the less idyllic it seems.

It saddens me to admit that there are times when I have been ashamed to show visitors the place where my hometown was founded. It's not that the surrounding neighborhood is a bit seedy; downtown in any major American city looks about the same. My problem is with the street itself. While merchants who run the tourist-oriented shops and restaurants have made an admirable effort to preserve its Mexican character, the street's ambience, by the most generous standards, is tacky.

A few stores sell genuine Mexican folk art. But too many are cluttered with Laker T-shirts, Hollywood-sign ashtrays and similar junk. There is not enough parking. And the place is not cleaned as often as it should be. It's a sign of how much Olvera Street still means to local Latinos that so many keep going there in spite of its many shortcomings.

Thankfully, most of the street's merchants know that it needs sprucing up. And those who doubt it need only ponder the effects of urban renewal in nearby Chinatown and Little Tokyo to see what could happen to Olvera Street if they do not take some initiative.

That's why merchants on the street began working two years ago to develop their own plans for upgrading and modernizing Olvera Street, with the cooperation of some Latino architects and several preservationist groups. Because of their self-interest and knowledge of Olvera Street's history, the merchants say, they have the sensitivity needed to carefully oversee its restoration. But their efforts have not been without infighting.

Earlier this year a dissident group called the Business Leadership of Olvera Street broke off from the long-established Olvera Street Merchants Assn. For the last few months they have been at loggerheads, each group insisting that it should take the lead in restoration of the street. Normally one might expect these factions to compromise, but the estrangement is actually growing worse. A key reason is that, despite smaller numbers, the Business Leadership has the advantage of close ties to Eastside Council-man Richard Alatorre. The strong-willed councilman has his own ideas of how Olvera Street should change and would prefer to work with whichever group is most amenable.

The coming year is likely to be pivotal for Olvera Street's future, for two reasons:

• By Jan. 1, the control of the land on which it sits will pass to the city from the state of California, which has owned it as part of El Pueblo de Los Angeles State Historic Park. That move will eliminate many bureaucratic roadblocks that delayed renewal and will speed the decision-making process.

• Next spring, the city will have a mayoral election, and the Olvera Street Merchants Assn. wants to use the opportunity to pressure Mayor Tom Bradley, and his opponents like Westside Councilman Zev Yaroslavsky, to take a stand on the street's future. So far, Bradley has let Alatorre take the lead rather than intervening on an issue that many people think has city-wide implications.

The Olvera Street Merchants Assn.'s strategy will not endear it to the mayor, who'd prefer to get reelected with as little controversy as possible. But it makes coldhearted sense. It's a sure sign that the era of naive innocence on Olvera Street is dead. Once the battle there spills over from the Eastside, whatever benign impressions about Olvera Street still exist in the rest of the city will surely die too.

My daughter is a teenager now and seems to have outgrown her childhood enjoyment of Olvera Street and its Las Posadas pageant. But I may take her one last time before Christmas. The way things are going, neither of us will be able to look at Olvera Street in quite the same way again.

NOVEMBER 13, 1995

# Latino Youth Rekindle the Spark of Activism

THERE'S A JOAN BAEZ SONG with a line in it about "little victories and big defeats." I'm not doing justice to her poetry by summarizing it, but the moral is that the former help make the latter more tolerable.

That's how I feel now that San Francisco voters have rejected a move to restore the old name of the city street that last January was renamed in honor of the late farm labor leader Cesar Chavez. The vote against Proposition O, which would have changed the name of the nondescript roadway that runs through the predominantly Latino Mission District back to Army Street, was 55% to 45%.

It was a symbolic victory for the 100,000 residents of San Francisco who are Latino. Having a street named after a revered Mexican American is a point of pride for them. And some Latinos I know in the Bay Area even see the Proposition O vote as one of those little victories that could help heal the sting of the big defeat California Latinos suffered a year ago.

I refer, of course, to the vote on Proposition 187, the muddled initiative that a relative handful of anti-immigrant extremists and political snake-oil salesmen sold California voters as a "solution" to the state's illegal alien "problem."

Not surprisingly, since the most visible illegal immigrants in California are from Mexico, the campaign for 187 had a decidedly anti-Latino tone. Politicians who used it to boost their own campaigns, from Republican Gov. Pete Wilson to Democratic Sen. Dianne Feinstein, aired countless TV spots showing illegal immigrants sneaking across our southern border.

Not surprisingly, 187 passed easily despite such an ugly campaign. Most Californians aren't as extreme in their views as 187's loudest proponents, but they do worry about the influx of immigrants to this state. Exit polls indicated that people voted for Proposition 187 because they wanted to "send a message" to Washington, where immigration policy is set.

Those same exit polls showed that Latino voters did not join the pro-187 consensus. Although pre-election polls found that Latinos are every bit as concerned as non-Latinos about illegal immigration, almost 80% voted against 187. Again, that is really no surprise. Latinos were put off by the tone of the 187 campaign.

Many Latinos remain angry about Proposition 187, but a year of hindsight makes it easier to see some good things that happened as a result of it. The most obvious is the fact that Latino immigrants, who have traditionally had the lowest naturalization rate of all immigrants to this country, are now applying for citizenship in record numbers.

Less obvious but potentially just as important is the fact that the campaign against 187 helped politicize a younger generation of California Latinos, many of them the children of immigrants. Those young people were well on their way to assimilating to life in this country and probably would never have thought of themselves as anything but Americans until Proposition 187 came along.

Even those who were too young to vote against 187 reacted to the campaign that portrayed their parents and neighbors so negatively by asserting their pride as Latinos. That is why there were so many anti-187 protests at high schools and colleges throughout California. And that is also why so many Mexican flags were visible at those protests.

To this day, veteran Latino politicos complain about those Mexican flags. They're convinced that such displays of cultural pride hurt the anti-187 campaign.

I'm not so sure. The momentum behind 187 was so great that nothing could beat it. So it is far more important that those young people expressed their pride by waving the flag of their parents' homeland than it would have been to leave the flag home for the sake of a few more votes. It was part of the consciousness-raising that will make them more dedicated community activists in the years to come.

What brings all this to mind is the fact that several Latinos I spoke to in San Francisco this week mentioned the highly visible role that young Latinos played in the campaign against Proposition O.

"I figured the vote would be close," said Juan Gonzalez, the publisher of El Tecolote, a weekly bilingual newspaper. "But then a lot of the kids got energized, not just by pride over Cesar Chavez Street but by the anti-curfew campaign."

He was referring to another ballot measure, Proposition L, promoted by Mayor Frank Jordan, to impose a tougher curfew on young people in the city as an anti-crime measure.

"I thought the curfew would pass with ease," Gonzalez said. "It was a law-and-order issue, and Jordan's an ex-cop." But Proposition L was defeated, and Gonzalez thinks young people were a key factor in that outcome.

Like Proposition 187, Propositions O and L "gave kids an impetus to get involved with politics," Gonzalez said, "Now that they see we can win some of these campaigns, I think many of them will stay energized."

Here's hoping Gonzalez is right and that these little victories — like that one big defeat — may portend better things, someday, for California Latinos.

MARCH 11, 1996

# All It Takes Is a Glimpse of Possibilities

**L**AST SATURDAY was NetDay. And if you have only a vague notion what that means, don't feel too bad about it.

Like me, you are probably among those who are still tiptoeing uneasily into that brave new world where the boundaries are only defined by the technical limits of personal computers and their links to the Internet. To hear computer enthusiasts talk, that means it is a world with virtually no boundaries.

NetDay was the idea of two such enthusiasts: John Gage, the chief scientist for Sun Microsystems in the Silicon Valley, and Michael Kaufman, director of information technology at a San Francisco TV station. They organized it as a "high-tech barn-raising." The goal was to have all 13,000 public, private and parochial schools in California linked to the Internet by community volunteers.

A wonderful idea, to be sure. So engaging that it even drew President Clinton to California to help out.

Clinton and Vice President Al Gore joined volunteers at a Concord high school in wiring the school's computers to accommodate access to the Internet. This was supposed to illustrate Clinton's recent pledge to invest $2 billion in federal money to have every classroom in the United States connected to the Internet by the year 2000.

Sound gimmicky? Of course. Which may account for the somewhat jaded news media reporting building up to the event.

The political press saw Clinton making yet one more pitch for support in the state with the most electoral votes. But even news stories that focused on NetDay and its laudatory goal seemed to accentuate the negative. The New York Times quoted educators who are dubious that putting an Internet-linked computer in every classroom will make much of a difference. A front-page article in this newspaper in advance of the event noted how many schools in Los Angeles couldn't even find sponsors to pay for the $400 NetDay wiring kits or the volunteers to help install them — a pity, given the magnitude of the challenge facing our Los Angeles schools as they try to prepare kids from poor minority or immigrant families for the high-tech jobs of the 21st century.

This challenge was underscored in an important report issued last month by the Tomas Rivera Center, a Latino public-policy think tank affiliated with the Claremont Colleges and the University of Texas.

Based on U.S. census data, the report estimated that African American and Latino youngsters lag four years behind their Anglo counterparts in having access to computers in school. Because of their parents' low incomes and limited educations, young Latinos are less likely than young Anglos to have access to a computer at home; only one Latino household in eight has a home computer, half the number in non-Hispanic white households. So if there is hope for Latino kids becoming computer-literate, the report concludes, it must start in the schools. They are "perhaps the central gateway through which Latinos can become full participants in the information society."

The report urges high-tech companies to market their products more aggressively, and where possible more inexpensively, to minorities. And it calls for government policies that would ensure the widest possible public access to new information technologies.

Sound recommendations. But if I have come to one conclusion about the information and technology revolution, it is that government policies and corporate decisions will inevitably lag behind the efforts of the thousands of computer enthusiasts who worked last Saturday trying to get all California schools on the Net.

A perfect example of what can be accomplished by giving a kid just a small glimpse of his own possibilities is the computer whiz closest to me — my 12-year-old nephew Hugo Gutierrez, a sixth-grader at Alisal Elementary School, a predominantly Latino school in Salinas.

Hugo was first exposed to computers at school because, a few years back, the local Latino activists who took control of the Alisal district school board made getting their students online a top priority. Hugo did so well on the school machines that his parents decided to make the financial sacrifices it took to buy him a home computer. Now, he not only helps his Uncle Frank through the maze of the Internet but some of his teachers too.

If little Hugo can do it, so can the many other Latino kids who are as much a part of this state's future as the high-tech industries that they will one day work for and run. Who knows? A youngster exposed to computers at school may become the engineer who someday designs the personal computer that even the poorest family can afford to have at home.

SEPTEMBER 21, 1997

# Mother Agnes Knew the Score

I WAS SADDENED to learn last week that one of the toughest and most influential teachers in my life — a Roman Catholic nun I knew only as Mother Agnes — is dead.

Saddened, but not surprised. I had not seen her in 30 years, since I graduated from high school in the San Fernando Valley. She was elderly even then. Elderly but still tough, with that deep reservoir of quiet strength that the truly faithful carry within themselves.

Mother Agnes was a native of Mexico and a member of an order of nuns called the Religious of Jesus and Mary. For two generations they have provided teachers for the Catholic school I attended from the fourth through the eighth grades, Guardian Angel in Pacoima.

That was in the early 1960s, and back then there were not many neighborhoods in Los Angeles tougher or poorer than the public housing project where I lived, the San Fernando Gardens. "The projects," as everyone called them, surround Guardian Angel. Yet Mother Agnes, who was both a teacher and the principal, and the other nuns strove mightily to keep crime and other dangers outside the schoolyard gates.

I telephoned Guardian Angel last week hoping to find Mother Agnes, if she was alive. I wanted to ask if she remembered an incident that is still vivid in my mind and that I planned to talk about at a dinner where I was to be honored as a role model for Latino youngsters by the Boy Scouts of America.

It happened when I was 13 and preparing to leave Guardian Angel for high school. Filled with adolescent hubris, a handful of eighth-grade classmates and I ditched class one day to eat at a nearby hamburger stand. Of course, we got caught and were severely disciplined.

But I will never forget how Mother Agnes singled me out for special attention. She took me into her office and gave me a tongue-lashing that still burns my ears after all this time.

"I'm more disappointed in you than any of those others," she said. "You're the smartest boy in school, yet you led your classmates wrong rather than right."

Toward the end of this stern lecture that seemed to last hours but was really only minutes, her voice softened. "If only you knew what you can achieve if you just set your mind to it," she said almost wistfully.

At that moment, feeling as if I'd let the whole world down, those words of encouragement from Mother Agnes resonated like a reprieve from heaven itself.

As she escorted me from her office, Mother Agnes handed me a paperback book — the Boy Scout Manual. I don't know where she got it, but she urged me to read it and consider becoming a Scout. "I know you have what it takes," she added with a wink.

Sadly, I was never able to join the Boy Scouts. My mother could find no Scouting program in the Pacoima area. And in retrospect, I now realize that a single mother struggling to raise six kids in a housing project probably could not have afforded it even if she had found one.

But I kept the manual, read it carefully and learned many things both practical and philosophical. Not least among them is how universal are those qualities of character that Scouting teaches — honesty, reverence, cleanliness, bravery and all the rest. They are so universal than even a Mexican nun in a barrio school knew that when she needed help keeping a potentially troubled kid straight, she could look to the Boy Scout Manual for assistance.

I did share that anecdote with the Boy Scouts' San Gabriel Valley Council the other night, when they honored me and two far-more deserving Latino businessmen, George de la Torre of Juanita Foods and Carlos A. Perez of Deloitte & Touche. For it almost perfectly illustrates the importance of what the civic leaders who run that Boy Scout council are trying to do.

Five years ago, they looked at the changing demographics of the San Gabriel Valley and saw a challenge. Although the Scouting-age population in local schools was roughly 53% Latino, there were only about 1,300 Latino Scouts. So they launched a recruiting and fundraising drive to make sure that any Latino youngsters who want to become Scouts can do so, and to help any boy who needs financial aid to do it.

Today the San Gabriel Valley has 9,000 Latino Scouts, and the local council is pushing to recruit even more. Amid all the statistics we hear about youth crime and gangs in Los Angeles County, that number is the most encouraging I've heard in a long time.

I share it with readers of The Times not just to give you some hope about the future of this city and its young people, but as a useful reminder.

All too often when we in the news media report on gangs, we do so with an eye toward what new programs and initiatives might be out there to solve a seemingly permanent problem. But let's not overlook the "old" solutions that are still out there — Boy Scouts, Boys and Girls Clubs and the like. They are still pretty darned effective too, if only we will support them and make them accessible to as many kids as possible.

JUNE 29, 1997

# Who Remembers the Invasion of Catalina?

THE SUMMER OF 1972 saw the waning of what Chicano activists refer to as *el movimiento*. But don't look for anyone to note the 25th anniversary this year, because, in the words of the poet, it ended with a whimper.

"The movement" was a period that began in the late 1960s when urban Latinos, inspired by Cesar Chavez's unionizing drive among farmworkers, tried to create a civil rights movement akin to that long waged by African Americans. From San Antonio's West Side to East Los Angeles, *el movimiento* had its moments but could not last as a pale imitation of the black civil rights struggle. The history of Mexican Americans and other Latinos in this country is too different from the African American experience.

But I'm less concerned with revisiting those distinctions than with recalling the two simultaneous events in September 1972 that marked both a high point and a nadir of *el movimiento* — the La Raza Unida Party convention and the "invasion" of Santa Catalina Island by the Brown Berets. A backward glance illustrates how difficult it is to tell, at the time, which news events will really matter in the long run.

I chose to cover La Raza Unida's convention instead of the Catalina incident, although colleagues at this newspaper questioned my news judgment. Some still may. But in the long run, we were all wrong.

I'd reported on La Raza Unida's electoral takeover of some mostly Mexican American towns in South Texas in 1970, so it seemed logical to be at the El Paso convention where the Chicano party was threatening to nominate its own presidential candidate, undermining an already uphill struggle by Democratic Sen. George McGovern to unseat Richard Nixon.

It later turned out (as a sidelight of the Watergate investigation) that the Nixon campaign secretly funneled money to some La Raza Unida activists. But even if La Raza Unida had not been dragged into national politics, it was newsworthy to cover one of the few occasions that Chicano icons like La Raza Unida founder Jose Angel Gutierrez, Colorado activist Rodolfo "Corky" Gonzalez and New Mexico's fiery Reies Lopez Tijerina came together to plan a common strategy.

They didn't get very far, of course. In the end, La Raza Unida did not nominate anyone for president and wound up a local party in Texas, with a few sympathizers elsewhere in the Southwest. But the Brown Berets' "invasion" of Catalina faded from memory even faster.

That bit of political theater was carried out by a few stragglers of what had once been one of the most visible Chicano groups of the *movimiento* era. Modeled after the Black Panthers, the Brown Berets dressed in military-style tunics and the head gear from which they took their name. But despite their militant stance, the group never amounted to much more than a self-styled Chicano security force.

Still, in the aftermath of the 1970 East Los Angeles riots, they became an obvious target for infiltration and intimidation by police and the FBI, which helped hasten their demise. When The Times' city desk telephoned me in El Paso to tell me about the Catalina incident, it was the first I'd heard of the Brown Berets for a couple of years.

Leaders of the "invasion" claimed that under provisions of the 1848 treaty ending the Mexican-American War, California's coastal islands were still Mexican property. So they sailed to Catalina on tourist boats, put up a Mexican flag and claimed the island on behalf of all Chicanos. Their bravado got no support in Los Angeles, much less in Mexico City. I told my colleagues not to panic and suggested they send another reporter to Catalina rather than bring me back from Texas.

Thus my colleague Dial Torgerson was there a couple of days later when sheriff's deputies marched into the small encampment the Brown Berets had set up near the town of Avalon, cited some for trespassing and took everyone back to the mainland.

The Catalina story wound up on Page 1. My stories from Texas were published on Page 3. While La Raza's story was more important, I can't fault my colleagues' news judgment. The "invasion" was one of those only-in-L.A. stories that deserve coverage.

In retrospect, I missed part of a bigger story in Texas. For even as La Raza Unida was getting ink from me, the New York Times and other national publications, other Texas Chicanos were quietly doing the dull behind-the-scenes work needed to make political progress for Latinos.

They included Willie Velasquez, who founded the Southwest Voter Registration Project by signing up thousands of voters all over Texas; Ernesto Cortes, who helped organize the barrios of San Antonio into a potent political force; and Henry Cisneros, a young college professor who would become San Antonio's mayor, then a Cabinet member in the Clinton administration and who now heads Univision, the Spanish-language television network. I would meet and write about them later; but only after all the sound and fury of La Raza Unida and the Brown Berets had faded.

MARCH 1, 1998

# Line Drawn in 1848 Shaped Who We Are

I FIND IT ODD that so many people in this country are taking note of the centennial of the outbreak of the Spanish-American war — the sinking of the battleship Maine was on Feb. 15, 1898 — while at the same time virtually ignoring an important anniversary in the Mexican-American War.

I refer to the 150th anniversary of the signing of the Treaty of Guadalupe Hidalgo, which on Feb. 2, 1848, ended hostilities in a much longer (22 months as opposed to four) conflict.

The Spanish-American War certainly merits attention. It made this country a world power when Washington wrested from Spain not just

Caribbean islands like Cuba and Puerto Rico, but key outposts in the Pacific like the Philippines and Guam.

But the spoils of the Mexican War are not to be denigrated. The peace treaty, named after the Mexico City suburb where it was signed, acknowledged the United States' annexation of Texas as a state and ceded half of Mexico's territory to this country — land that today includes all or parts of California, Arizona, New Mexico, Utah, Colorado and Montana.

Other effects of the Treaty of Guadalupe Hidalgo also resonate to the present day. Its echoes are heard in debates over everything from illegal immigration to NAFTA to which national team Mexican-born soccer fans in Los Angeles should root for.

To begin with, the Treaty of Guadalupe Hidalgo created the first generation of Mexican Americans by guaranteeing the Mexicans who inhabited the ceded territories the right to their property, language and culture. To this day there are Latino activists who cite the treaty, and not more recent civil rights laws, as the legal basis for programs like bilingual education. I personally think such arguments are on shaky ground, given how much things have changed in the Southwest since 1848. But that doesn't make the argument any less interesting or provocative.

Of more relevance, to my mind, is that the Treaty of Guadalupe Hidalgo put the western end of the U.S.-Mexico border in an utterly illogical — and ultimately rather futile — place.

As the final details of the treaty were being hammered out by diplomats in Mexico City, there was uncertainty almost to the last moment over where exactly to draw a new U.S. border with Mexico. The Mexicans wanted to draw the line at the 37th parallel, just south of Monterey. They assumed the United States would be satisfied with the two fine harbors offered by the San Francisco and Monterey bays. But U.S. negotiators also wanted the harbor at San Diego included in the deal.

According to a San Diego State University historian, Richard Griswold del Castillo, the Mexicans tried to keep San Diego by insisting that the mission there had long been considered the northernmost outpost of Baja California. But their claim was disproved when a young military officer in the U.S. delegation, a Virginian named Robert E. Lee who would go on to fame in the Civil War, researched the Mexican archives and came up with proof that the mission San Diego de Alcala was actually the southernmost outpost of the province of Alta California.

With the conquering army of Gen. Winfield Scott still occupying Mexico City, the U.S. argument carried the day and the U.S.-California border was set at "one marine league due south of the southernmost point" of San Diego Bay. That is where it runs today, between the San Diego suburb of San Ysidro and the Mexican metropolis of Tijuana.

And for all the controversy that still flies around that border, over drug smuggling and other crimes, immigration, pollution and the like, there is no denying that both San Diego and Tijuana have prospered from the relative openness of their mutual frontier.

One suspects that is how Lee and the other U.S. negotiators wanted it. For if the U.S. had really wanted a virtually impenetrable border with Mexico, it would have drawn the line somewhere else in 1848. Maybe not below Monterey Bay but perhaps along the spine of California's rugged coastal mountains, leaving the ocean side to Mexico.

Imagine a border running from where the Santa Ynez Mountains rise north of Santa Barbara, to the San Gabriel and San Bernardino Mountains that loom above the Los Angeles Basin. From the terminus of those mountain ranges all the way to the Rio Grande in southern New Mexico, the Mojave and Sonora deserts provide another formidable barrier. Even in modern times, such a border would have been virtually impassable by anyone who didn't have a legitimate reason to cross.

But in 1848, a victorious United States wanted all it could get from Mexico and pretty much came away with it. In the process it got a little more than it bargained for, not least a whole lot of Mexican Americans whose distant cousins continue to live and work in the Southwest, and far beyond it, to this very day.

There are plenty of U.S. citizens who worry about that, I know. But it does help explain why, to most Latinos, the migration of Mexicans back and forth across our southern border seems a perfectly natural and normal part of life. And for all our efforts to change it through immigration restrictions and bigger border fences, we shouldn't expect it to change very much.

{ CHAPTER FOUR }

# Unions and the Grass Roots

*The struggle for rights, wages and a future itself*

FRANK DEL OLMO HAD A GREAT appreciation for the work of Saul Alinsky, the passionate Russian Jewish author of the 1946 book "Reveille for Radicals" and his "people's organizations" in the slums of Chicago.

Frank believed in going beyond the traditional political parties to inform readers about alternative forms of community-based action. Using Alinsky's organizing methods, groups like UNO (the United Neighborhoods Organization) made their mark in Los Angeles, San Antonio and other cities. Better known nationally was the organizing work in the fields by the United Farm Workers and its Alinsky-trained leader, Cesar Chavez.

Through del Olmo, readers also learned about grass-roots leaders such as Father Greg Boyle, the Jesuit pastor of a poor Los Angeles church, who focused his ministry "on people shunned and feared by many, Latino gang members."

Frank reveled in telling the often-ignored social justice stories of the working poor becoming empowered to change their lives.

# Killing of Farmworker
# Casts Shadow on Sacramento

WHO IS TO BLAME for the death of Rene Lopez? The 21-year-old farmworker was shot to death two weeks ago, after a union representation election at the Sikkema Family Farm dairy in Caruthers, near Fresno. But the ramifications of his death reach all the way to the state Capitol in Sacramento.

The young Mexican American had been employed at the Sikkema dairy for eight months and had a reputation as an outspoken worker who often "confronted the bosses," according to colleagues. Lopez was one of the workers who asked the United Farm Workers union to represent the Sikkema employees after they had been told that their wages would be lowered as an economy measure.

The dairy's employees walked off the job Sept. 15, and the United Farm Workers petitioned the state's Agricultural Labor Relations Board to hold a union representation election. The vote was scheduled for Sept. 21 and was conducted by two agents from the board's Fresno office.

Just after the voting had been completed, two men who had been working as strikebreakers at the dairy drove up to the company-owned housing where Lopez lived, about 100 yards from the polling place. The two men, Dietmar Ahsmann, 30, the brother-in-law of dairy owner Ralph Sikkema, and Donato Estrada, 26, called out to him from their car. As Lopez approached the vehicle, he fell to the ground with a bullet wound in the head.

Lopez died two days later. Estrada and Ahsmann were charged with murder.

Cesar Chavez, president of the United Farm Workers union, has charged that others share the responsibility for Lopez's killing, regardless of what is determined in the Estrada and Ahsmann case. He blames the California growers who have vehemently, even rabidly, opposed his unionizing efforts for almost 20 years. And he blames Gov. George Deukmejian for weakening the Agricultural Labor Relations Board.

Chavez has a point. For all the strikes, boycotts and other disruptions that preceded its creation in 1975, the board has been remarkably successful in settling farm labor disputes peaceably. It has conducted almost 800 elections involving 75,000 workers, according to a spokesman. And the Lopez shooting marked only the second time that an election has been marred by violence.

Not all California growers object to their workers belonging to unions. But anyone who knows agribusiness in this state knows that there are farmers who still cannot resign themselves to the fact that the days are long gone when they could rely on an uncomplaining and pliable farm labor force, like the braceros brought in from Mexico during the 1940s. One San Joaquin Valley politician once sadly told me that for these growers "even the 1940s would not be far enough back in time."

The hostility of these rigidly anti-union farmers toward their workers is reflected in the way in which they often react to strikes or organizing drives. As a reporter I covered the United Farm Workers' activities during the 1970s, and I can recall dozens of instances in which growers hired local thugs, or ill-trained security guards, to keep an eye on striking farmworkers.

The very presence of such rugged characters in already tense situations could lead to violent incidents. Afterward the union would blame it on the grower's "goons," and the grower would blame it on union "radicals." While I was rarely able to sort out which version was the truth, I know who usually lost those confrontations. The four persons who have died as a result of strike-related violence in California agriculture in the last decade were all with the United Farm Workers.

"I don't think they tell these rough men to come out and shoot us," Chavez said after Lopez's funeral. But he warned that there can be no lasting peace in California's fields until growers "refrain from hiring the kind of violent men who shot and killed Lopez."

But that will happen only if government strictly enforces the state's Agricultural Labor Relations Act, which not only guarantees farmworkers the right to decide whether they want to belong to unions but also includes provisions to protect them against violence and intimidation.

This is where Deukmejian's attitude comes in. While the governor has never shown the overt contempt for farmworkers that some California farmers express, he has shown little respect for the law designed to protect farmworkers' rights. Last year Deukmejian made it clear to growers, who were major supporters in his election campaign, that he would change the way in which the Agricultural Labor Relations Board operated once he was in office. Since then he has appointed a chief counsel for the agency, David Stirling, who says that he must correct its pro-union slant. Deukmejian has also cut the board's budget 27%, forcing staff reductions and delays in the adjudication of worker complaints.

By cutting at it so drastically, Deukmejian is undermining the board's ability to effectively enforce the law that it was created to uphold. The director of the board's Fresno office, for example, says that without the recent budget cuts he would have had more agents to oversee the Sikkema dairy election.

Deukmejian built his political career by being a tough law-and-order man. So he should know better than anyone what happens when laws, and their enforcement, are taken lightly. People start thinking that they can ignore them. And that, I fear, is the message that some California farmers are getting these days from the state's chief executive about the Agricultural Labor Relations Act.

Deukmejian should set them straight, before Chavez and the United Farm Workers have any more martyrs.

NOVEMBER 21, 1985

# Olympic $ Should Be Shared With the Ghetto and Barrio

THERE IS AN INTERESTING CONTEST left over from the 1984 Olympics that will go into its first round today: a test of wills over how to spend the estimated $90-million profit from the Games.

On one side is the Los Angeles Olympic Organizing Committee, the well-connected local business and political leaders who brought the Summer Games to this city over the objections of many doubters and cynics, and made them a success. They have regrouped as the Los Angeles Organizing Committee Amateur Athletic Foundation in order to distribute the local share of Olympic profits.

On the other side are the United Neighborhoods Organization of East Los Angeles and the South-Central Organizing Committee, two of the largest and most influential groups in the city's Latino and black neighborhoods. In recent years, UNO and SCOC have also accomplished things that doubters and cynics thought were impossible, helping to bring disciplined community action and civic improvements to poor ghetto neighborhoods.

A confrontation between such formidable contestants would, appropriately, be of Olympian proportions. On both sides are strong-willed people used to having their way. Nobody can question the clout and determination of the Olympic organizers. And it would be a serious mistake to underestimate the staying power of UNO and SCOC.

The two sister organizations were created using the techniques of the late radical Saul Alinsky, which have been carried to new levels of sophistication by his successors in the Industrial Areas Foundation. Using local churches as their main organizing unit, IAF staff members have had great success in creating mass-membership community groups in cities throughout the country, particularly among Latino Roman Catholics in the Southwest.

These groups empower people who are not only poor but in some cases not even citizens. The organizers show them that they can have a say in matters that affect their lives, from where a city government decides to put a stop sign to whether a supermarket chain enforces high standards for its outlets in poor neighborhoods. Community leaders trained in small struggles like these usually move on to tougher issues, like improving public education or controlling gang violence.

It is precisely those fundamental concerns, UNO and SCOC leaders say, that led them to focus on the $90 million that will be left for local use after other proceeds from the Olympics are distributed. Leaders of UNO and SCOC remember all the good things that the Olympics brought to Los Angeles in the summer of 1984 — particularly a drop in crime in the neighborhoods around Exposition Park, where many of the Olympic activities were centered.

Having decided some time ago that drug use and the crime associated with it are the basic causes of many problems in East Los Angeles and the Southside, UNO and SCOC leaders scoured poor neighborhoods to find programs that kept young people away from drugs and crime. They listed them in a funding proposal sent to the athletic foundation, asking that $6.6 million in Olympic funds be given to 136 groups ranging from small Roman Catholic and Protestant churches to major programs like the Community Youth Gang Services Project.

It was a typically ambitious effort by UNO and SCOC. But it hit the athletic foundation like another Soviet boycott.

Spokesmen for the foundation reacted defensively to the UNO and SCOC shopping list. They pointed out that the foundation has at least 70 other proposals pending from worthy agencies. They noted that many of the programs on the list, such as rape hotlines, don't meet the main purpose for which the Olympic money was to be used: youth sports programs. (This glosses over the exception already made when the foundation granted $2 million for an arts festival similar to the Olympic Arts Festival of 1984.) They also point out that the foundation has not even decided how much of the $90 million it will give away now and how much should be saved for later years. All reasonable objections. But they overlook what UNO and SCOC leaders are really getting at.

None of them expect all 136 programs on the UNO/SCOC shopping list to be funded. Their main concern is that Los Angeles neighborhoods that have historically been neglected get a significant share of what athletic foundation officials like to call the "Olympic legacy." As one SCOC leader told me, "We'll be happy no matter what groups they fund on the Eastside or in Watts, even if they hand-pick them themselves. We just want our neighborhoods included when that money is divided up." In other words, just as they have in their past campaigns, UNO and SCOC want to have some say in the matter when Los Angeles' movers and shakers make decisions that affect their communities.

The latest moving and shaking will begin today, when the Olympic foundation's grants committee meets to begin screening proposals in preparation for a full board meeting Dec. 9. Among two dozen proposals to be considered are 10 from the UNO/SCOC shopping list. Whether or not they are accepted will determine if the standoff between the two community groups and Olympic committee leaders ends in compromise or confrontation.

They should, of course, compromise. In their own unique ways, the Olympic organizers and UNO and SCOC leaders have shown the rest of us that with hard work, good organization and confidence, Los Angeles can be a better city. That is important common ground to share.

# UNO, at 10, Enjoys Key Role in Region's Decision-Making

I T IS HARD, nowadays, to think of a major public issue being dealt with on Los Angeles' Eastside without participation by the United Neighborhoods Organization, the biggest and most respected grass-roots community group in the area. But it is even harder to believe that when UNO first came onto the scene 10 years ago, many Latino activists were resentful of the new group.

That was because they did not understand the subtle but effective organizing theory behind UNO and the other important Latino community group that preceded it, Communities Organized for Public Service (COPS) in San Antonio, Texas. A few probably also felt uneasy because UNO had tapped into a segment of the Latino community rarely heard from before — the conservative, church-going people of the barrio.

There has always been activism on the Eastside, of course, but it focused on specific crises like the urban-renewal battles of the 1950s or the Zoot Suit Riots in the 1940s. By the 1960s, most Latino activists were from a new generation. They called themselves Chicanos and were inspired by the black civil rights movement, the antiwar movement and Cesar Chavez's drive to unionize field workers. For a brief, dramatic period, the Chicano movement shook up the Eastside and the rest of the nation. But by 1977 it was, for all intents and purposes, dead.

It died of impatience and impetuousness. The young men and women deeply involved in it had energy that was good for organizing street protests but not for building institutions to last. They were aggressive too, which drew the attention of the FBI and other police agencies, which coldly and efficiently suppressed outbursts by the most hot-headed activists.

Within a few years after *el movimiento* began, most of the activists who had demonstrated against the barrio's many problems — police brutality, high unemployment, poor education and so on — were exhausted and frustrated. The handful of activists still waving Viva la Raza banners worked in community-action programs spawned by the Johnson administration's War on Poverty. As they tried to deal with the community's problems, they also had to struggle against constant cuts in the government funding that supported anti-poverty programs. Meanwhile, some of the brighter young Chicanos of the 1960s had been co-opted by more powerful forces. They were becoming part of the establishment that they had once protested against — working their way up in politics and government, major corporations and the professions.

That is when UNO came along and carried Latino community activism to a new level of discipline and sophistication. UNO, COPS and other organizations established with the help of the Industrial Areas Foundation apply the teaching and organizing methods developed by the late radical Saul Alinsky, refined and updated by IAF's professional staff. IAF organizers create community groups using local churches as a basic organizing unit. They take the family and neighborhood networks already there and train their leaders, whether clergy or laity, in how to deal with public issues. It is a slow process that does not attract frenetic activists. The Chicanos who misunderstood UNO when it started up were so used to protesting on behalf of "the people" that they forgot that the people can do a lot for themselves, given a chance.

One need only think back on the roster of issues that UNO has raised in the last 10 years to realize that its leaders have done remarkably well in identifying and attacking issues of importance to barrio residents:

They helped lower auto insurance rates on the Eastside, pressured supermarket chains to clean up stores in ghetto areas, closed down a toxic dump in Boyle Heights, fought for better police deployment in inner-city neighborhoods and helped create an innovative project to help reduce violence by the city's youth gangs. Now they seek to help immigrant families that may be torn apart by the nation's new immigration law.

With a track record like that, it should come as no surprise that UNO has expanded from the Eastside into the small cities southeast of Los Angeles and spawned two sister organizations — the South-Central Organizing Committee in South Los Angeles and Compton and the East Valleys Organization covering the San Gabriel and Pomona valleys.

The three groups came together Sunday to celebrate UNO's decade of success in teaching poor and working-class people (and not just Latinos) how to organize themselves. It was an impressive show — 7,000 people who were cheering tributes from city leaders and a keynote address by Sen. Edward M. Kennedy (D-Mass.), who promised to join UNO and its sister organizations in their campaigns to liberalize the new immigration law and raise the minimum wage. San Antonio Mayor Henry Cisneros praised the IAF affiliates for having trained a new cadre of Latino leadership.

The turnout of political, religious and business leaders was proof that, after 10 years of methodical work, UNO is accepted as a key player in this region's decision-making process. No longer do a handful of Latino elected officials or power brokers speak for "the people" of the barrios. The people speak for themselves.

And, lest anybody think that UNO is resting on its laurels, the final announcement made Sunday was that UNO and its sister organizations are looking to build a fourth community organization in the San Fernando Valley. I grew up in Pacoima and know how cautious and even conservative barrio leaders in the Valley can be. But I have little doubt that when UNO celebrates another decade of work in 1997 there will be a fourth organization in my old neighborhood — and maybe in a few other places as well.

AUGUST 26, 1988

# Cesar Chavez Suffers for and Revives the Cause of Farmworkers' Contracts

DELANO, Calif. — About 25 years ago, two very different Californians, Ronald Reagan and Cesar Chavez, burst onto the national scene. Reagan was successful in making the transition from former actor to governor and then to president. Chavez had more ups and downs in building the United Farm Workers of America into a viable labor union, but he remains a potent symbol in the consciousness of the nation — much to the chagrin of his critics.

These days Chavez is waging another battle against agribusiness — a boycott of table grapes to press for stronger protection against pesticides. As he has done before, Chavez presented his case with a dramatic act: a 36-day water-only fast, which seriously endangered his health.

When that fast ended here on Sunday, with dozens of journalists to report it, the moment was heavy with symbolism. The family of the late Sen. Robert F. Kennedy was with Chavez, just as Kennedy had been when Chavez ended another long fast in 1968. Also present was the Rev. Jesse Jackson, who began a three-day fast once Chavez's had ended. The former presidential candidate said that other prominent UFW supporters would take up the fast in a "chain of suffering" aimed at persuading people to stop buying grapes.

It was a brilliantly staged media event. And the media have always helped Chavez keep his union visible, even during its periodic downturns. In the last 10 years the UFW has lost 100 contracts that it had with grape growers, the biggest employers in California agriculture.

But even if Chavez's fast and its dramatic ending were irresistible to the media, one cannot dismiss him as just a media manipulator. No one who saw the 61-year-old union leader being carried into the rally where 7,000 silent union members and supporters waited, then watched him sit weakly through a Mass, grimacing in pain, can doubt that Chavez suffered during his self-imposed ordeal. Argue with his tactics, but the deep sincerity of his beliefs is obvious.

That is why Chavez has been so successful over the years in winning sympathy for his cause. He believes in what he is doing so fervently that he is willing to do anything to keep his movement alive — even nearly kill himself. Such conviction sways people, even when the facts of an issue are gray rather than black and white.

In this respect Chavez and Reagan, who have agreed on few issues over the years, are very much alike. They're both "Great Communicators," to use the cliché often applied to Reagan. Reagan does it with a well-delivered phrase. Chavez, a former field hand who dropped out of school in the seventh grade, uses his body to make the point.

But Chavez is just as effective. He has got people thinking again about farmworkers, even if he may be overstating his case. This time he is urging consumers to boycott grapes by raising the possibility that they are tainted with the same pesticides that cause health problems for farmworkers.

Growers and supermarket executives say that there is no threat to consumers from pesticides, which are used on many kinds of produce. Perhaps not. But some of the pesticides that Chavez is worried about are under investigation for toxic side effects. And all of them are dangerous if improperly used. In the last five years, according to the California Department of

Food and Agriculture, almost 350 field hands have been poisoned after entering fields or storage areas where the toxicity of pesticides was thought to be at safe levels.

Then there's the frightening pall that hangs over the San Joaquin Valley, the heart of this state's large agricultural industry. A few years ago children in McFarland, about 10 miles south of Delano, began suffering higher-than-normal rates of cancer. What causes the "cancer cluster" is still unknown, but one possibility being studied is that the illnesses are caused by water supplies contaminated by pesticides. Some of the affected McFarland families resent being used by the UFW for its anti-grape propaganda. But there is no denying the reality of their plight.

And there is no denying that farm laborers were among the lowest-paid and most easily exploited workers in this country until 1970, when, through strikes and boycotts, Chavez brought large-scale unionization to agriculture for the first time in history. Among other things, those first UFW contracts forced grape growers to eliminate or curtail their use of pesticides like DDT long before the federal government banned them as dangerous.

That little-noted fact is at the root of Chavez's current boycott. For, while government tries to protect workers from the potential dangers of pesticides, Chavez is convinced that the best protection is provided by unions and labor contracts that give workers an equal say with growers regarding how pesticides are used.

As Ronald Reagan has been telling us lately, facts are stubborn things. The fact of this matter is that Chavez has a stronger case against grapes than growers like to admit. And he is conveying it so effectively that the growers will have to respond.

It's hard to argue with someone who is willing to risk death to make a point. So the growers' best bet is to sit down with Chavez and talk about new labor contracts.

# A Latino at the Top of the Ladder

IGUEL CONTRERAS, the new executive secretary-treasurer of the Los Angeles County Federation of Labor, would be busy enough if his only responsibility were to be the designated Labor Leader of Greater Los Angeles.

After all, the County Fed, as it is widely known, has been a political force here since the 1960s, when former Mayor Tom Bradley first ran for citywide office with the help of organized labor. Although Bradley lost that round, he finally won the mayor's office in 1973, and for the next 16 years, one of his most reliable supporters and trusted advisors was William R. "Bill" Robertson, head of the County Fed.

Robertson's hand-picked successor was James M. Wood, who died earlier this year of lung cancer at the age of 51. Wood had been a mentor to Contreras, even naming him to head the County Fed's political committee, so Contreras ran for election to serve out the remaining two years of Wood's four-year term.

In May, representatives of the County Fed's 325 unions elected the 43-year-old Contreras to the executive secretary-treasurer's post by acclamation. He is the first Latino to head the federation in its 102-year history. And now, as he introduces himself around town, Contreras finds himself being asked not just about the future of organized labor, but about the future of this region's biggest ethnic group. For, whether Contreras wants it or not, he has taken on an unofficial responsibility that could prove almost as important as his day job: "Latino Leader."

Fortunately, the soft-spoken Contreras learned about being both a labor and a Latino leader from someone who did a good job of handling both responsibilities during his lifetime: Cesar Chavez.

Contreras was a 17-year-old fruit picker in the San Joaquin Valley when his family joined Chavez's United Farm Workers. That was in 1970, when Chavez signed his union's first labor contracts with California table grape growers at the end of the five-year strike and grape boycott that made Chavez famous.

Three years later, when grape growers refused to renew their UFW contracts and Chavez launched another strike and boycott, Contreras became a picket line captain. His leadership abilities caught the attention of Chavez, who put Contreras on the UFW staff.

That second big UFW strike culminated in the California Agricultural Labor Relations Act, which set up procedures for union representation elections on California farms that are still in effect.

After helping Chavez in some of those early elections, Contreras left UFW in 1977 to become an organizer of hotel, restaurant and casino workers in California and Nevada. He spent 10 years working his way up in the Hotel Employees and Restaurant Employees Union, coming to Los Angeles in 1988 to help rebuild HERE's Local 11, which had been put under the trusteeship of the union's national office. It was here that Contreras met the union activist who would become his wife, Maria Elena Durazo, the leader of a dissident faction who would eventually be elected president of Local 11.

An outspoken and vivacious woman, Durazo is the best-known labor leader in Los Angeles these days. She is also the most controversial. Her organizing tactics have included not just strikes and protests against some of the city's biggest hotels, but also a negative publicity campaign against the city's important tourism industry. Durazo's brief anti-tourism campaign, including a videotape that highlighted Los Angeles' problems after the 1992 riots, still rankles many local business and political leaders. But Durazo remains unapologetic about the tactic, as does her husband.

"If we [in organized labor] do our jobs, we can keep what happened in 1992 from happening again," he says flatly.

I must agree. For, even as thousands of high-paying union jobs left Southern California with the end of the Cold War and the transfer of heavy manufacturing to other regions, Los Angeles remains an industrial powerhouse thanks to Latino workers. A recent UCLA study estimated that there are more industrial jobs in Los Angeles County than in the Chicago area — roughly 650,000 positions in light manufacturing, food processing, the garment trade and related industries.

Half of those jobs are filled by Latinos. And the best way to keep those workers, and their families, content with life in this city is ensuring that they get paid decent wages and benefits. And, for better or worse, one good way to do that is by having them bargain collectively with their employers.

As important as an emerging middle class of Latino business people and professionals is to the future of Los Angeles, we would be foolish to overlook the well-being of an equally large Latino population that is the blue-collar backbone of the region's emerging economy.

With a labor — and Latino — leader like Contreras around, I don't think we will.

NOVEMBER 23, 2003

# He'd Prefer a Helping Hand to an Ovation

I T IS NOT SURPRISING to see Father Gregory Boyle widely celebrated these days. He may be, after all, the closest thing to a living saint that anyone in modern Los Angeles will ever know. And now that doctors have found that Boyle has leukemia, the sad reality that a saint in our midst may soon be gone has added a touch of anxiety to the admiration Boyle has justly earned since 1986.

That is when the 49-year-old Jesuit became pastor of one of the city's poorest churches, Dolores Mission, in one of its toughest housing projects, the Aliso-Pico Village. Almost immediately he began to focus his ministry on people shunned and feared by many, Latino gang members. Since then, Boyle sadly notes, he has presided at the funerals of more than 100 of those young men and women.

However, he also founded Homeboy Industries, the nonprofit agency that has helped 500 former gang members find the jobs and self-respect to turn their lives around. And that has inspired thousands of Angelenos to ponder the possibility that the street gangs so many of us accept as an unpleasant fact of L.A. life could someday be eliminated.

That day is still a long way off, which is why Boyle inspires emotional outpourings like the one I witnessed at a recent fundraising dinner for the Mexican American Legal Defense and Educational Fund. MALDEF, based in Los Angeles, is one of the nation's major Latino civil rights groups. Its annual dinner draws L.A.'s Latino elite.

Yet among this year's high-powered honorees, it was Boyle who inspired the most adulation. And his remarks, urging the audience to never give up hope for his young charges no matter how hopeless it might seem, had many in the audience in tears.

The sad fact is that even if Greg Boyle were to live another 30 years, instead of the five his doctors have told him to expect, he would make only a small — if inspiring — dent in L.A.'s gang problems. The latest estimates by gang experts is that between 100,000 and 200,000 young men and women in Los Angeles County alone are now affiliated with local gangs, if only as hangers-on and wannabes.

That sobering statistic was cited a few days after the MALDEF dinner by Los Angeles Police Det. Marc Espinoza. He was addressing Latino business leaders invited to learn more about the city's gang problems by the Latin American Law Enforcement Assn., or La Ley, the organization of Latino LAPD officers. It was the first of what La Ley leaders envision as a series of conferences to bring non-experts up to date on the reality of L.A.'s street gangs, as opposed to some misperceptions in the popular media. Gangs are, for instance, not just a Latino problem. Although there are more than 500 Latino gangs, there are also more than 300 black gangs, more than 100 Asian gangs and at least 28 white street gangs, Espinoza said.

Follow-up sessions of the La Ley conference will focus on successful strategies to combat gangs, according to La Ley President Art Placencia, a veteran Hollywood Division detective. Significantly, the group will not just focus on getting more law enforcement resources. It also will push for intervention programs like Homeboy Industries that offer young people alternatives to gang life. "There are people smarter than us who are grappling with this problem," Placencia said. "We are talking to business people because they are the movers and shakers who influence public policy, the folks to whom the politicians and bureaucrats listen."

They are also the people who have the wherewithal to create, and make available, more of the kinds of entry-level jobs that Homeboy Industries offers.

There were only about 60 people at the La Ley conference. Nearly 1,200 people gave Boyle a standing ovation the night of the MALDEF dinner. If only a quarter of that larger group followed up on that show of support with specific efforts aimed at offering at-risk youngsters alternatives to gang life, it would make life easier not just for La Ley's members and their colleagues in law enforcement. It would help carry on the admirable work begun by Father Boyle. Anyone who knows Boyle knows that he would want no other legacy.

# CHAPTER FIVE

# Journalism and Mass Media

*The image of the Latino, from Ruben
Salazar to Star Fleet Command*

ON MARCH 19, 1995, Frank del Olmo went where he had never gone before: boldly describing himself as a "Star Trek" fan. He did it to make a point: the importance of increasing accurate Latino portrayals so often missing in news coverage and entertainment. Exhibit A was "Star Trek," which took decades to include Latinos in lead roles, a development Frank humorously chronicled in his column.

Del Olmo believed that media should accurately reflect the entire community and that increasing diversity in media employment was critical to providing quality coverage.

He wrote movingly about his mentor, the late Times columnist Ruben Salazar, killed in 1970 while covering an antiwar demonstration. Del Olmo, 22 when Salazar died, was haunted by the tragedy. He became fiercely determined to carry on the work Salazar began: lifting the cloak of invisibility about a community then mostly ignored or misunderstood by media.

# Ruben Salazar: Los Angeles' Misunderstood Martyr

TEN YEARS AFTER it happened, the death of Ruben Salazar is still a sensitive subject to those of us who were his colleagues and friends in journalism. We have been doing a lot of reminiscing about him lately, and about his work as a columnist for The Times and as news director at KMEX, Channel 34. This Friday will be the 10th anniversary of his death.

Partly it was the way he died — his head shattered by a heavy, bullet-shaped tear gas projectile fired by a deputy sheriff during a major riot in East Los Angeles on Aug. 29, 1970. Ruben was there doing his job, and there wasn't a reporter in town who had not covered similar incidents. We could all envision ourselves the victim of the same quirk of fate that found Ruben in the wrong place at the wrong time.

But in the aftermath of his death, something else happened that made many journalists who knew Ruben even more uncomfortable. To the Mexican American community activists whose problems and protests he had been writing about, Ruben became a martyr.

And that aura has grown with the passage of time. Awards are now granted in his memory. There are parks, community centers and even schools named after Ruben in places as far away as Texas and as close as Lincoln Heights. There are murals and Chicano posters that bear his likeness.

There is one poster in particular, a copy of a silk-screen by the famous Mexican painter David Alfaro Siqueiros, that I am uncomfortable looking at to this day. The likeness of Ruben that Siqueiros painted is saint-like, with a distant, long-suffering look to the eyes. It is not the earthy man I knew.

Ruben was, above all else, a pro. He was a seasoned newsman who had worked for years as a journalist in El Paso, San Francisco, Vietnam and Latin America before he came to Los Angeles in the late 1960s to do the work he is most remembered for by Chicanos.

Ruben would not have fit any stereotypes of the typical Chicano (whatever that is). He was married to an Anglo woman and lived a comfortably suburban middle-class life, complete with a swimming pool, in Orange County.

The journalists who knew Ruben and worked with him say they thought of him as a reporter first and a Chicano second, which is why they were so surprised at the outpouring of rage and grief in the Chicano community that followed his death.

By training and tradition, journalists are uncomfortable as activists or advocates, so I can understand my colleagues' uneasiness at the heroic image many Chicanos have of Ruben. But I think the community's reaction would be easier for my colleagues to understand if they just remembered a couple of things about Ruben and the community that took him as its martyr, almost in spite of himself.

First, one has to remember the traumatic events that led up to Ruben's death. The Chicano protest he helped to cover that hot, smoggy Saturday afternoon was the largest Mexican American demonstration ever held in this country. It was billed as a Chicano moratorium against the Vietnam War, in which Latino soldiers were dying in proportionally greater numbers than any other ethnic group.

In Los Angeles, that demonstration had been preceded by two years of militant Chicano protests against bad education, police brutality and even the Roman Catholic Church's insensitivity to Latino problems.

Throughout the rest of the Southwest, other Chicano groups had been springing up with similar protests, so that when 20,000 people gathered for the Aug. 29 Moratorium, it was the high point of a movement that had been building for some time. People came not only from California but from throughout the country to march down Whittier Boulevard, the main street of the biggest barrio in the Southwest. I still vividly remember the fiesta atmosphere surrounding the whole event. Many people even brought their families.

After a long, hot march, the demonstrators arrived at Laguna Park (renamed Salazar Park after Ruben's death). There the antiwar rally planned for that day began, but never finished. The trouble began when several Los Angeles County Sheriff's Department patrol cars, responding to reports of looting at a liquor store near the park, became the targets for rocks and bottles thrown from the fringes of the large crowd.

A decision was made to clear the park, and a skirmish line of riot-equipped officers moved in, followed by a barrage of tear gas. Many protesters fled, some stayed and fought, and others headed back down Whittier Boulevard, taking out their anger on the businesses along the way.

For Los Angeles, it was the biggest, bloodiest riot since Watts exploded five years earlier. For the Eastside, it was the most violent upheaval since the Zoot Suit Riots of 1943. Millions of dollars worth of property was destroyed, dozens of people were injured and arrested and three people died, including Ruben Salazar.

All three deaths were tragic and useless, and the community would have mourned the victims no matter who they were. But the fact that Ruben was among the dead compounded the tragedy.

Most of the activists who mourned Ruben did not know him, but they knew of him. His reporting did not cater to them. Indeed, a few of them considered him a sellout Tio Taco because it didn't. But they knew he paid attention to them, which gave their protests importance.

To this day there are Chicanos who believe Ruben's death was not accidental, as official investigations later concluded. There are some who will always be sure that his death was an assassination — carried out by dark, sinister forces fearful of the influence and power Ruben could wield from his new position as a columnist and news executive.

While I do not subscribe to those theories, I do know that his death was a devastating loss to a community just starting to find its voice. He was one of the few Chicano journalists then working in this country, and the only Chicano columnist. Given the circumstances and timing of his death, it comes as no surprise that the emotions it stirred among Chicanos ran so deep and spread so far. A second thing I think Ruben's former colleagues forget about his last few months is that he was changing during that time. They may understand those changes as part of a process all people go through upon reaching middle age (Ruben was 42 when he died), but I don't think they fully comprehend how Ruben's changes coincided with a time of remarkable ferment in the Mexican American community.

Ruben had resigned his reporting job at The Times in January 1970, after 11 years on the staff. He left to become news director of television station KMEX, Channel 34, the city's first Spanish-language outlet. Working there, he told me once, he felt that for the first time he was talking to his own people instead of trying to explain Chicanos to Anglos. He was enjoying immensely the independence and authority this new job gave him.

His new job also gave him the opportunity to immerse himself more

Frank was born in 1948 and grew up in the San Fernando Valley. As a baby in 1949, above, on horseback in the 1950s and as an elementary student in the early 1960s.

Frank graduates from Bishop Alemany High School in the San Fernando Valley. He is flanked by his younger sister, Theresa, and his mother, the late Margaret del Olmo.

Working on a story as a Metro reporter at the Los Angeles Times in the early 1970s.

Frank with Mexican President José López Portillo in 1977.

Frank with his sisters and brothers, early 1970s. Back row, from left: Theresa Previtire, the late Rey Garcia, Margie Maldonado and Frank. Bottom: Gabriel Garcia and Elisa Garcia.

Frank with members of the California Chicano News Media Association Board of Directors at a meeting held at USC's School of Journalism in the early 1980s.

Frank and United Farm Workers leader Cesar Chavez at a California Chicano News Media Association meeting in June 1986.

Frank del Olmo, second from right, celebrates with other members of the Los Angeles Times team that won the 1984 Pulitzer Prize gold medal for meritorious public service. Seated at center, holding a reprint book on the articles about Southern California's Latino community, is Frank O. Sotomayor.

Frank and Magdalena at a Plaza de la Raza celebration in Los Angeles honoring former Times reporter Ruben Salazar in the summer of 1990.

Frank and his daugher, Valentina, at age 11, in 1986.

Avid "Star Trek" fans, Frank and Frankie play the part on Halloween night 1993 in Salinas, Calif.

Frank in Spain, where he lectured at the famed El Escorial University near Madrid in 1992.

"My dad's work never kept him from being a devoted father. Shared time was one of the most precious and abundant gifts he gave Frankie and me."

—

*Valentina del Olmo*

The del Olmo family in Pacific Grove, Calif., in 1993. From left: Valentina, Frank, Frankie and Magdalena.

Key early members and founders of the Chicano News Media Association at an anniversary celebration in the 1990s. From left: Joe Ramirez, KNBC; Frank; Henry Alfaro, KABC; Bob Navarro, KCBS; and Frank Cruz, now a board member for the Corporation for Public Broadcasting.

Frank provides the commencement address at his alma mater, California State University, Northridge, in the mid-1990s.

President Clinton welcomes Frank and Magdalena del Olmo at the White House in October 1995 during a visit by Mexican President Ernesto Zedillo.

Frank at the California Chicano News Media Association's Job Opportunities Conference in 1997 with leaders of several journalism groups. From left: George White of the National Association of Black Journalists; Nancy Yoshihara of the Asian American Journalists Association; attorney-activist Angela Oh, guest speaker; Marc Brown of NABJ and Sid Garcia of CCNMA.

Los Angeles Mayor Richard J. Riordan, Frank, Los Angeles Galaxy soccer team co-owner Danny Villanueva and former HUD Secretary Henry G. Cisneros at the Los Angeles Times celebration of Frank's 25th year with the newspaper in 1997.

Frank joins other inductees into the National Association of Hispanic Journalists' Hall of Fame in June 2001. From left: Dr. Félix Gutiérrez, USC School of Journalism; Frank O. Sotomayor and Frank.

PAUL CONRAD, 2004

LALO ALCARAZ, 2004

Frank, Frankie, Valentina, Magdalena and family pet Chocolate in November 2002, in their last family portrait.

Frank and Frankie at the Monterey Bay Aquarium in 2003.

than ever in the ferment that in those days had the Chicano community in such intellectual and cultural flux. As in the rest of American society, there had been protest and activism in the barrios before, but never on the scale of the late 1960s.

It was because this ferment was so widespread that The Times gave Ruben the opportunity to write his weekly opinion column about Chicano affairs. And I think many of Ruben's friends have forgotten how unsettling they sometimes found that column. More than once I heard Anglo reporters express surprise at the angry tone of something Ruben had written about barrio problems.

He never hesitated to criticize Mexican Americans when our own shortcomings were to blame, but he didn't mince words when he thought the cause was Anglo racism, either.

Only once do I remember hearing an Anglo friend of Ruben's say he thought the man was changing, maybe even finding himself, in his new role. But, with 10 years of hindsight, I now think that is exactly what was happening.

I will always remember the last conversation I had with him, the day before the Chicano Moratorium. It was already looming as the biggest Chicano protest ever, and he was frankly hoping for a large crowd.

"We have really been covering it here," he said, referring to Channel 34's newscast. "I hope the *gente* [people] really turn out for it. We have to show the Anglo what we can do."

I am not saying Ruben had become an activist Chicano, but he was certainly not the same man he was when he left The Times' reporting staff. I am convinced that in his own personality, Ruben was going through the same turmoil the entire Chicano community was dealing with in those days.

Like a relative handful of successful Mexican Americans, Ruben had made it in the Anglo world, playing by the Anglo's rules. Years later, other Chicanos came along, mostly young people inspired by the civil rights and Black Power movements, the protests against the Vietnam War and Cesar Chavez's campaign to unionize farmworkers. They began to question the assimilationist path that had proved so successful for Ruben and others like him.

And they did not raise these questions quietly, but aggressively, demonstrating and protesting on a scale their elders had never attempted.

Impelled by his professional responsibility, Ruben began to report on this phenomenon. But it affected him. He was disciplined enough to report on it accurately and fairly, but human enough to wonder about the questions these young militants were asking, and to begin asking similar questions himself.

I think he often wrote his columns explaining things like "Who is a Chicano, and what is it that Chicanos want?" as much to clarify things in his own mind as he did to clarify them for his Anglo and other readers.

And one of the saddest things about his death is that Ruben died never having fully answered many of those questions for himself, or for the Chicano community.

My own feeling is that neither his journalistic colleagues nor his Chicano admirers, and I include myself in both those groups, fully knew the man who died that fiery Aug. 29 on Whittier Boulevard.

I know he was not a Chicano saint. But I also know he was not just another Mexican American, either. What he was, and what he might have become, can never be fully answered. And while that is not the greatest tragedy of the Aug. 29 riot, it remains, for me, the most profound.

The greater tragedy, of course, is that the riot happened at all and that much of the anger and so many of the social problems that spawned it fester in the barrios to this day.

SEPTEMBER 9, 1982

# El Pachuco Deflates the Pachuco Image

IT IS PROBABLY UN-CHICANO of me to admit it, but I never really liked the El Pachuco character in Luis Valdez's hit play "Zoot Suit," which had such a long, successful run in Los Angeles a couple of years back.

The mythical character is fascinating, to be sure. El Pachuco speaks as both the play's narrator and the conscience of its protagonist. As portrayed by Edward James Olmos in an acting tour de force, El Pachuco dominated the state and seemed at times to stand 10 feet tall.

Olmos made El Pachuco the epitome of barrio cool. He didn't walk so much as he glided in and out of the shadows. He spoke the old pachuco slang with the eloquence of Laurence Olivier reading Shakespeare. And he was switchblade-sharp in his trim, black zoot suit and wide-brimmed hat.

El Pachuco was a wonder to behold, but he troubled me.

All cultures produce their swaggering antiheroes, of course, but what worried me most about El Pachuco was the adoring reaction that he got from so many of the young Latinos who flocked to see "Zoot Suit."

The gang lifestyle that El Pachuco represented is still too real, and too uncomfortably close by, for him to be dismissed as simply a fictional character. I feared that some impressionable young people might see in El Pachuco a living symbol of a tragic mode of behavior that in still all too common in the barrios and that they might be tempted to emulate.

I was not the only Chicano who felt that way. Olmos, who played El Pachuco perhaps 300 times on stage in Los Angeles and on Broadway, was another.

Olmos went out of his way during the play's run, and since then, to impress on young Latinos the point that El Pachuco was just a fictional character artfully interpreted by a soft-spoken actor. He has taken that message almost 100 times to Chicano groups "in high schools and grade schools, in youth camps and juvenile halls."

"I tell them that El Pachuco's style of pride and self-assertion may have been necessary for his time" (the early 1940s, when wartime hysteria had prejudice against Mexican Americans running especially high), Olmos says. "But it's a negative pride, a defense mechanism — a shield against the outside world that Chicanos don't really need anymore."

The 35-year-old Olmos believes that seeing the man who played El Pachuco portray significantly different roles can also help young Latinos put the El Pachuco character into perspective. Olmos has made several motion pictures since "Zoot Suit," but only recently has he appeared in a film aimed specifically at a Latino audience.

Olmos' latest role could not be more different from the hip defiance of El Pachuco. He plays the title role in "The Ballad of Gregorio Cortez," a Western based on a true incident that took place along the Texas-Mexico border in 1901 — one that is still sung about in corridos, Mexican American narrative folk songs.

Cortez was a Mexican American farmhand who shot and killed the sheriff of Gonzales, Texas, in a dispute that arose because of a misunderstanding over the translation of a single word. Fleeing for his life at a time when Mexicans were regularly lynched in the Southwest, Cortez outran a posse and the Texas Rangers for 11 days. He was captured only after another Mexican American turned him in for a reward. He was tried and sentenced to life in prison but was pardoned 12 years later.

It is not a happy story, and the characters and their motivations are ambiguous. Not all the Latinos are heroes, and not all the Anglos are villains. It is a lovely film to watch, a gritty and authentic depiction of the American West at the turn of the century.

Most important, Olmos portrays Cortez not as a swashbuckling El Pachuco-on-horseback but as he must really have been — a frightened, confused and exhausted man fleeing for his life. It is a startling contrast in roles for Olmos and must be a shocker for anyone who is used to thinking of Olmos as El Pachuco. So it may be a gamble for the young actor.

But it is not the biggest gamble that Olmos is taking. He agreed to co-produce the film with Moctezuma Esparza and is taking a risk that only superstars like Robert Redford and Clint Eastwood normally take, using his own money to package "Cortez" for distribution to theaters as a feature film.

"Cortez" was originally a project of the National Council of La Raza, a Latino advocacy group based in Washington, D.C., which obtained funding for the production from the National Endowment for the Humanities.

The first of a projected series of film on the Latino experience in the United States, "Cortez" was screened earlier this year on the Public Broadcasting Service, receiving favorable reviews.

Olmos now wants to carry it into theaters, and he has held sneak-preview screenings in San Antonio and Los Angeles to test audience reaction. "I want to prove that Latino-themed films can be successful," he says, raising an issue that is sensitive with the small but growing number of Latinos in the film industry. "I want to show the major studios that a Latino film can be a success without focusing just on gangs and violence," the only themes that Hollywood studios seem willing to treat in films about Latinos.

While films like "Boulevard Nights" and "Walk Proud" received same favorable reviews, they were unanimously — and justifiably — blasted by Latino activists as blatant misportrayals. Even worse from the studios' standpoint, none of them did well commercially.

Even a stage hit like "Zoot Suit" has not been as successful on film as Universal Studios would have liked. Produced on a modest budget of $2.5 million, the film has thus far grossed only $4.5 million, not nearly enough by the high-stakes standards of modern moviemaking.

If Olmos succeeds with his gamble on "The Ballad of Gregorio Cortez," it may change a few minds in Hollywood's executive suites.

But it's more important to me that it change a few minds in places like East Los Angeles and San Antonio's West Side. The more widely Olmos' latest film is played, the more chances there will be for young Latinos to see another side of El Pachuco.

APRIL 24, 1987

# Changing World: Latinos and the Media

DURING MY YEARS AT THE TIMES I have often heard from Latino activists complaining about the kind of coverage that ethnic minorities and minority-related issues get in the news media.

In honesty, I often find the complaints unjustified. People misread straightforward news reports and conclude that journalists are biased against them simply because reporters don't take their views on some controversial subjects. But there have been times when I've read news clippings that were unbalanced, incomplete or just sensationalistic. Not the kind of journalism that I want to be associated with.

But I am associated with it by the very nature of my work. As a professional journalist, I am acutely aware of the strengths and weaknesses of my craft. While I take considerable pride in our achievements, I must answer for our shortcomings too. And one area in which we need to improve is how we report on Latinos and other minority groups.

Almost 20 years ago, the Kerner Commission's report on the urban rioting of the 1960s placed part of the blame on the news media, which had ignored America's ghettos until they exploded. As a result of that criticism, many news executives pledged to help integrate the nation's newsrooms. Yet journalism remains a highly segregated profession; only about 8% of the professionals working for newspapers are members of minorities, while 18% of the nation's population is minority.

On the whole, I would argue that the news media are covering the problems and aspirations of this nation's minorities better than they did before the 1960s. But I worry that, with the minority population growing and the issues becoming more subtle and complicated (equal economic opportunity as opposed to racial segregation, for example), we risk falling behind again.

I make no secret of my concern to colleagues in the news business. But when I talk to Latino activists on the subject, I offer what must seem like very conservative advice. I urge them to try to understand the inner workings of the media and to cooperate with reporters and editors rather than criticize them. I also advise against confrontation-style tactics, such as boycotts, which can be counterproductive.

If the news media are going to change, the most effective pressure for change will come from inside the profession, among journalists themselves, rather than from outside pressure groups. And the best way to make the news media more sensitive to minority groups is to have more Latinos and other minority people in the newsroom.

When more Latinos, blacks and other minorities are writing and reporting the news, or making decisions about what will be covered as news, there will be a better balance in the reporting about minority communities. Controversial stories about gangs, illegal aliens, drugs, welfare and the like will still be written and broadcast, because these issues are too important to be ignored. But they will be balanced by positive stories, the kinds of upbeat features that now are sometimes overlooked.

What prompts these musings is the fact that this week hundreds of Latino journalists from across the nation are in Los Angeles to participate in the annual conference organized by the California Chicano News Media Assn. and the National Assn. of Hispanic Journalists. A key topic will be getting the media to hire more Latinos and improving the career opportunities for those already in the field.

But while those meetings are going on, a group of local activists, calling itself the National Hispanic Media Coalition, is using the occasion to publicize its complaint against television station KCBS, which, it says, has a poor record in the hiring and promoting of minorities. It expressed its feelings by holding a demonstration outside the station.

As noted above, these '60s-style protest tactics are not that useful. On the other hand, a cynic could argue that conferences where minority participation in the news media is discussed in moderate, measured tones aren't doing that much good, either. But I persist in believing that pushing from the inside is preferable, not just because it is more likely to succeed but also because outside pressure on the media jeopardizes freedom of the press.

After all, if angry Latinos pressure a TV station one day, the shoe could easily be on the other foot the next day. This week, for example, the news department at KNBC is getting lots of angry phone calls from English-speaking viewers who don't like the fact that its series on a new immigration law is being broadcast in Spanish as well as in English. KNBC refused to change the decision to broadcast in two languages, to its credit. It can do that because the First Amendment guarantees the news media's independence. And that independence is the source of some of the media's finest achievements. It is what allows reporters to challenge government authority, or society's conventional wisdom, when necessary.

Editorial independence does not mean that the news media can ignore criticism, of course. If they do a poor job, we must be willing to listen to protests. And if the criticism is valid, we must be willing to change. But there is enough good sense in this profession to make those changes without outside pressure.

Of all people, journalists know that freedom of the press carries with it responsibilities. One of them is a duty to be fair and balanced in our work, and when it comes to minorities in U.S. society, we still fall short on both counts. That will change when American newsrooms better reflect American society. We're working on it.

MARCH 19, 1995

# *Donde Muy Pocos Latinos Han Ido\**

HOW DO YOU SAY "Beam me up, Scotty" in Spanish?

I ask only half-jokingly. Because word is getting out among Latinos who are also fans of "Star Trek" — like me — that we're finally a big part of the science-fiction universe envisioned by the late Gene Roddenberry.

I have been a loyal Trekker ever since the very first "Star Trek" TV series in the late 1960s, but I confess that it was sometimes a bit painful to note how the racially mixed crew on the original Starship Enterprise hardly ever included Latinos.

Jesus Salvador Trevino, a veteran screenwriter and director, wrote to The Times' Calendar section some years ago that he was still waiting for the "Star Trek" episode that would explain how all the Latinos in the universe had been " wiped out by some horrible intergalactic disease."

Luis Reyes, author of "Hispanics in Hollywood: An Encyclopedia of Film and Television," made the same point in discussing his authoritative new book. " 'Star Trek' was supposed to be the future and there were no Latinos," he said in a Calendar article. "Now what does that say about us?"

In fairness to Roddenberry, who died in 1991, and the many other creative people who have continued his endeavor, Trevino and Reyes were overstating things — but not by much. I can recall a pivotal episode in the original NBC series in which Mr. Spock, the science officer from the planet Vulcan, is court-martialed and the presiding officer is a Starfleet commodore named Mendez. Ricardo Montalban played a villain in the old TV series — the renegade scientist Khan. And there were references in the more recent TV series, "Star Trek: The Next Generation," to a starship named Zapata, apparently in honor of a hero of the Mexican Revolution.

So it's not like Latinos were invisible on "Star Trek." But they had no continuing role until the premiere in January of the new series, "Star Trek: Voyager." Robert Beltran portrays the starship's first officer, and the chief engineer is named Torres. So finally Latinos are on a par — if not exactly of the same rank — with Capt. James T. Kirk, the macho American who commanded the original Starship Enterprise, and Capt. Jean Luc Picard, the erudite Frenchman who took over the bridge on "The Next Generation."

Some TV reviewers noted that the "Voyager" crew, with a female captain, a Korean communications officer and a black Vulcan, may be the most politically correct since the cast of the original "Star Trek" series. That crew had a Japanese navigator, a Russian helmsman, a ship's engineer with a thick Scottish burr (Scotty, of the oft-repeated gag line) and an African communications officer named Uhuru.

At this point, fellow Trekkers are probably thinking that I am making too much of the Latino presence on "Star Trek: Voyager." After all, Roddenberry's idealistic vision was of a future where humans overcome their racial, ethnic and nationality differences to make peace on Earth and move on to explore the stars. But these things do add up in their small way. No less a fan than the Rev. Martin Luther King Jr. once told actress Nichelle Nichols that her continuing role as Uhuru was an important milestone for African Americans.

If an actor named Beltran and a character named Torres give some Latino kids the idea of having a career in space science — or even science-fiction — they will represent a breakthrough that Gene Roddenberry, who once worked as a Los Angeles cop and knew this city's tough barrios, would surely have appreciated.

----

\* Where Few Latinos Have Gone Before

AUGUST 27, 1995

# Salazar: a Pioneer, Not a Martyr

IT HAS BEEN 25 YEARS since one of my mentors in the news business, Ruben Salazar, was killed during a riot in East Los Angeles on Aug. 29, 1970. And while it's gratifying to see him finally getting his due as a groundbreaking journalist, it's disappointing to note how incomplete many of the commemorative retrospectives of his work are.

That was probably inevitable, because the retrospectives are mostly being done in English and understandably focus on the work Salazar, who was 42 when he died, did in his 15 years as a reporter, foreign correspondent and columnist for The Times and other newspapers in Texas and California. (A good compilation of that work is "Ruben Salazar, Border Correspondent," by UC Santa Barbara professor Mario T. Garcia, published by UC Press.)

Yet some of the most powerful journalism Salazar did was in Spanish. It was his Spanish-language journalism that most irritated Los Angeles' power structure — even frightened segments of it — in the weeks leading up to his untimely death. And unless you take his Spanish-language work into account, you really can't understand why Salazar is more revered by Latino activists than by his fellow journalists.

Salazar did that work as news director for KMEX-TV, Channel 34, the city's first Spanish-language station. This fundamentally important fact of Salazar's career is often overlooked. Although his weekly column on The Times' Op-Ed page was influential — indeed, some of his columns were downright prescient — it was just a sideline.

The job that really gave Salazar a sense of power was at KMEX. There he oversaw a staff of just three reporters and one cameraman. But that small staff did local reporting that was every bit as significant, in Salazar's mind, as anything he wrote for The Times. He sent his KMEX news team into East L.A. and other barrios to cover stories that the English-language media ignored. He made sure that his crew covered most, if not all, of the protest demonstrations held by Chicano activists — no small thing in an era when the schools, police and even the Roman Catholic Church were the targets of such protests.

None of the events the Salazar team covered was more controversial than the fatal shooting of two unarmed Mexican cousins by Los Angeles police in July 1970. In a tragic case of mistaken identity, Guillermo and Gildardo Sanchez were killed in their apartment when officers burst in looking for a criminal suspect. Their tactics were so questionable that seven LAPD officers would later be indicted on federal charges of violating the victims' civil rights. The officers were ultimately acquitted.

The killing of the Sanchez cousins stirred a major outcry in the Latino community back when the LAPD was not accustomed to being publicly criticized. KMEX's reporting on the case was largely responsible, which is why LAPD officials called on Salazar "to express their concern" about KMEX's coverage, as he wrote in a column afterward.

Despite the LAPD's concern, Salazar did not let up on KMEX's aggressive news coverage. A month later he was dead, his head shattered by a bullet-shaped tear gas projectile fired by a Los Angeles County sheriff's deputy at the height of a riot along Whittier Boulevard. Seen in this context, it is understandable why more than a few Latino activists are convinced to this day that Salazar's death was no accident. I have never shared that view, but I don't expect the controversy over his death to ever be fully resolved.

As much as anything he wrote, the circumstances of Salazar's death made him a martyr to the Chicano *movimiento*, a role no one would have found more ironic than Salazar himself. For above all, he was a principled journalist who saw his job as reporting the news, not making it. And one of his most important, if most overlooked, contributions was bringing high standards of journalism to the Spanish-language media just as they were beginning to proliferate in this country. Some Latinos claim KMEX news has never been as good as it was in Salazar's day.

Perhaps. All I know is that it was so good that I even wanted to work there. The last talk I ever had with Salazar was over the telephone, the day before he died. I told him that my summer internship at The Times was ending and asked if I could spend a few days at the KMEX newsroom before going to journalism graduate school. I wanted to see if I found journalism in Spanish more edifying than at The Times, which in those days was not always a comfortable place for minority reporters.

Salazar said I was welcome to visit but warned that he would try to talk me into staying at The Times. This newspaper also had an obligation to report on Latinos, he said, so that Anglo society would better understand the barrio and its problems. I told him we needed to talk more.

We never talked again, of course. But I knew that Salazar had won his point the very next night, when I stood on a burned-out Whittier Boulevard and watched his body being loaded into the coroner's hearse.

FEBRUARY 9, 1997

# Radio Bows to a Different World

*All is change with time.* — Stevie Wonder

POPULAR AS STEVIE WONDER IS, I doubt if many readers have heard the song from which I took the quote above. It's called "All in Love Is Fair."

Even in my own eclectic collection of phonograph records, tapes and CDs, I have only one version, on a jazz album by Carmen McRae and Cal Tjader.

Those words seem an appropriate way to comfort fans of popular radio station KSCA-FM (101.9), which last week became the most recent victim of Los Angeles' changing demographics. It signed off the air, to be replaced by the city's newest Spanish-language radio station.

Of course, the way local news media played the story, you'd have thought radio stations had never changed formats before. Many have, sometimes quite dramatically.

Take KFWB-AM (980), the city's only 24-hours news station. It was once the rock station in town. In the 1950s, to hear the latest Elvis, Buddy Holly or Fats Domino hit, youngsters like me tuned to KFWB.

KFWB's downfall as a rock station began in the 1960s, when a rival AM station, KHJ (930), got itself named the "official" outlet for an interesting new group called the Beatles.

But even KHJ's reign as the top station in town ended, and a few years ago it became one of the first English outlets to switch to Spanish. Which brings us back to KSCA.

One reason for all the news coverage KSCA's changeover got, I suspect, is the demographic profile of the station's former listeners. It was a small audience, the station's marketing director told The Times, but "very upscale … and virtually all white." In other words, the kinds of folks who will express their displeasure when something they like is suddenly changed and who have the clout to make themselves heard — even if they can't roll back the change that has them upset.

For weeks, loyal KSCA listeners have been sending letters of protest — not just through the mail but via computer — to the station. But its new owner, Heftel Broadcasting Corp., was not about to change its plans for KSCA. Heftel already owns the most popular radio station in Los Angeles, KLVE-FM (107.5), and wants to expand in the fast-growing Latino market.

"K-Love," as its executives prefer to call it, features an easy-listening Spanish format, mostly romantic ballads by singers like Julio Iglesias. That makes it popular with enough Latinos to be the highest-rated radio station in Los Angeles, according to the Arbitron ratings service. But KLVE is not every Latino's cup of *te*.

What is happening to Spanish-language radio here is what has long been the rule in the English-language market. A big population that looks homogenous to outsiders is really a collection of segments with varied tastes and interests. The new format of KSCA, for example, is what radio marketers call "regional Mexican." I'd define it as Mexican country music. Many KLVE listeners probably think of it as the kind of music rural hicks listen to. But it will surely find an audience, as nine other Spanish-language radio outlets have in Greater Los Angeles.

I don't want to seem unsympathetic to KSCA's former fans. I live with one of them. My wife, Magdalena, is a rock aficionado and will miss what she calls the "smart, adult music" KSCA played. It was a mix of what she considers the best rock music of the past 20 years, featuring groups like U2 and vocalists like Sting.

So to empathize, let me relate a final anecdote about the one local radio format change that I did take personally. About the time the Beatles broke up, I became a jazz buff. I'd always liked big bands, having been raised by a mother who liked not just Latin American artists like Lola Beltran and Perez Prado, but also Count Basie. In the early '70s, I began listening to KBCA-FM, a jazz station that carried me from Basie to Miles Davis, John Coltrane and other great artists. I've never looked back, but have been forced to look for other stations.

After changing its call letters to KKGO-FM (105.1) a few years ago, my favorite radio station also switched formats, to classical music. According to news stories at the time, we jazz buffs have less attractive demographics than other radio audiences. So the only outlet that tried to pick up the slack was the radio station at Cal State Long Beach, KLON-FM (88.1).

Thankfully, KLON also hired my favorite KBCA deejays, and together they have carried on, albeit with a much weaker radio signal. Sometimes they'll even play an obscure Stevie Wonder tune, as performed by Cal Tjader and Carmen McRae.

FEBRUARY 22, 1998

# Watergate Inspires in Any Language

CARTAGENA, Colombia — I came to this historic city on the Caribbean Sea to talk to a group of Latin American journalists about a 25-year-old political scandal that everyone still refers to with a single buzzword: "Watergate." In the process, I learned some hopeful lessons about an ongoing political scandal in Colombia that has also come to be known by a simple but all-encompassing label: *Ocho Mil*.

In Spanish that means 8,000. It was the case number assigned two years ago by the Colombian attorney general to his investigation into allegations that drug lords contributed $6 million to the 1994 election campaign of President Ernesto Samper.

Watergate, of course, eventually came to mean more than the Washington office complex where a "second-rate burglary" in 1972 launched the political scandal that brought down President Richard Nixon two years later. There are many Colombians who still harbor hopes that "the 8,000 process" will bring down Samper and lead to wholesale change in Colombia's political system — or at the very least end the corrupting influence of drug money in an otherwise proud and democratic nation.

Despite admissions by Samper's former campaign manager and finance chairman that drug money did flow into his campaign coffers and that he was fully aware of it, the Colombian Congress voted last summer to end its investigation into the scandal for lack of evidence. Not surprisingly, the 265-member body is dominated by members of Samper's party. Samper is now expected to complete his single four-year term, and Colombians will elect a new president later this year. The seminar I addressed was organized to help Colombian journalists better report on that campaign.

That the 8,000 scandal refuses to die is in no small part due to aggressive reporting by a young new generation of Colombian journalists, many working for historic but revitalized newspapers like Bogota's El Tiempo. Congress may have cleared Samper, but journalists simply refuse to let up on the case. They have been encouraged — indeed, even inspired — in this campaign by the 1982 Nobel laureate in literature, Gabriel García Márquez.

The author of such modern literary classics as "One Hundred Years of Solitude" and "Love in the Time of Cholera" began his writing career as a reporter for Bogota's other leading daily, El Espectador. He waxed nostalgic about his reporting days at the seminar, telling the 25 Colombian print and broadcast reporters in attendance that they must "strive to recapture the excitement of those heady days," for their own good and for the betterment of Colombian democracy.

The seminar was the latest organized by the Foundation for a New Iberoamerican Journalism, established by García Márquez in 1995 in this coastal city where he makes his home. Faculty for the seminars include senior journalists from all over the world drawn here by his stature.

García Márquez asked me to come not because I'm any kind of expert on Watergate. But I was a second-string reporter for The Times during the 1972 presidential campaign, and I also helped our great investigative reporter, Jack Nelson, in the early days of Watergate, when he needed a Spanish-speaking reporter to go into Miami's Cuban exile community to learn whatever could be learned about the four Cuban Americans who were involved in the Watergate burglary.

García Márquez wanted young Colombian journalists to hear the Watergate story from someone who lived through it and through the remarkable changes that American journalism has undergone since. Indeed, as I briefed my Colombian colleagues about the campaign finance reforms that have come into effect since 1972 and about the legal access that journalists now have to probe such records, I couldn't help but admire them for working so doggedly without any of the tools U.S. reporters have at their disposal.

There are many well-meaning Americans, I know, who think the proverbial pendulum has swung too far since Watergate and that the press has far too much power (and too little self-restraint) in reporting on scandals like President Clinton's alleged sexual escapades.

But, as I told my Colombian audience, the reporting we have done since 1972 has helped make Americans more knowledgeable about their political process and perhaps even more mature about it. So mature that, according to most public opinion polls, they are now willing to forgive sex scandals as long as public officials are honest on the job and effective.

Of course, whether Bill Clinton is honest and effective is what underlies the more careful reporting about the current White House scandal. It is also what underlies the best reporting about the other Washington scandal that could go a lot further in undermining Clinton's presidency: the heavy-handed fundraising that preceded his reelection campaign.

When I told my Colombian colleagues that they have not heard the last about "Donorgate," they were reassured that U.S. journalism has not lost its way and is still a model for them.

# CHAPTER SIX

# Education

*Striving for schools that again
can 'stand and deliver'*

IT IS NO SURPRISE that Frank del Olmo's first column dealt with education. Graduating magna cum laude from California State University, Northridge, del Olmo saw education as his route out of the San Fernando Valley barrios, as well as a way to make a difference.

In one column, he praised the achievements of calculus teacher Jaime Escalante and his Garfield High students in East Los Angeles. As portrayed in the film "Stand and Deliver," they showed what Latino inner-city students — motivated by a teacher with *ganas* (desire) — can achieve. Del Olmo wanted excellent schools to be accessible to all residents but lamented what he saw: California's education system, once the nation's model, was crumbling. He made a strong case for less talk and more action.

# Bilingual Education Works — Just Ask Connie Jimenez

I T'S NOT AS IF WE NEEDED more controversy in California over bilingual education, but we're going to get it. U.S. Secretary of Education Shirley Hufstedler guaranteed that recently when she announced the bilingual education guidelines that her department, for the first time, wants to require all school districts receiving money from the federal government to meet.

Among other things, the guidelines would require schools to test students to see if they should be taught in a language other than English. Any school with more than 25 students within two grades who speak the same foreign language would be required to set up a bilingual program; students would have to leave such programs within five years, regardless of English proficiency.

The proposed guidelines will be the subject of public hearings across the country in the next few weeks, and bilingual education's many critics should have a field day. A whole series of them, in fact.

California has already received a taste of what is coming. It has taken the Legislature almost two years of wrangling to come up with guidelines for bilingual education in this state. And the compromise bill that would enact them into law must still be approved by the state Senate before Gov. Jerry Brown, who supports it, can sign it.

In all the arguing about bilingual education, it would help to keep in mind just what it is and how it's supposed to work.

More than anything else, bilingual education is designed to keep children who do not speak English in the educational mainstream. It does this by not letting them drop behind their peers and by acknowledging their home language and culture as valuable. It is when students fall behind, or feel alienated from their school, that there begins the downward spiral leading to the high dropout rates and low test scores often found in minority schools.

In Southern California, this involves mostly Spanish-speaking children, although the current influx of Asian refugees may create challenges similar to those facing San Francisco's schools in dealing with the children of that city's Chinese population.

Bilingual education has had a bad rap in the last decade not because the theory is bad but because it has been poorly executed in many districts. At least one reason is that there are not enough bilingual teachers to carry out even the best-planned programs.

I wish that all the people who will come forward in the next few weeks to criticize bilingual education could have been with me a couple of months ago when I visited Bridge Street Elementary School in Boyle Heights. It is one of the older schools in Los Angeles and, like many an inner-city school, does not wear its age well.

A two-story building dating back to the 1930s, its mustard-yellow exterior is faded and chipped. On a bad day the school could blend in with the smog but for the small murals painted along one side of the building and the children playing on its barren asphalt playground.

I went to visit the third-grade class taught by an old friend of mine — a bright, capable young woman named Connie Jimenez. She had asked me to talk to her class about my work at The Times. She met me in the hallway outside to tell me about the 27 children I was about to greet.

"Some of them will ask questions in English, and some in Spanish. Just remember to answer in the language they ask the question in, then translate to make sure everyone understands," she said.

Now, English is my primary language, but I work hard at maintaining my Spanish and take some pride in being bilingual.

I have conducted many interviews in Spanish, on some sensitive and complicated subjects. But I don't think the first few minutes of any such session were as nerve-wracking for me as what those third-graders put me through.

Maybe it was the utter lack of inhibition with which they asked their questions. No diplomatic formalities or measured words here, just "Do you like to go to fires?" "How much do they pay you?" "Do you fly on airplanes?"

I worked hard to keep my wits, answering each question clearly and succinctly, determined not to counteract, by some thoughtless slip of the tongue, the work that Connie had done.

But I began to relax when I realized that something was different in this classroom. As the questions kept zipping at me like so many fastballs, I realized that for the first time in several years of teaching and visiting classrooms, from grade school through university levels, I was talking to a class in which everybody was participating.

In many schools, especially minority schools in poor communities, there are stragglers — youngsters who seem lost. Not here. Even at the rear of the classroom, every time I looked toward one child with a raised hand, two or three nearby shot up their arms also. Either I was besieged by the smartest bunch of little Chicanos in the world or I had stumbled onto one of those special places where the much-maligned bilingual experiment was working well.

I am convinced that it was the latter, because I know Connie Jimenez. She is hard-working and enthusiastic, like many a fine young teacher. But, equally important, she is a Chicana who has spoken some Spanish all her life and knows how it can be as wonderful to use as English, and she conveys this feeling to her students.

Connie has been a bilingual teacher six years and knows that it can work "if people will just give it a chance."

"A lot of other teachers I meet, who aren't working at bilingual schools, are negative about it." she adds. "Maybe they feel threatened by it. But some parents are skeptical too. I think they all just don't know enough about it."

"It's not just Spanish, but English too. It works both ways. What we lack is teachers, people who know what they're doing."

When it came time for her class to break for lunchtime, Connie walked me out of the classroom and thanked me. "I think they got a lot out of it," she said.

So did I. A renewed conviction that bilingual education can work, and inspiration at how beautiful it can be when it does.

This is the first column by Frank del Olmo published in The Times.

# Scoring Controversy Tests Latino Community Pride

THE EDUCATIONAL TESTING SERVICE is probably so accustomed to national controversy by now that the current dispute involving 14 Garfield High School students must seem like a minor irritant. But its officials should not underestimate the depth of feeling in Los Angeles' Chicano community over the way events unfolded.

The testing service, a nonprofit corporation based in Princeton, N.J., administers standardized tests for everyone from high school juniors to applicants for law school and other professional and graduate programs. Two years ago, no less a consumer watchdog than Ralph Nader charged that the service's college admission tests were biased in favor of students from upper-income families and had little value as a predictor of future performance.

Last year, service officials were red-faced when defective questions were found in four different tests — including the all-important Scholastic Aptitude Test, which helps determine where thousands of high school students will attend college.

Given this context, it's easy to see why the service might not pay much attention to the protests of the Mexican American Bar Assn., the Mexican-American Education Commission and other groups over the treatment of 14 youngsters from East Los Angeles. But the service's actions have touched a raw nerve in a community that is understandably sensitive about unwarranted slights against its young people.

The gist of the Garfield High incident is this:

Last May, 18 students took an advanced-calculus placement test administered by the testing service. All passed — seven with a perfect score of 5 points, four others with 4 points. A few weeks later, according to Jaime Escalante, their mathematics teacher, 14 of the students received letters from the testing service asking questions about their performance. The service wanted to know why the students solved a particular problem in exactly the same way and why they had similar answers on the multiple choice portion of the examination.

Escalante, a demanding instructor who insists that his advanced-math students work after school hours and use college-level textbooks, said that the explanation can be found in his highly structured teaching methods. He emphasizes a step-by-step approach to problem solving and a methodical answering process that often involves graphs.

While he concedes that the technique might seem rigid, it has proved remarkably successful in preparing Garfield students to take advanced math classes. Escalante began using his method at Garfield in 1979, and each year since the number of students taking trigonometry and calculus classes has increased. At the same time, the number who passed the testing service's standardized tests increased from four in 1979 to eight in 1980 to a high of 15 in 1981.

That explanation was not good enough for the testing service. It insisted that the students either forfeit their high scores or take the test again. Twelve chose the latter option (the other two had already left school). On the retest, all 12 passed again — with five scoring 5 points and four scoring 4. All but one of the students have graduated and are attending such colleges as Columbia, Princeton, UC Berkeley, USC and UCLA.

Not surprisingly, many members of the school staff suspect that these students were subjected to such a forceful challenge because they were Latinos attending an inner-city school.

Spokesmen for the testing service deny that the incident had anything to do with the students' ethnic background. They offer credible explanations as to why test scorers might have noted the similarity in answers and passed on a query to the testing service's review boards, which handle all dealings with individual students.

But if the testing service's caution is understandable, so is the anger at Garfield. Teachers and parents are so used to hearing about problems at Eastside schools — such as gangs, graffiti and dropout rates — that when there is cause for genuine pride it is doubly frustrating to have its validity questioned. Here were 14 smart Latinos doing extra work in a difficult subject and holding their own with the best young minds in the country. And how does it get into the news? When some faraway testing agency suggests that somebody may be cheating.

As if that were not enough, the testing service has also refused to discuss the Garfield case with anyone but the students and their families on privacy grounds. So far, the service has ignored requests for explanations and apologies from Escalante, other Garfield teachers and counselors and the principal, Henry Gradillas.

Gradillas wants the students' original test scores reinstated, and not just as a matter of principle. By scoring well, some of the former Garfield students received college credit for the advanced work that they did in high school. Those who didn't score as well the second time may have to take a freshman math course that they could have avoided. Also, he wants an apology, because he believes that Garfield's reputation has been unfairly maligned.

Escalante also wants the original scores reinstated, although it was he who finally urged his students to retake the calculus test lest further delays affect their chances of attending the colleges of their choice. He is uncomfortable with all the publicity and worries that the continuing controversy may begin to impair his teaching.

That seems unlikely. He teaches a hard subject and is very demanding of his students, but his enthusiasm for his work is obvious. And, as many other math teachers were succumbing to the lure of private industry, Escalante gave up a position with a major engineering company to return to teaching, his field in his native Bolivia.

One can't help but admire Escalante's energy in the classroom as he rapidly writes equations on the blackboard, prodding his students while he addresses them with playful nicknames like "Secret Agent" and "Marching Band." He is clearly one of those special teachers who deserve far more support and encouragement than they get. It's too bad that when recognition came he wasn't allowed to enjoy it.

# Cathedral Alumni Show They Learned Lessons Well

OFFICIALS OF THE Los Angeles Archdiocese may have anticipated some community disappointment over their recent decision to close Cathedral High School, a predominantly Latino boys' school just north of downtown. But they were clearly taken aback by the scope and vehemence of the criticism. Apparently they were unaware of what Catholic schools like Cathedral have come to mean to Latino families over the last few decades.

Cathedral has been operated since 1924 by the Christian Brothers, a teaching order that is probably better known to most people for its winery in Northern California. Profits from the winery heavily subsidize Cathedral and nine other schools that the brothers operate throughout the country. More than a third of Cathedral's 500 students get some scholarship or work-study assistance to help pay the $1,000 annual tuition. Part of the cost of education at Cathedral is also borne by the archdiocese, which gave $6.3 million in the 1983-84 school year toward the support of Catholic schools in Los Angeles, Ventura and Santa Barbara counties.

The cozy cathedral campus sits on a knoll just below Dodger Stadium. One does not have to be a real estate speculator to appreciate the market value of such a site, close to the central business district and with a fine view of the downtown skyscrapers. Unofficial estimates run from $8 million to $14 million. So it is easy to understand the logic of archdiocesan officials: They figured that other Catholic high schools nearby could absorb cathedral's students, while the property's revenue would benefit all. The transaction was considered routine, and by July, when it became known that Cathedral would be closed next June, sale of the property was already in escrow.

The storm broke immediately. Students, parents and alumni launched a campaign to save the school, generating a remarkable degree of political support. Within days, there were more purple-and-white "Save Cathedral High" bumper stickers on cars in East Los Angeles than "L.A. '84" strips.

Latino politicians, from U.S. Rep. Edward R. Roybal (D-Los Angeles) on down, began calling on church officials, asking that the school be spared. And the Los Angeles City Council voted to declare the school a cultural monument, which could delay its demolition for years (but will not affect the decision to close the institution).

What has everyone upset, even angry, is that church officials didn't bother to consult the people most affected before deciding to close Cathedral. They would have learned that to many Latino Catholics, the school is a community resource. For, at a time when the quality of education that minority students get in the public schools can most charitably be described as uneven, Catholic schools have played a key, perhaps even decisive, role in training and developing Latino leaders in this city.

Many of the Latino college students involved in the Chicano activism of the 1960s, for example, who today are among the city's up-and-coming lawyers, doctors, teachers, businessmen and politicians, graduated from Catholic high schools like Cathedral — or Loyola, or Bishop Alemany in San Fernando, or Salesian in Boyle Heights, Pater Noster in Glassell Park, Mount Carmel in Montebello.

And Catholic schools educated many of the leaders of the United Neighborhoods Organization of East Los Angeles. UNO is the largest and most effective Latino community group in the city, and one of its key strengths lies in its being organized around Catholic parishes and Protestant churches on the Eastside.

Anyone who knows U.S. history realizes there is nothing new to this pattern. It is the same thing that parochial schools in other large American cities did for the children of previous generations of Roman Catholic immigrants, like the Irish in Boston, Italians in New York or the Polish in Chicago. Catholic schools helped acculturate those new Americans, keeping their ethnic identity and religion strong while preparing them to deal socially and politically in a pluralistic society.

Cathedral High School was built on the fringes of what was then an Italian neighborhood to serve children of workers who lived there. Apart from the wedge of Chinatown, the area has been mostly Latino for two generations, a fact reflected in the makeup of Cathedral's student body.

It is because so many of Cathedral's alumni were well-taught by the Christian Brothers that they are now leaders of this city, active in business, politics and the church. And deeply concerned about public issues affecting the Latino community — such as the campaign to save a high school that for 60 years has taken boys from the inner city and turned them into young men ready to face the outside world.

FEBRUARY 14, 1985

# Bad Teachers: Putting the University on the Spot Too

IN 1969, I was one of a handful of Chicano students attending San Fernando Valley State College who persuaded a respected Mexican American historian to give up his job at a private college in order to build a Chicano studies department at our school.

We all believed that if anyone could make Valley State — or Cal State Northridge, as it is now called — more sensitive to Latino students it was Rodolfo Acuña. After all, Acuña, who holds a Ph.D in Latin American history, was as well known for his political activism as for his academic research into the history of the Southwestern United States and the Mexican Americans who helped build the region.

Fifteen years later I know that we made the right choice, but I am just as sure that university officials wish that we had picked someone else.

For, despite his academic credentials, Acuña also is a gadfly who freely criticizes the shortcomings of the system that nurtures him. Only his reputation as a teacher and the fact that he has tenure protect him when he gets into internal brouhahas with his academic peers and superiors. The latest round began when Acuña criticized Chancellor Anne Reynolds' proposal to raise student admission standards for the state university system.

Reynolds believes that Latinos and other minority students will have a better chance of success in higher education if they are better prepared by the state's high schools before they arrive at Cal State's 19 campuses. She sold the idea to the university board of trustees, who decided that, starting in 1988, high school students applying for admission must have completed at least four years of English, three years of mathematics and social sciences, two years of science and foreign languages and one year of fine arts.

"Improved high school preparation is the single most important element in expanding minority access to and persistence in higher education,"

Reynolds wrote recently.

But when they try to explain how their new admission requirements will get the state's high schools to improve the quality of instruction that they offer, state university officials never seem to mention one important fact: The state university produces 50% to 70% of the teachers now working in California's schools. If those schools are doing a less-than-satisfactory job, one wonders if part of the problem might be that the institution training most of our teachers also is doing a less-than-satisfactory job.

Acuña said as much in a recent letter to The Times. Warning that the new requirements might keep many otherwise-qualified Latino students from getting into the state university system, Acuña acerbically suggested that Reynolds "should pay more attention to improving conditions for students and professors within [her] system" before trying to improve schools that are someone else's responsibility. Now he is getting flak from fellow faculty members and haughty letters from the chancellor's office.

In one of those letters, Associate Chancellor John W. Bedell cites some "decisive steps" that Reynolds has taken to improve the quality of teacher training in the Cal State system, "such as raising the requirements for completion of the programs, adding incentives for master teachers and strengthening the student teaching experience."

I find it sadly revealing that Bedell's letter does not mention other steps that would be just as useful in helping student teachers prepare to deal with minority students, who have now become a majority in Los Angeles' public schools as well as in those of other large cities.

How about ethnic studies classes to sensitize teachers to the hard realities of life in this nation's barrios and ghettos? The Chicano Studies Department was set up at Cal State Northridge precisely because state colleges train so many teachers, and those future teachers must be prepared to work in Latino communities.

Or how about teaching them foreign languages? Perhaps it would lessen Anglo teachers' hostility toward bilingual-education programs and for the bilingual teacher aides who work in many schools with large immigrant populations.

Acuña has been arguing for such remedial steps for years, and he's still fighting the good fight despite pressure from his peers, and on high, to keep quiet.

When he was hired at Cal State Northridge, the school had fewer than a dozen Chicano students. University officials cite the fact that 1,300 are now enrolled there as a sign that things have improved. But that represents less than 5% of a student body of 28,000.

Meanwhile, statistics released last week by the Los Angeles Unified School District indicate that Latinos represent 52% of the public school students in Los Angeles and 63% of those in kindergarten. In light of those numbers, 5% is not good enough. And when Acuña raises the discomfiting question of whether new admission requirements will keep the number of Chicanos in the Cal State system low, he deserves more than icy, pro forma letters in response.

Cal State officials had better be sure that their own house is in order, as Acuña suggests, before shifting the responsibility for improving public education to the state's high schools.

NOVEMBER 4, 1988

# Schools Don't Need More Talk, They Need Action

I'M NOT SURE precisely when it happened, but sometime between that fall day in 1953 when I first entered a California public school and a fall day in 1980 when my daughter did the same, people in this state seemed to stop caring about education. It saddens me, as a son of this blessed commonwealth, that we have reached a point where our state education budget is so tight that California, which once led the nation in spending on public schools, is now among the states that spend the least amount of money per pupil. We ranked 47th in a recent survey that measured per capita spending on schools.

Many people can share the blame for this state of affairs.

Start with former Gov. Ronald Reagan and the student protesters whom he campaigned against when he first ran for office in 1966. Reagan promised to make students in the state's colleges pay tuition for the first time in history, arguing that they should have to "pay to carry their picket signs." He got voters to take an us-against-them attitude toward teachers too. Public education in this state has yet to recover from the resulting alienation.

Former Gov. Jerry Brown didn't help, either. After a generation in which Republican and Democratic governors alike supported public schools and built a great state college and university system, Brown made little or no effort to reverse Reagan's negative trend. In fact, his "small is beautiful" philosophy may have fed the public perception that California, a state built by people who thought big, had done enough for its young people.

Howard Jarvis, the godfather of Proposition 13, the property tax limitation initiative approved by state voters in 1978, put his heavy hand into the mix too. With its meat-ax approach to government expenditures, Proposition 13 forced public officials all over California to cut not just the fat in their budgets but meat as well. Among the most badly hurt were public schools, which were the most dependent on property tax revenues.

Paul Gann delivered a second devastating blow in 1979, when voters approved his initiative that took Proposition 13 a step further, limiting the amount of tax money that the state can spend each year. Its formula has proved so restrictive that the state is now spending too little not just on schools but also on health care and other vital services. Even people who still think that Proposition 13 was useful have doubts about the "Gann limits" that are strangling California's ability to provide public services.

Educators are to blame too. School administrators have not done enough to reform the education system that they oversee. And many teachers' unions seem more interested in pressing their demands through strikes than in improving the quality of their members' work.

The tragedy of all this is that public support for California's schools dried up precisely when it was needed the most — just as many urban school districts started struggling with an influx of students whose parents are immigrants from Latin America and Asia, and when schools everywhere began preparing young people to work in a changing world and national economy.

It has become a cliché for political and business leaders to talk about the challenges facing California in the 21st century, of the riches that await us if we exploit our ties to the Pacific Rim, and of the harm that could befall us if we let aggressive competitors like Japan continue to outpace us. The latest such effort, a report titled "Return to Greatness," was put together by a commission that included representatives of high-tech companies like Apple Computer and Hewlett Packard and AT&T.

Unfortunately, that's all that California's current crop of leaders have done about schools so far — talk.

We can start getting action on Nov. 8 if state voters approve one of the least publicized but most important initiatives on the state ballot. Proposition 98 would lift the Gann limits on the state's education budget, requiring that schools get no less support than they received in 1986-87, roughly 38.6% of the general fund.

Proposition 98 is controversial. Because it would leave the Gann limits in place on the rest of the state budget, its opponents argue that other services might suffer in order to pay for our schools. They call for trying to repeal the Gann limits across the board. But how long is that going to take? And what happens to this state's children in the meantime? Leaving a few thousand more kids to a few more years of mediocre education smacks of cruelty.

Ever since a lame Franciscan friar, Junipero Serra, had the courage to start building a chain of missions in what was then a desolate outpost of the Spanish empire, this has been a state of doers. That's how '49ers made their fortunes. That's how San Franciscans built a jewel of a city from the ashes of a terrible earthquake. That's why, despite the Depression, Angelenos banked on a film industry to send celluloid dreams all over the world. That's how our aircraft and ship builders helped win the biggest war in history. It's how we built a freeway system that's the envy of the nation and a public school system that used to be — by doing rather than just talking.

We'll revive some of that get-it-done tradition if we approve Proposition 98.

# The Ghosts of Bustop Haunt LAUSD, This Time Speaking Spanish

**W**HEN MY SOURCES at the Los Angeles Unified School District told me they'd seen a ghost wandering the halls of district headquarters, I figured it was a Halloween prank. But then the reformers who recently took control of the LAUSD board ousted Supt. Ruben Zacarias and put the ghost in charge.

That's what happened Tuesday when the LAUSD board quite suddenly — and quite sloppily — created the new post of chief executive officer, reducing Zacarias to a figurehead. The 33-year veteran of the school district has not taken kindly to the coup and is marshaling his political support in the increasingly assertive Latino community. As a result, I can foresee a scenario for both public education and ethnic politics in this city that — to extend the Halloween metaphor — gets pretty scary.

The ghost is Howard Miller, the Century City attorney who (for the time being, at least) is the LAUSD's new CEO. This is the same Howard Miller who, as president of the L.A. school board, was recalled from office in a bitter election 20 years ago over the issue of busing for racial balance.

Those of us who cover politics in L.A. wrote Miller's political obituaries after that 1979 vote. He was, after all, the first (and still the only) public official recalled by citywide vote since 1938, when the notoriously corrupt Mayor Frank Shaw was run out of office.

To be sure, Miller's sins were not like Shaw's. Indeed, some still consider Miller, a USC law professor when he was first appointed to the LAUSD board in 1976, one of the smartest people to ever hold public office in Los Angeles.

But in politics, Miller had a tin ear. He came onto the LAUSD board publicly skeptical about mandatory school busing, then looming over the district as a result of a 1963 desegregation lawsuit. But when the courts ordered busing to begin in 1978, the dutiful law professor took the lead in trying to implement their mandate.

And that sealed Miller's doom. In less than a year, Bustop, the San Fernando Valley-based group that led the opposition to busing here, launched the recall campaign that drove Miller from office. Elected to his seat on the board was a Valley anti-busing activist, Roberta Weintraub.

Weintraub wound up serving on the board until 1993. But the ripple effect of the Valley's rebellion against school busing lingered far longer, and far more profoundly, than that.

Bustop, and all that it accomplished politically — the defeat of a judge involved in the desegregation case and at least one liberal congressman — gave Valley voters a sense of just how much political clout they could wield. Its echoes resonate in the Valley secession movement of today, a movement that will almost surely force a vote to break up the city sometime early in the next century.

Now, in their zeal to shake up the LAUSD, the well-meaning but hamhanded reformers who brought Miller back to political life may have set the same kind of political dynamic in motion. Only this time, thousands of newly enfranchised Latino voters are in the position of the Valley suburbanites: Their children are a majority in the schools, and while they tend to like their neighborhood schools, they are increasingly worried and frustrated over what they see going on at LAUSD headquarters.

This is the simmering discontent that Zacarias and his many political allies can tap into if they choose to make a fight of the current impasse. For, whatever his flaws, the superintendent has done a very thorough job of cultivating his support not just among Latino parents but among Latino public officials and the middle-class Latino voters who provide the backbone of their political support. And let no one forget that many of those middle-class Latinos owe their social status to jobs in the public sector — including the public schools.

Zacarias is not blameless for the bureaucratic mess at the LAUSD. The district's biggest single problem, the scandal-plagued Belmont Learning Complex project, began long before his watch. But in his three years on the job, Zacarias has been far too tolerant of the painfully obvious shortcomings of his colleagues in the schools' administration. He pats too many a head that would be better lopped off — which is why the LAUSD board voted 4-2, with one abstention, to bring Miller in.

But like the political neophytes and zealots they are, the board majority got ahead of itself. They did not do a good job of laying the groundwork for Zacarias' ouster. Indeed, a smarter strategy would have been to find a way to make Zacarias part of the solution. The good cop to Miller's bad cop.

Instead, the reformers now have as the foremost symbol of their great experiment at the LAUSD a man whose name is forever linked to the last great failed experiment in L.A.'s public schools — forced busing.

And if Zacarias' ouster creates the political firestorm I fear, with a newly empowered Latino majority facing off against downtown business leaders, liberal Jews and African Americans, I can foresee the LAUSD being broken up into smaller districts, with the city of Los Angeles itself to follow not long afterward.

My sources at the school district have good reason to jump at the sight of political ghosts. For even as Howard Miller and Ruben Zacarias struggle, looming over both of their heads is the specter of Bustop — speaking in Spanish.

FEBRUARY 24, 2002

# Latinos Have Waited Long Enough for the Belmont Complex

THE POOR NEIGHBORHOODS around Belmont High School have been waiting 20 years for another secondary school to relieve student overcrowding. But that school has never opened, at least partly because the narrow agendas of politicians and interest groups keep getting in the way. So why should things be any different now?

On Tuesday, Los Angeles schools Supt. Roy Romer will ask the Board of Education to approve a plan to finish the new Belmont Learning Complex. That should be a no-brainer, since the new site is just a few blocks from 79-year-old Belmont High, where 5,000 students are jammed onto a campus designed for half that many.

With the can-do optimism that has characterized his brief tenure in Los Angeles, Romer is confident a school board that voted to shut down the project two years ago will give it another try. But rumors continue to circulate that powerful players in local school politics may try to delay the school's opening for many more months, if not years. Such rumors cannot be easily dismissed.

The latest twist in the Belmont saga involves a possible standoff between the nonprofit group that wants to finish the Belmont Learning Complex and the district's teachers union, United Teachers of Los Angeles.

Alliance for a Better Community, or ABC, is the nonprofit that says it can finish the already costly ($154 million) complex for an additional $68 million to $88 million, mitigating safety issues that halted the project in 1999.

ABC is a Latino education reform group organized two years ago by local community activists and corporate executives. It was created to protect the interests of Latino students — who make up 70% of the Los Angeles Unified School District — even as a newly elected school board majority began to shake up the LAUSD by, among other things, firing a popular Latino superintendent.

Rather than pushing to break up the district, as some angry Latino activists wanted, ABC opted to work for education reforms that would keep the interests of Latino kids foremost. The plan to complete the Belmont complex is ABC's first big effort. The ever-pragmatic Romer will recommend ABC's plan to the school board as the best of the proposals to finish the project.

Romer has done such a good job of laying the groundwork for reviving the project that some school board members who voted to close it down in 1999 now may vote to reopen it. That only makes the discordant note sounded by UTLA all the more jarring.

Teachers union officials are not opposed to finishing the new high school but worry about another part of ABC's reform agenda: charter schools. The Latino reform group says it hopes to use the Belmont Learning Complex, when it finally opens, to experiment with charter schools — campuses supported by public funds but run like private schools under state charters.

UTLA President Day Higuchi says his union is not against charter schools per se but is "totally opposed" to Edison Schools Inc., the New York-based company advising ABC on how to set up charter schools, because of labor problems it has had in other cities.

This is a risky stance for the UTLA. It will not look good for a white-collar union to stand as the last roadblock to a project desperately needed by the children of working-class immigrants whom many other local labor unions are trying to sign up as members.

But UTLA's leaders are no fools. And the Latino leaders who founded ABC are as pragmatic and politically well connected as Romer, a former Colorado governor and former chair of the Democratic National Committee.

So I suspect a way will be found around UTLA's objections — like putting off any discussion of charter schools until construction of the Belmont complex is finished.

But I can't help but wonder if this final skirmish in the long fight to get the Belmont Learning Complex built isn't also the first battle in an even bigger war: the fight to get Latino kids in Los Angeles the quality education they deserve, no matter who gets in the way.

SEPTEMBER 7, 2003

# Mechistas?
# It's *Mucho* Ado About *Nada*

I T SHOULDN'T SURPRISE ANYONE who reads this column that I was active in the again-controversial Latino student group MEChA during my college days.

MEChA is an esoteric Spanish acronym that translates as Chicano Student Movement of Aztlan. That final word refers to an ancient legend that places an Aztec homeland somewhere in the north. A few Mexican Americans use the word to refer to the U.S. Southwest, and extremists on both ends of the political spectrum interpret that as a desire by Chicanos to reclaim that region — somehow, someday — for Mexico.

But such a far-out idea was never on my agenda in the 1960s, when I was one of the few Mexican Americans at UCLA or, later, at Cal State Northridge. I just wanted to help get more Latinos into college.

Thankfully, MEChA was successful in reaching its goals by focusing on such practical matters.

So successful that thousands of young Latinos in college have created about 300 MEChA chapters, and similar groups, aimed at Latino students on campuses from San Diego to Boston. And most of them are even more benign in their aspirations and activities than the Mechistas I went to college with.

But that has not stopped some folks from trying to equate MEChA with hate groups like the Ku Klux Klan. Some of these claims are based on genuine confusion, such as attributing offensive political slogans once used by other Chicano groups ("For the race, everything. Outside the race, nothing") to MEChA.

Of course, the rhetoric some then-Mechistas used was overblown. But they were immature activists who — ignorant of a long history of Mexican American activism — really thought they were the community's political vanguard.

That is why Lt. Gov. Cruz Bustamante should not renounce his affiliation with the MEChA chapter at Fresno State in the 1970s, when Bustamante was a student there. A rival candidate in the campaign leading up to the Oct. 7 recall election, Sen. Tom McClintock (R-Thousand Oaks), made that demand recently, repeating the canard that MEChA is a racist militant group.

But if the normally diligent senator had done better homework he'd have found that MEChA is no more militant and racist than the Young Republicans clubs on many campuses.

Bustamante is not the first Latino politician to be attacked for his MEChA ties. A few supporters of Los Angeles Mayor James Hahn attacked City Councilman Antonio Villaraigosa for the same thing during a tight race for the top job in City Hall three years ago, although Hahn did not join in.

And it's a safe bet other Latino politicians will face similar attacks as they run for higher office.

Despite the bigoted undertones of these attacks, I find them humorous. They simply don't jibe with the mundane reality of the largely social organization I belonged to.

There is no national MEChA organization, just clubs on campuses where students want to organize. I never filled out any application to join or paid dues. I just showed up at occasional meetings (and more often at off-campus parties) and helped at fundraising events or tutored fellow students. Not very radical.

Which is not to say that some MEChA members were not involved in radical politics. This was the '60s, after all, and some Mechistas also belonged to genuinely militant groups like the Brown Berets, a small Chicano group that aped the militancy of the Black Panther Party. But the overwhelming majority of Mechistas I knew, as is the case today, were hardworking kids of blue-collar backgrounds. And because they were usually the first in their families to attend college, they were not about to undermine their futures by getting into radical politics.

In fact, one of my most vivid memories of college is of a large antiwar protest on the CSUN campus where I and a handful of other senior MEChA members moved through the crowd looking for younger Latinos or Latinas, urging them to leave. We didn't want them to jeopardize their slots in college or any scholarships by getting arrested. And most of them complied.

As this anecdote may reveal, I was a pretty conservative Mechista. I even opposed changing the name of what once was called United Mexican American Students, or UMAS, to MEChA in 1969 but lost out to majority opinion. But so did a loudmouthed transfer student from UC Berkeley, who wanted to change the name to Partido Popular Estudiantil (the Students' Peoples Party). I knew that leftist proposal would lose after I got a big laugh by pointing out that UMAS would be mocked if it started referring to itself as PPE — deliberately pronouncing the acronym.

When adults who should know better try to demonize a legitimate student group — and the idealistic young people who join it — they're just PPEing in the wind too.

# CHAPTER SEVEN

# Sports

*The pride of the Angelenos, from*
*Fernandomania to* futbol

DODGER BASEBALL FANS fell in love with Fernando Valenzuela in 1981 when the rookie pitcher from Sonora, Mexico, led
them to a World Series victory.

An avid sports fan, Frank del Olmo admired Valenzuela's
pitching prowess too but said he rooted for him because "I love
Los Angeles and appreciate anything that helps give this megalopolis a sense of community. I also appreciate anyone who helps
this community better understand and appreciate its largest ethnic minority, 3 million Mexican Americans."

For similar reasons, del Olmo wrote about the symbolism
represented by other Latino sports heroes, such as former Raiders
Coach Tom Flores, quarterback Jim Plunkett and 1984 Olympic
gold medalist Paul Gonzales. And when the Rams and the Raiders both abandoned Los Angeles, del Olmo knew that Latino fans
had an answer to the loss of pro football: Are you ready for some
*futbol*?

# Latino Pride Comes Served in a Bowl, and It's Super

OAKLAND — It is estimated that some 100 million people will watch, listen to or read about this year's Super Bowl game between the Oakland Raiders and the Philadelphia Eagles. So it's a safe bet that in the coming two weeks the Raiders' head coach, Tom Flores, and the team's starting quarterback, Jim Plunkett, will be the most publicized and talked about Chicanos in the world. At least this side of Cesar Chavez.

Just how significant that will be to American Latinos hit me the Monday morning after the Raiders won a berth in the Super Bowl by defeating the San Diego Chargers for championship of the American Football Conference. (Philadelphia emerged at the top of the National Conference.)

First there was a telephone call from a reporter with a Spanish-language newspaper. Admitting he knew "next to zero" about American-style football, he wanted to know where he could get information about these two Mexican American sport heroes.

Then came another telephone conversation, this time with a friend who is not an avid pro football fan. He had not even planned to watch the Raiders play the day before because he was taking his children to a birthday party. But he was surprised to arrive at the party and find many of the guests, all Latinos, gathered around a television set watching the football game and reveling in Plunkett's exploits.

My friend said his host was a native of Mexico who coaches soccer, the most popular sport in Latin America, where it is the only *futbol* that people talk about. Nevertheless, my friend said, here was this soccer fan rooting for Plunkett and "talking about him as a Chicano, just like he was a homeboy from East L.A."

I suspect that it's going to be hard to find many Mexican Americans — or other Latinos, for that matter — who will not be rooting for the Raiders on Super Bowl Sunday.

Interviewed at the Raiders' training facility here, Flores and Plunkett both said they were pleased that their participation in the game would probably increase Latino interest in it. But they were also quick to point out that being a Latino has little meaning on the football field.

That is precisely why their success is so significant to Latinos. Whether the Raiders win or lose the Super Bowl game, millions of Latinos will be proud simply that Flores and Plunkett are there. For they will be there not as representatives of their people but as competent professionals whose skill, determination and hard work have brought them to the pinnacle of success in their field.

There have been many Latino football stars at the high school and college level, but only a handful have ever made it to the pros. In most cases the size requirements of professional football have worked against Latinos. The one position where most Latino professional football players have excelled has been as kickers — usually soccer style.

Which is what sets Flores and Plunkett apart. Both were quarterbacks — and stars, at that.

Plunkett's has been a Cinderella story not once, but twice. He came from a poverty background in San Jose. His blind parents, a Mexican American mother and Irish father, supported three children by running a newsstand in a public office building, and occasionally had to go on welfare.

The strapping young Plunkett began working at an early age to help support the family and won a scholarship to Stanford. In his senior year, he won dozens of accolades, including the Heisman Trophy, and led Stanford to the Rose Bowl. His first year as a professional was a success too, but then a series of injuries almost ended his career.

Two years ago he was dropped by his last team, written off as a has-been at age 30. But the Raiders, particularly then-assistant coach Tom Flores, thought he still had potential. They nursed him along for a year so he could regain his health and confidence. Earlier this season the Raiders' starting quarterback was injured. Plunkett took over the team's leadership and has not looked back since.

Flores grew up in the San Joaquin Valley, the son of a farmworker from Chihuahua. He worked in the fields as a young man and says he might still be there but for a couple of lucky breaks.

When Flores played quarterback for the Raiders in the early 1960s, his teammates called him The Ice Man because of the extraordinary poise and patience that he displayed while being rushed by would-be tacklers.

The nickname was more than a little ironic. For, when Flores was 15, one of his breaks was getting a job in a Sanger ice factory. Lugging around 300-pound blocks of ice put muscles on his tall, lanky frame. "It was good for me," he says now of that job. "I saw that later, but it was hard to see then. The only thing I was sure of then was that it was better than working in the fields."

Flores was a popular star with the Raiders and other professional teams, and went into coaching when his playing days were over. He worked in relative obscurity for seven years as an assistant coach before being promoted two years ago. He is the first Latino to hold the high-visibility, high-pressure job of a pro football head coach.

"It's nice to be a first," he said. "I especially hope young people can identify with me. But I hope most people see me as just a Mexican American who worked hard, was optimistic and overcame some adversity to get where I am."

It's kind of hard for anybody to root against someone with an attitude like that.

Latino activists get very angry with those of us in the news media for not paying more attention to Latino heroes such as Plunkett and Flores, and less to Chicano gang members, illegal aliens from Mexico and other Latino "problems."

I can sympathize with that point of view, even while I know that our job is to report on society's ills, no matter what ethnic group is involved.

Which is why my next column will probably be on some Latino problem in East Los Angeles, along the Mexican border or in Central America. But in the meantime, like many a Latino, I'm going to enjoy the Super Bowl. No matter who wins.

# The Espinozas Join the Stankiewiczes in the Most All-American of Sports

**N**OT TO TAKE ANYTHING from Fernando Valenzuela's achievements last season, but it was hardly surprising that a Mexican eventually would be the No. 1 hero of the national pastime. Baseball has had a hold on Latin American and Caribbean countries for decades. But imagine the reaction we'll see when a Latino quarterback takes Notre Dame to a national championship.

That possibility is not too far-fetched. Every football fan can name blacks, Italian Americans and Polish Americans who have starred as the "Fighting Irish."

Although many people think that all Latino youngsters either belong to street gangs or have just sneaked across the border, most of them are typical teenagers and many of them play football, that most All-American of sports — and play it quite well.

Granted, relatively few of them, like few of all the other youngsters playing high school football, will ever attend "football factory" universities. Fewer still will enter the ranks of professional football. But, as they grow in size and number, Latino kids' chances for playing the high-visibility football of the pros and big colleges will increase in the coming years.

But to me that is not really what's important about all the Latino kids who prefer football to baseball, soccer and boxing — sports more closely associated in the public mind with Latino athletes.

What is noteworthy is that so many of these youngsters are quietly attending school, participating in extracurricular activities and will eventually graduate without having caused anyone much trouble — except for an occasional off-sides penalty.

Some will go on to junior colleges or lesser-known universities. Many will go right to work. They will raise families, pay taxes and, generally, become as typically American as the sport they played in high school. Just as the children of previous immigrants did.

A good example of this can be seen at St. Paul High School in Santa Fe Springs. The Roman Catholic school has a long tradition of winning football teams, and last week it defeated Colton High School, 30 to 9, to win the major conference championship of the California Interscholastic Federation, which represents most Southern California high schools outside the cities of Los Angeles and San Diego.

This year about two-thirds of St. Paul's football roster was made up of students with Spanish surnames — Morales, Espino, Oviedo, Pina, Mondaca, Palacios, Olmedo ... . Only in America, as the old saying goes, could a football team have a star quarterback named Espinoza throwing passes to a star receiver named Stankiewicz. (Latinos were well represented on the Colton team too; its leading ball carrier was a tailback named Mendoza.)

Like many private high schools, St. Paul draws its students from a wider geographic area than most public schools. Father Aidan Carroll, the school's principal, says most of the students come from within a five-mile radius of the campus — from cities including Pico Rivera, Whittier, Norwalk and La Mirada.

For at least the last 20 years, those cities and other suburbs southeast of downtown Los Angeles have seen a steady growth in Latino population. There always were small barrios in cities like Pico Rivera and Montebello, but most of the new Latino population has spread from Los Angeles' Eastside, as second- and third-generation Mexican Americans work their way up the economic ladder and out of the barrios. According to the 1980 census, for example, Santa Fe Springs' Spanish-surnamed population grew from 47% to 60% in the last decade, and Pico Rivera's from 61% to 76%.

The effect that this population growth has had on local football can be seen in the all-star team selected for the area this year by reporters in The Times' Southeast suburban section. Ten of the 22 young men listed are Spanish-surnamed, representing public high schools in Downey, Bell Gardens and Norwalk as well as St. Paul.

This year there are also Spanish-surnamed players on the all-star teams selected for the San Gabriel Valley, the Glendale/Burbank area and the San Fernando Valley.

This interest in football is not found only in suburban schools. One of the least reported major events that happens every year on Los Angeles' Eastside is the big game between Roosevelt and Garfield high schools.

Most non-Latinos in Los Angeles probably think that the only time these two schools confront each other is when rival gangs face off. Yet each year the game attracts upwards of 20,000 fans to an event that is as much a community celebration as a friendly football rivalry.

I am not trying to make more of this phenomenon than is really there, but I do think it represents something that we in the media often overlook. As this country's diverse and growing Latino population assimilates, many positive things are happening that may not be as dramatic or as troubling as the problems of the border or the barrios, but that are significant. One of them is the natural evolution of second- and third-generation Latinos into plain, ordinary Americans.

Father Carroll of St. Paul makes a valid point when he says that the young people at his school "have no real sense of any ethnic differences. They play sports, date and intermingle quite freely."

Which is just the way it should be. As natural as a quarterback named Espinoza lobbing touchdown passes to a receiver named Stankiewicz.

MARCH 11, 1982

# Valenzuela Is Knocked Out of the Box as a Role Model

ITH THE REAGAN ADMINISTRATION cutting back on bilingual education, calling for restrictive immigration laws and rattling sabers over Central America, one would think that Latinos had better things to worry about than whether Fernando Valenzuela will sign a new contract to pitch for the Dodgers.

Yet last week representatives of several major Latino organizations went to the trouble of holding a news conference to announce that, contrary to press reports, many Latinos are supporting the young Mexican left-hander during his spring training holdout.

Granted, things are not looking good on the Fernando Front these days. Talks between Dodger management and Valenzuela's agents have stalled with the two sides far apart in the salary figures they are talking about.

But is the most important issue facing Latinos in this community really a popular athlete's attempt to get more money out of his employers? Not really. And, if you cut through some of the overblown rhetoric, that is not what the Latino leaders were trying to say last week. They were reacting somewhat angrily to a problem transcending Valenzuela and his contract negotiations. They see the Latino community losing a hero. Not surprisingly, their anger at this turn of events is aimed not at the fallen star but at the other parties involved — Valenzuela's agents and the Dodgers. It is also aimed at the media, which are in the process of destroying one of the few positive role models for Latinos in recent years.

I won't argue one way or the other about how much money Valenzuela is worth to the Dodgers. I am enough of an idealist to be troubled that star athletes and other entertainers are paid more than teachers and nurses, yet I am enough of a realist to know that professional athletes have relatively brief careers and must earn what they can in a short time compared to other workers.

I am also not a Dodger fan. I lost interest in them, and in baseball in general, when I was 12 and they coldheartedly banished my boyhood idol, first baseman Gil Hodges, to the New York Mets.

I do not know Valenzuela's controversial agent, Antonio de Marco, and have never reported on the Latin American entertainment extravaganzas he promotes. His reputation in the Latino community is not favorable — he's considered egotistical and pompous. But then I don't know of any show business agents here who are really popular.

I do like Valenzuela, and toward the end of his rookie season I found myself rooting for him in a quiet sort of way. He is a pleasant and approachable young man, although really no more talkative or articulate than most other athletes I have ever interviewed, either in Spanish or in English.

The reason I rooted for him last year is because I love Los Angeles and appreciate anything that helps give this megalopolis a sense of community. I also appreciate anyone who helps this community better understand and appreciate its largest ethnic minority, 3 million Mexican Americans.

That's why it's sad to see what is being made of his holdout by the Dodgers, De Marco and by my colleagues in the press.

Latinos at last week's press conference, leaders of reputable groups like the American GI Forum and the League of United Latino American Citizens, came to the young pitcher's defense because they see him getting the same treatment that other Latinos get from the news media. At best, he is misunderstood. At worst, he is the victim of insensitive reporting and stereotyping.

They pointed to a Los Angeles Herald Examiner column boldly proclaiming that Valenzuela had lost the support of the barrios that rooted him to fame — this after the writer interviewed half a dozen Latinos.

They also pointed to a column in The Times full of south-of-the-border clichés and stereotypes. It tastelessly concluded that Valenzuela "should thank the Virgin of Guadalupe he's working." Would the same columnist, they asked, make light of the Wailing Wall, the Koran or other religious-cultural symbols that some people consider beyond satire?

Dr. Armando Navarro, one of the spokesmen at the press conference, said the reporting on Valenzuela "indicates the insensitivity of the press not only to this man but to the Latino community. We take no position on whether he [Valenzuela] is right or wrong. But these articles are certainly wrong."

Nobody at the conference had anything good to say about De Marco. Most refused to comment publicly, and the private remarks were all negative.

It was De Marco who first tried to use Valenzuela's popularity among Latino fans as a bargaining point in his talks with the Dodgers. And it is he who has done most of his negotiating through the press, calling on the Latino community for support.

"De Marco is treating this thing as though he were trying to get a contract for some singer at the Million Dollar Theater," a prominent Chicano attorney said privately this week. "The Dodgers don't deal that way. They are, quite literally, in a different league than De Marco is used to."

As for the Dodgers, they are handling the holdout with their usual cool efficiency. They have renewed Valenzuela's contract with a hefty raise and are sticking to it.

That businesslike attitude has clearly helped make the Dodgers a successful enterprise. But they are not the only top corporation in this city that has a hard time understanding the Latino community. They have been insensitive to Latinos before, mainly in not making a serious effort to sign top Mexican ballplayers until Valenzuela came along.

The Dodgers seem to be in command for now, but they should be careful lest their handling of Valenzuela's holdout cost them the loyalty of otherwise ardent Latino fans.

When I think back to how I worshiped the Dodgers as a boy, it surprises me how quickly my enthusiasm died when they shipped an aging slugger off to the Mets without a second thought. I hope the Valenzuela affair doesn't end the same way for present-day Dodger fans.

AUGUST 16, 1984

# A Boxer's Eyes Are on the Kids Still Trapped in the Barrio

WHILE TALKING RECENTLY with another Chicano journalist about Latino youth gangs, I was touched when my companion wearily commented: "If there were a war on, we'd be writing about those kids as heroes. But we're at peace, so we write about them as problems."

That comment was a painfully apt expression of what many Latinos feel when they look at the persistent problem of gang violence in barrio communities. The number of young Latinos attracted to what in my day was called *la vida loca*, the crazy life, is diminishing. But until the problem is eradicated we will always sadly wonder at its terrible waste of lives.

That's probably why, among all the fine Latino athletes who took part in the recent Olympic Games, the one closest to the heart of Los Angeles' Mexican American community was 20-year-old Paul Gonzales, a light-flyweight (106 pounds) boxer from Boyle Heights. There were other medal winners among the 16 Latinos on the U.S. Olympic team, including swimmer Pablo Morales, gymnast Tracee Talavera and weightlifter Mario Martinez. But none of their triumphs brought the tears of joy that Gonzales' gold medal did.

Latinos, especially young men and women, are hungry for role models in this media-oriented and image-conscious society. They have had more than a few phonies foisted on them in recent years, average jocks and ambitious starlets who proclaimed themselves "Hispanic" because it could help their careers. But Gonzales is not one of them. He's for real — a boxing phenomenon from the Aliso Village housing project, a former gang member who left his *clika* to fight by Marquess of Queensbury rules instead.

After his final boxing victory of the Olympics, Gonzales met with reporters, most of them sportswriters who, naturally, focused on his boxing achievement. But some of us there were more impressed by his other achievement — beating the odds of barrio life. Gonzales showed that he understood what that means.

Gonzales said that he had received an outpouring of letters and other tokens of support from young Latinos since the Olympics began, and he wanted his gold-medal victory "to give them a positive image so that people won't label us because of our background."

That is a provocative thing for an athlete to say.

And the more I listened to this tough but soft-spoken young man, the more I believed the sincerity of his commitment to be an inspiration for every gang kid who yearns to find a way out of a life of trouble.

"When you're always being labeled as a hoodlum it's easy to start believing it," he said. "You want to fire back at people and say, hey, I'm just a kid who needs a chance, who needs a break. I'm living proof that if people do try to help them, they can reach their dream too."

But, I asked, how can you help people anywhere but Aliso Village? Somebody from The Flats (the nickname that Chicano gang members gave Aliso) can't go into Maravilla, Pacoima, Wilmington and all the other barrios in this city and expect the *clikas* there to listen, can he?

"I can go anywhere I want," he replied. "There are people with dreams there too, and they'll listen to me even if some others don't. The ones that don't can stay in their shell. The ones with dreams, they'll see they can make it out."

One might be tempted to dismiss those sentiments as well-meaning but naïve. By every sociological measure, Gonzales should be in the category of Problem Kid, not Olympic Hero.

He grew up in one of the toughest housing projects in the city and was raised on welfare by a single mother. By the time he was 9 he was in a gang, and decided to change his ways only after being wounded in a drive-by shooting — a standard tactic in barrio gang wars.

Even then change wasn't easy. The boxing ring where Gonzales got his first experience was in the basement of the Los Angeles Police Department's Hollenbeck Division. He had to sneak in to work out, lest the local gang think that he turned snitch. And, of course, getting battered day after day in a boxing ring is one hell of a way to become famous.

There are still too many Chicanos in this city who are like Gonzales was before he found a dream to pursue in the Olympics — young men and women with little going for them except youthful energy and raw courage. They can't all be Olympic champions, but they can't ignore what Gonzales has shown them, either. There can be more to life than defending a patch of barrio turf.

Paul Gonzales is one tough young Chicano who didn't have to go to war to become a hero.


AUGUST 18, 1995

# *Futbol* Is the Ticket for the Coliseum

THERE WAS A BIG GAME at the Los Angeles Memorial Coliseum last Sunday, but you didn't see one word about it in the sports pages of English-language newspapers.

You didn't see any taped highlights on English-language TV, either, although an estimated 35,000 fans showed up to watch soccer teams from Mexico and El Salvador play.

That is almost as many people (38,017) as showed up at Dodger Stadium the same day for a big game in which the Dodgers beat the Pittsburgh Pirates to move into first place. It may even be more people than actually paid to attend a football game last Saturday in Oakland between two former Los Angeles teams, the St. Louis Rams and Oakland Raiders.

Several local news outlets sent reporters north to cover that event. That's understandable. It was the first game the Raiders played in Oakland after spending the last 13 years in Los Angeles, where the Rams also played for 34 years before moving to Anaheim in 1980 and then St. Louis this year. But in spite of all the hoopla surrounding the Raiders' return, Oakland's stadium did not sell out. The announced attendance was 50,000, but that number was padded with many tickets sold at discount or on a 2-for-1 basis.

But my purpose is not to revisit the recent departure of the Rams and

Raiders. It is to point out that their former home stadium, the Los Angeles Coliseum, does have a future in spite of being more than 70 years old. It could even be a prosperous future, and not just because of college football — although the six games that USC plays in the Coliseum every fall do help keep the publicly owned stadium afloat.

The Coliseum should become a venue for the fast-moving game we call soccer, known in Latin America and the rest of the world as football.

Sunday's match was an exhibition between one of Mexico's most popular and historic teams, Club America of Mexico City, against the team that was last season's national champion in El Salvador, Club Deportivo FAS. Despite ending in a scoreless tie, it was more interesting than many Raiders and Rams games I saw at the Coliseum.

And it was as much fun. As anyone who attended the World Cup matches held in the United States last year can attest, soccer fans have an infectious enthusiasm more akin to the crowd at a college football game than at a pro football contest. And, no, the crowd was no more troublesome than a similar-sized crowd at a baseball or American football game. There were only two arrests at Sunday's match, according to the Los Angeles police. There were several Raider games in recent years where the arrest count was higher.

But despite the obvious success of Sunday's soccer match, conventional wisdom hereabouts is that the Coliseum is a good-for-nothing white elephant. A perfect example was the recent front-page headline in a local newspaper (not The Times): "Losses Multiplying at Empty Coliseum."

Empty? It wasn't empty Sunday. Nor at a Latino music concert two weeks earlier that drew 35,000 people. And it won't be empty this coming Sunday when another soccer match is played between a popular Salvadoran team, Aguila, and Mexico City's Atlante team.

Still, that article went on to quote local politicians like Mayor Richard Riordan and County Supervisor Zev Yaroslavsky bemoaning the lack of a pro football tenant for the Coliseum. Yaroslavsky said that without football, the Coliseum may wind up with "soccer and some religious revivals." What's wrong with soccer and religious events? The biggest Coliseum crowd ever (more than 130,000) was drawn to a revival featuring the Rev. Billy Graham in 1963.

This week, Riordan appointed a 28-member task force to help bring pro football back to Los Angeles, if not to the Coliseum. It is called Football LA and includes civic leaders, some former athletes and actor Arnold Schwarzenegger.

Why not appoint a task force to bring more big soccer matches to the Coliseum? I have seen many soccer stadiums in Latin America and Europe, and the Coliseum compares quite favorably. And even the biggest foreign soccer stars would jump at the chance to play matches a few miles from Hollywood, the world capital of glitz and glamour.

Despite its age and location — not nearly so bad a neighborhood as suburbanites think, but that's another subject — the Coliseum could have a bright future. But this city's leaders must focus on its potential as a venue not for the bloated corporate entity American pro football has become. Let's go for a whole new ball game: *futbol*.

JANUARY 18, 1995

# No Farewell Tears Here for the Rams

THE LOS ANGELES RAMS were the first hometown team I ever rooted for; they were here before the Dodgers, before the Lakers and well before the Raiders. In fact, the Rams, having moved from Cleveland in 1946, had been the only pro game in town for two years before I was born here. So why am I — indeed, why is most of L.A. — so indifferent to the announcement that the Rams will be leaving after 49 years to play in St. Louis?

Maybe it's because California's other professional football teams all had good-to-great seasons. Two of them, the San Diego Chargers (who started out in 1960 as the Los Angeles Chargers) and the San Francisco '49ers, will play for pro football's championship in the Jan. 29 Super Bowl. The Raiders also had a winning record and came within a game of making the playoffs. The Rams won only four games all season and lost their last seven in a row, which did make me a little nostalgic for the Rams I rooted for as a youngster.

The Rams had good teams when they first moved west, and even were National Football League champs in 1951. But when I started following them closely, they were something of a joke. From the mid-'50s well into the 1960s, they consistently had losing seasons and were best known for trading away players who helped other teams win championships, like Bill Wade, Norm Van Brocklin and Zeke Bratowski.

But somehow that never mattered to an uncritical young fan like me. Losers though they were, the Rams were still L.A.'s team. And my loyalty was repaid eventually, when the Rams became consistent winners in the 1970s under coaches like the late George Allen. Their last season in Los Angeles proper, 1979, remains one of their best. They reached the Super Bowl at the end of that season, losing to the mighty Pittsburgh Steelers.

In 1980, the Rams moved to Anaheim Stadium and became, like the baseball Angels, an Orange County team. They were replaced in the Los Angeles Memorial Coliseum, and in the hearts of many Los Angeles football fans, by the Raiders, who moved south from Oakland.

I never begrudged the Rams their move to Orange County, for I was an adult by then and saw the logic of it. The city and county of Los Angeles had allowed the Coliseum to deteriorate, and even with recent earthquake repairs, it may not be satisfactory enough to keep the Raiders from leaving.

Anaheim's city fathers had offered the late Carroll Rosenbloom a generous deal to move his Rams to the bright, new stadium the city had built for the Angels. The first sign of trouble, to my mind, was when Rosenbloom insisted that his team was still the "Los Angeles" Rams.

Then the Rams mangled Anaheim Stadium. They took a fine baseball park open to the stars and sunshine like Dodger Stadium, Fenway Park and other classic fields, and turned it into an enclosed concrete mausoleum. To no one's surprise, that made the Angels unhappy. And within a few years, Rams' management was whining too.

In fact, Rams owner Georgia Frontiere and her underlings haven't stopped complaining about the alleged shortcomings of Anaheim Stadium, while at the same time carrying on public flirtations with St. Louis, Baltimore and just about any other city desperate enough for pro football to pay through the nose for it. So her announcement that they are actually leaving was anticlimactic.

It was also insulting to Orange County, given everything local leaders did to bring the Rams there and all they tried to do to keep them. At least they still have the Angels and an exciting young hockey team in the Mighty Ducks.

They could even wind up with the Raiders, now that Anaheim Stadium has room for a football tenant. That is something L.A.'s political and business leaders should keep in mind the next time Raiders owner Al Davis points out everything that still needs fixing at the Coliseum.

As for those of us in Los Angeles who still occasionally pulled for the Rams, having been spurned once makes getting dumped a second time fairly painless. But that doesn't mean we can't learn something from the end of a 49-year relationship. Just having nice weather (most of the time, anyway) is no guarantee of success in any business, including the coldhearted world of pro sports, where dollars talk louder than fans can ever cheer.

A headline in the old Los Angeles Herald Examiner comes to mind. 1970 was the first year that teams from the former American Football League played the older teams of the NFL after the two leagues had merged. In their first meeting ever, the Rams beat the Chargers, 37-10. "Right Team Left Town," the Herald stated. The same words would work today.

FEBRUARY 9, 1996

# Can Behring Walk on Quicksand?

LOOKS LIKE LOS ANGELES may get another pro football team whether we want it or not.

A lot of legal and political infighting is likely before the planned move of the Seattle Seahawks actually happens. And Pasadena's Rose Bowl, where Seahawks owner Ken Behring wants his team to play temporarily, and the city of Anaheim, where he wants it to practice, may be dragged into the fray.

But they'll have the satisfaction of sharing the misery with a group of folks who truly deserve it: the owners of the 28 teams that comprise the National Football League and the league's befuddled and seemingly powerless leadership.

Behring, a Northern California land developer, announced last week that he was moving his team out of Seattle, the fifth NFL team owner to relocate a franchise in less than a year. In every instance the excuse for fleeing is the same: The team needs a new stadium so that it can increase revenues by leasing luxury boxes and selling not just season tickets but "personal seat licenses" for the right to buy those season tickets.

This insane game of musical stadiums began in Southern California when the Rams left for St. Louis in April, followed by the Raiders returning to Oakland in June. A few months later, the Cleveland Browns announced a move to Baltimore and the Houston Oilers fled to Nashville. And the game isn't over yet. Teams in San Francisco, Cincinnati, Phoenix and Tampa also are unhappy with their current accommodations.

This turmoil is badly undermining the NFL's popularity. Heretofore, the league had been so successful that it recently began proclaiming, with characteristic hubris, that pro football is "the new national pastime."

The former national pastime is still around, of course. But baseball is desperately trying to regain fan loyalty after the bitter 1994 players' strike. Franchise shuffling in pro football is having the same effect because it sends the same message to the hard-working stiffs who buy most of the tickets: Fan loyalty doesn't count as much as our bottom line.

That is why the NFL now finds itself being sued by angry fans and cities from Ohio to the Pacific Northwest. And why, in Greater Los Angeles, Behring has been greeted by a skeptical, even suspicious, community.

Behring says he will approach the Los Angeles market like the owner of an expansion franchise, with a completely fresh start, including a new team name. The Seahawk name, logo and even the team colors will remain in Seattle, presumably to be assumed someday by some other team.

If only it were that simple. For in L.A., Behring is venturing into a public relations minefield left behind by the two NFL owners who preceded him, the Rams' Georgia Frontiere and the Raiders' Al Davis.

During their last few years in Orange County, the Rams made absolutely no effort at public or community relations. Frontiere even stopped helping a struggling Boys and Girls Club in Lincoln Heights that the Rams had supported since the 1950s.

The Raiders did a little better, but only by comparison to the Rams, and largely because of the unappreciated efforts of one man, their director of marketing and community relations, Gil Hernandez.

If Raiders players couldn't, or wouldn't, make it to a public appearance, Hernandez did. If news stories linked the Raiders' silver-and-black pirate logo to youth gangs, Hernandez wrote letters to the editor pointing out the team's (actually his) support for anti gang programs in the community. And when Davis decided to raise ticket prices, Hernandez tried to talk him out of it.

Hernandez understood better than anyone in Raider management the unique dynamics of the Los Angeles market, with its suburban sprawl and many ethnic enclaves. He got Raider games on Spanish-language radio before any other NFL team had thought of it — including the Rams, who had been here 30 years before the Raiders arrived. To me, that remains the single most important symbol of Hernandez's efforts to promote the Raiders among the millions of Latinos who are the blue-collar backbone of this region's economy.

Considering how lackluster the Raiders played toward the end of their stay here, Hernandez may have been the best thing Davis had going for him in Los Angeles. And now Hernandez is not sure he will move north when the team's administrative offices are transferred to Oakland later this year.

"Al [Davis] has always been supportive of me," the El Paso native says, "but L.A.'s my adopted home, and I'm really torn about leaving."

In a meeting this week with Los Angeles Mayor Richard Riordan, Behring said that he wants "to earn the respect and support of the community" with his new team, whatever it winds up being called and wherever it winds up playing its games. Fine words. But given all that has gone before, harder than Behring realizes.

Mr. Behring, meet Mr. Hernandez.

JANUARY 12, 1997

# Is It O'Malley's Last Out or First Down?

AS FAR AS MANY LATINOS ARE CONCERNED, the possible sale of the Dodgers baseball team is just the latest twist in the Battle of Palo Verde.

That is what Latino activists call the final expulsion, in 1959, of the 20 or so homeowners who still lived in Chavez Ravine before the last homes there were razed to make way for Dodger Stadium.

Once, a thousand families lived there, in a barrio called Palo Verde. By 1958, most had been forced out by the city, which planned to build public housing in the area. But when the Dodgers arrived from Brooklyn that year, drawn with a promise that city officials would cooperate with Walter O'Malley's dream of building his team a new baseball stadium, those plans changed.

Impressed with Chavez Ravine's access to the freeways that converge downtown, O'Malley asked for the 300-plus acres of property. In exchange he offered an old minor league stadium and its nine acres, which he had bought as a possible temporary home for his team.

The exchange was made, but not without controversy. It passed as a citywide ballot measure by only 25,785 votes. Shortly afterward the Chavez Ravine holdouts were forcibly removed — some dragged kicking and screaming from their houses by sheriff's deputies as the bulldozers moved in.

While many other barrio residents were displaced by urban renewal in the 1950s, the Battle of Palo Verde took on a special symbolism. Perhaps it was because the rest of Los Angeles — even many Latinos — embraced the Dodgers and the leap to major league status they represented for the city. Whatever the reason, genuine bitterness lingers among those who remember Palo Verde.

You heard it last Monday, when Peter O'Malley announced that the Dodgers are for sale. Former Chavez Ravine residents tracked down by a Times reporter spoke of never having gone to a Dodger game and of sad memories of "deceit and lies and trauma." Those strong words were uttered by the Rev. Juan Santillan, who grew up in Palo Verde and is now pastor of a Catholic parish in nearby Lincoln Heights.

When I began researching this column, I thought it might be time to bury memories of Palo Verde. For the financial challenges O'Malley now faces can be traced at least partly to his father's land deal. And isn't there at least some measure of satisfaction in that for the former residents of Palo Verde?

Walter O'Malley got a real bargain in 1959 when he acquired all that prime real estate overlooking downtown. But his son found some downsides to the deal by the 1990s. They first became evident when he expressed an interest in building a football stadium on his property to attract a new National Football League franchise to Los Angeles. Dodger Stadium's neighbors reacted with such hostility that O'Malley was quickly forced to back down. More than a few Angelenos were surprised to learn that the Dodgers and their popular, soft-spoken owner were considered something less than good neighbors by folks in Elysian Park and Echo Park.

O'Malley's NFL flirtation also confirmed a problem that some observers had begun to suspect: Dodger Stadium, completed in 1962, is outdated. Not architecturally, to be sure, but by the financial standards of modern pro sports. It will be difficult for the Dodgers to compete with other teams for high-priced players without the added revenue produced by luxury boxes and the other amenities new stadiums offer.

Many of those new baseball parks, like Baltimore's Camden Yards, were built with public funds. But since O'Malley owns his own stadium and the land it sits on, he can't ask taxpayers to pay for renovations. And paying for a stadium upgrade privately is harder than it seems at first glance.

It was little noted amid the hoopla when O'Malley expressed interest in an NFL franchise, but some financial experts warned that he might not be able to afford it. With most of his wealth tied up in the Dodgers and their properties, analysts questioned whether O'Malley could leverage a deal that might cost more than $500 million without the help of partners with very deep pockets.

I think those skeptics were right. Which is why I've also come to the conclusion that it is still too early to forget the Battle of Palo Verde.

For I am just skeptical enough to now wonder if O'Malley's dramatic for-sale announcement wasn't a ploy.

After all, O'Malley could have found out what his team and real estate are worth, and could even have approached possible buyers, before making any announcement. But by going public so suddenly, O'Malley stirred up civic concern that the Dodgers will change for the worse, or maybe even leave town. And that could give him leverage to pressure the community activists and elected officials who opposed his football expansion plans to back down.

I could be wrong, of course. O'Malley may truly want out, as he said, because the legal and financial complexities of modern pro sports are just too daunting for a family-owned business.

But for now I'm keeping Father Santillan's words in mind. Not just as sad memories, but as words of warning.

# Our Two Boys of Summer

I N THE NOT-ALWAYS-FRIENDLY rivalry between the Los Angeles area's two major league baseball teams, it's unlikely that Artemania can top Fernandomania. That's probably why just as Arte Moreno's Anaheim Angels finally emerge from the shadow of the L.A. Dodgers by winning last year's World Series, the Dodgers have responded by calling Fernando Valenzuela out of history's bullpen.

Of course every baseball fan in town — and many non-fans — knows who Valenzuela is and what he represents in recent L.A. history. Any who don't need only catch a performance of the new play at the Music Center's Mark Taper Forum, "Chavez Ravine."

The play relates the complex tale of how some old Mexican barrios near downtown Los Angeles were bulldozed in the 1950s to make way for Dodger Stadium. It unfolds as a series of historical vignettes being retold, in 1981, to a Dodger rookie from rural Mexico, Valenzuela, as he stands astride the pitcher's mound in Dodger Stadium.

Anyone who doubts the resonance of that dramatic device to a Latino audience need only note the attention the Dodgers got last week in L.A.'s Spanish-language media when they announced that Valenzuela was returning to his old team as a commentator on Spanish-language radio broadcasts. "¿Fernandomania II?" La Opinion headlined. If only it were that easy to bring back.

Fernandomania, of course, was the term coined by the media to describe the fiesta-like atmosphere that descended on Dodger Stadium, and eventually the whole town, every time Valenzuela pitched during that spring of 1981. The young left-hander helped feed the frenzy by pitching brilliantly and capped that dream season by helping the Dodgers win the World Series.

For the Dodgers, 1981 was one of those magical years that baseball essayists, and the nostalgic fans who read them, often return to as symbols of larger social and cultural trends.

As "Chavez Ravine," the play, correctly surmises, Fernandomania helped heal a rift between the Dodgers and a big part of Los Angeles' Latino community that refused to forget Chavez Ravine, the neighborhood.

Having rooted for the Dodgers when they played in Brooklyn, I was not among the Latinos who rejected the team when it came to town. But as a native-born Angeleno, my loyalties were severely torn when the Los Angeles Angels were born in 1960 and joined the American League. And my affection grew despite their poor record in the early years and persisted even when the late Gene Autry moved his team to Orange County.

Sadly, it took the Angels decades to gain real respectability. And a big reason for their slow ascent to success was their failure to aggressively recruit Latin American baseball players. I was not surprised that when the Angels finally won the World Series last year, their roster included players from Mexico, Puerto Rico and the Dominican Republic and a talented Latino rookie pitcher — Francisco Rodriguez — from Venezuela.

Also not surprising was the multitude of Latino fans in the stands, many of them residents of the increasingly Mexican neighborhoods around Anaheim Stadium.

But for local Latinos, the biggest Angel surprise came last month, when the team was sold to Moreno, a Mexican American businessman from Tucson. As Valenzuela was in his heyday, Moreno is now one of the hottest Latino celebrities in L.A.

Just what Moreno will make of fame in the big city remains to be seen. Reviews were mixed, for instance, on his vow to lower the price of beer at Anaheim Stadium. Sportswriters found it a fan-friendly gesture, but a vocal group of Latino activists were critical, concerned about the high incidence of alcoholism among Latinos.

It would do Moreno well to remember that even Fernandomania had its downbeat moments. Although the pitcher went on to have a fine career, Valenzuela never quite recaptured the magic of those early months of the '81 season. And after he finally retired from the majors in 1997, Valenzuela would never visit Dodger Stadium.

Dodger spokesmen say Valenzuela was invited to old-timers' games and other events but never showed up — until last week's press conference on his new broadcasting duties.

What with Artemania looming down the freeway, the Dodgers' reconciliation with Valenzuela comes at just the right time.

# CHAPTER EIGHT

# Immigration

## *Amid the rhetoric, taking a firm stand*

REVERSING A 20-YEAR POLICY, the Los Angeles Times decided to support a candidate for governor in 1994. As deputy editorial page editor, Frank del Olmo and the Times editorial board had fought the newspaper's endorsement of California Gov. Pete Wilson for a second term. Del Olmo considered resigning but instead fired a salvo at Wilson in what became his best-known column. The Republican governor was cynically backing Proposition 187, which targeted illegal immigrants, by playing the divisive ethnic politics card, he wrote.

As with all his columns on this topic, del Olmo argued that immigration was far too complex — and too valuable to this nation of immigrants — to reduce it to alarmist rhetoric. Proposition 187 passed, but most of its provisions later were declared unconstitutional. And a year later, as del Olmo noted, it was learned that Wilson had once employed an illegal immigrant maid.

# A Look at the Border — and at Past and Present Lookers

U.S. ATTY. GEN. WILLIAM FRENCH SMITH took his obligatory firsthand look at the U.S.-Mexico border this week, and to his credit resisted the temptation to turn the brief visit into a media event.

Like innumerable VIPs before him, Smith toured the U.S. Immigration and Naturalization Service facility at San Ysidro, the nation's busiest port of entry in terms of both legal and illegal crossings. He spent less than two hours there talking with immigration officers and U.S. Border Patrol agents but said very little to them or to the many reporters who converged on the facility for his visit — which seemed to disappoint everyone there.

After all, it always makes for colorful articles and dramatic TV footage to have a VIP looking on as Border Patrol agents in Jeeps round up illegal Mexican aliens.

Unfortunately, such staged events do very little to inform the public about the long history of migration between Mexico and the United States, and the complicated social and economic factors behind it. If anything, such news coverage makes illegal immigration seem like little more than an international game of cops and robbers.

In the last decade, as the so-called "illegal alien problem" has become hot news, too many public officials have used border media events to gain some quick and easy publicity.

One of the first to try this gimmick was the late Rep. Leo J. Ryan, the San Francisco Democrat who later found greater fame, and great tragedy, by investigating the Rev. Jim Jones and his People's Temple cult in the jungles of Guyana. In 1973, Ryan informed several news media that he was planning to take a "secret tour" of the border, to uncover corruption in the immigration service and to determine the extent of illegal immigration from Mexico.

Ryan was before his time, however. Only a handful of reporters was interested in immigration in those days, and those knowledgeable about the issue saw Ryan's ploy for what it was and declined his invitation.

Dozens of congressmen have followed Ryan to San Ysidro or El Paso, though they rarely, if ever, visit places such as Nogales, Ariz., or Calexico, where television cameras are scarce. And they never seem to pay their calls at night, when illegal border crossing activity is at its height.

Probably the most dramatically overplayed visit to the border was made in 1977 by Leonel Castillo, the prominent Chicano politician from Houston who was President Carter's commissioner of immigration.

During his stopover in San Ysidro, where the immigration service has been known to detain 30,000 illegal entrants in a busy month, Castillo joined some Border Patrol agents on their nightly rounds.

Castillo made his contribution to the immigration service's illegal entry statistics by manning the searchlight of a Border Patrol helicopter while it hovered over a group of Mexican nationals who were trying to sneak into the country from Tijuana. Among Latino activists, his reputation has never fully recovered.

Which is too bad, because Castillo has never received the credit that he deserved for helping streamline and humanize the operations of the immigration service and the Border Patrol.

After that initial visit to the border, Castillo was able to look beyond the cops-and-robbers aspect of illegal immigration. He began to see that issue as a historic phenomenon with no easy solutions, especially no easy police solutions.

He reallocated his agency's resources so that the emphasis was not simply on catching more illegal immigrants but on minimizing the exploitation that they face because of their illegal status, whether that exploitation comes from people-smugglers, border bandits, unscrupulous employers or even insensitive immigration officers.

Castillo put more money into special Border Patrol anti-smuggling units. He encouraged other government agencies to enforce existing worker-protection laws, and he pointed out how they could crack down on employers who abuse illegal workers. He urged immigration officials in big cities to spend less time trying to locate suspected illegal aliens and more time servicing those immigrants whose status could be legalized.

Castillo's approach, it almost goes without saying, alienated longtime immigration service officials and angered advocates of immigration restrictions. But his was a better way of dealing with illegal immigration.

At bottom, the real problem is human exploitation, not the movement of people back and forth across the border. That migration has been going on for more than a century with no great harm either to Mexico or the United States, and more than a few benefits to both nations.

Simply increasing the number of men and machines watching our side of the border will not stop that migration. Greater enforcement efforts may reduce the number of people who get across, but not very much. And the people who continue to make it across will be all the more fearful and exploitable, which will only exacerbate the real problem.

Whether this is the conclusion that Smith reached after looking into the immigration dilemma will not be formally known for a few more weeks, when the final report of the task force that President Reagan appointed to recommend reform of the country's immigration laws is made public. News accounts based on early drafts of the report indicated that the task force will propose a large-scale guest-worker program for up to 1.5 million Mexican workers in this country.

In, the meantime, Smith has returned to Washington to brief Reagan on illegal immigration before next week's summit meeting with Mexican President Jose Lopez Portillo at Camp David.

Smith and Reagan may both want to keep in mind that, like Castillo, Lopez Portillo has often said that illegal immigration is not amenable to police solutions.

# A Circular Ripple of Justice

*"Regardless of what the future holds for our union, regardless of what the future holds for farmworkers, our accomplishment cannot be undone. The consciousness and pride that were raised by our union are alive and thriving inside millions of young Hispanics who will never work on a farm."* — Cesar Chavez in a 1984 speech to San Francisco's Commonwealth Club

I WAS RELUCTANT, initially, to join the chorus writing obituaries for farm labor leader Cesar Chavez.

The president of the AFL-CIO United Farm Workers Union was one of the country's best-known labor leaders, the nation's best-known Mexican American and, in some circles, among the most admired men in the world. So when Chavez died last Friday at the age of 66, it was no surprise that tributes and remembrances flowed in not just from the powerful political and religious leaders he knew, but also from the weak and poor, especially the field laborers he spent the better part of his life trying to help.

I also expected that, somewhere amid the many interviews given and speeches delivered by Chavez during his more than 30 years of public life, he would have delivered his own most eloquent eulogy. He did, in the speech cited above.

UFW officials dug that speech out of the union's files a day after Chavez's death was announced. They cited it as evidence the union and its work will continue even though its founder and longtime president is gone. But it has more significance than that.

For while it's arguable whether the UFW will ever again have the influence it had in its heyday — indeed, many of the obituaries have pointed out that both its membership rolls and the number of labor contracts it has negotiated have shrunk dramatically since the 1970s — no one can dispute the fact that Cesar Chavez had a profound influence on literally millions of people, especially Mexican Americans.

Consider the roster of Latino leaders who began their community activism working for UFW. Politicians like state Sen. Art Torres (D-Los Angeles), a former UFW attorney, are only the most obvious. Movie director Luis Valdez launched his career with El Teatro Campesino when it was UFW's agitprop arm, performing skits on picket lines and at union rallies. Ernesto Cortes, the community organizer who has helped create effective grass-roots citizens groups from East Los Angeles to San Antonio's West Side, began his career organizing the UFW grape boycott in his native Texas. Like a circular ripple in a pond, Chavez's influence lives on in people like that.

Just as important, the focus of Chavez's work — lifting up the poor by helping them organize unions — remains a challenge for the current generation of Latino leaders. But it is a widely misunderstood challenge, as it was when Chavez was alive.

Growers often criticized Chavez for trying to make the UFW more than just a union, for trying to turn it into a social cause, *La Causa*, and thereby drawing to the UFW an assortment of well-meaning volunteers who knew nothing about administering labor contracts. He replied by saying the UFW's volunteers would be gone once the union had enough members and contracts to support itself without them. If farmworkers were given a living wage and decent working conditions, Chavez argued, they were perfectly capable of taking care of themselves without do-gooders or, for that matter, the government.

But even some of Chavez's most ardent Latino admirers misunderstood that. He burst onto the scene in 1965 with the biggest, most successful unionization drive California's powerful agricultural industry had ever seen. In the process, he brought national attention, for the first time, to Mexican Americans as a minority group with a unique history and problems. Some Latinos became frustrated that, as the most visible Chicano leader in the world, Chavez didn't do more to help the 80% of Latinos who live in cities. Chavez replied that UFW could never afford to give up the rural focus of its work. So in recent years, a new generation of urban Latino leaders considered Chavez and his union quaint anachronisms.

Yet when one ponders the problems facing many urban Latinos, it is not unreasonable to conclude that they could be solved through unionization as effectively as the social needs of farm laborers. As some researchers have pointed out, most recently in the aftermath of last year's Los Angeles riots, the problems facing inner-city Latinos are not those of people who are utterly destitute. They are the problems of the working poor: not a lack of jobs, but of jobs that pay enough; not a lack of housing, but of decent housing; not a lack of education, but of schools to prepare children for better jobs than their parents have.

Most Latinos, even the poorest, know what their problems are and want only the chance to strive for what is best for their families, unencumbered by the burdens of poverty. It is not insignificant, I think, that the most vibrant organizing going on right now among Latinos in the Los Angeles area is within labor unions like those representing janitors, hotel and restaurant workers and drywallers in the housing industry.

Chavez was not an admirable anachronism. Just as in the early '60s, he may well have been ahead of his time without anyone quite realizing it. The greatest tribute the current generation of Latinos can pay him is to continue his work, as the quote above clearly implies, not just on our farms but in our cities.

AUGUST 23, 1993

# Wilson Risks His Latino Support

GOV. PETE WILSON is getting abundant political flak from leaders of California's Latino community for having lent the prestige of his office — and his credentials as a moderate Republican — to controversial proposals to deter illegal immigration. He probably expected it. And he probably doesn't worry about it too much.

That's why Wilson went all out last week promoting an open letter he sent to the White House urging President Clinton to do something, and fast, about the illegal immigrants who have California "under siege." Wilson, normally so low-key as to be somnolent, waxed almost hysterical in that letter, blaming most of his state's financial troubles on immigrants who he claims are driving up the cost of welfare, education and public health care.

Wilson's letter also endorsed several proposals put forward by anti-immigrant groups and backed by a few politicians. Among the proposals is one to repeal the 14th Amendment to the Constitution to deny U.S. citizenship to the children of illegal immigrants, which should bar illegal immigrants from receiving all but emergency medical care at public hospitals and keep their children out of public schools. Wilson also urged Clinton to hold the pending North American Free Trade Agreement hostage to force the Mexican government to cooperate with the United States in cracking down on the border.

Now, forget for a moment that each of those proposals can be challenged as illegal, counterproductive or simply impractical. And forget that most immigration experts doubt that any of them would have an impact on illegal immigration, which results from economic factors and not any desire for U.S. citizenship by foreigners. Wilson's stance is supposedly good politics, especially given the fact that he has lately received the lowest popularity rating (15%) of any California governor in the history of public-opinion polling.

The conventional wisdom among political professionals, like those on Wilson's staff and in the state Republican Party — who are gearing up for his 1994 reelection campaign — is that illegal immigration is a "hot button" issue with Californians who vote (that is, older, white and suburban voters). So if Latinos don't like anti-immigrant appeals, that's no real problem because they don't vote or, when they do, don't vote in numbers big enough to outpoll the frightened Anglos that Wilson is appealing to.

That's why Wilson probably won't be fazed by harsh criticism from Latino activist groups like San Diego's Committee on Chicano Rights. Herman Baca, head of that group, predicted that Wilson's anti-immigrant stance "would guarantee the loss of the 40%-45% of the Hispanic vote" the Republican Party has aimed for since former President Ronald Reagan made inroads among Latino voters in the 1980s.

But Baca is not alone in his anger. Ana Barbosa, head of Los Angeles' Latin Business Assn., has expressed the fear that every Latino-owned business in the state "now faces the backlash of racism fueled by the derogatory statements of … elected officials" like Wilson. Strong stuff, considering that LBA members are mostly small-business people who have been as staunchly pro-Republican as any Latino group in California in recent years.

When a Chicano activist like Baca finds common ground with a businesswoman like Barbosa, there is indeed potential political danger in Wilson's stance.

Of course, immigration restrictionists are fond of quoting public-opinion polls that find many Latinos concerned about illegal immigration, and

Wilson is surely counting on some of that quiet sympathy to work on his behalf. I don't doubt the accuracy of those polls, but I don't think that anti-immigrant sentiment runs deep among Latinos. It's one thing for a Latino to tell a pollster that he doesn't like illegals. It's a stretch to assume that he would deny citizenship to an illegal immigrant's child. When you remember how many ties there are between Latinos in this country and relatives in Latin America, such a "modest proposal" can hit pretty close to home.

Wilson and his advisors may yet find that he has maneuvered himself into an untenable position not unlike that of a policeman who tries to resolve a family dispute and winds up with the husband, wife and kids all ganging up on him.

Consider this: A poll taken this month by La Opinion, Los Angeles' respected Spanish-language daily, found that 81% of 286 Latino respondents disapproved of Wilson's anti-immigrant stance. The obvious question is, will they vote that way?

Wilson had best hope they don't — or next election day he could wind up with a political frying pan upside his head.

OCTOBER 31, 1994

# A Dissenting Vote on the Endorsement of Pete Wilson

THE TIMES ON SUNDAY published an editorial endorsing Gov. Pete Wilson for reelection, the first time this newspaper has endorsed a gubernatorial candidate in more than 20 years.

As deputy editor of the editorial pages, I played a role in the deliberations that led up to its publication. Unfortunately, my deeply felt belief that Wilson does not deserve The Times' endorsement did not carry the day. Under normal circumstances, I would quietly accept that decision and move on. This time I cannot. Because this is not just another political campaign. And the Wilson endorsement is not — as a senior colleague whom I respect tried to convince me — just another endorsement.

For me, a Mexican American born and reared in California and a journalist here for more than 20 years, this campaign is unprecedented in the harm it does — permanent damage, I fear — to an ethnic community I care deeply about and a state I love. The reason, of course, is its weapon of choice: the complex and emotional issue of illegal immigration.

In the form of Proposition 187 — the mean-spirited and unconstitutional ballot initiative that would deprive "apparent illegal aliens" of public health services and immigrant children of public education — the immigration issue has become the cornerstone of Wilson's desperate and cynical effort to win a second term.

I say cynical because Wilson has chosen to discuss the immigration issue not on the high plane one would expect from the governor of the nation's largest state — a man who could be president someday. Instead he has taken the low road, using alarmist rhetoric and frightening television ads that portray illegal immigrants in the ugliest, most negative terms. He is making illegal immigrants scapegoats for larger economic problems, like the defense cutbacks that so devastated the California economy.

So I must protest against this awful, and unnecessary, campaign in the strongest way I know how — if only to live with my conscience after the voters render their judgment on both Wilson and Proposition 187 on Nov. 8.

Please note how I link the two campaigns — Wilson the candidate and 187 the ballot measure. That is pivotal to my reasoning and to the fundamental difference I now feel with some of my superiors. For I am speaking as a Mexican American, and in the eyes of the vast majority of Mexican Americans — California's largest single ethnic group at 6.1 million people — Wilson's campaign and Proposition 187 cannot be separated. Lord knows, the Wilson campaign has made no effort to separate the two in the minds of anxious voters.

I say that with the confidence of someone who has covered Mexican American politics in this state for many years. And sources I trust have told me that the same can be said of this state's fastest-growing minority, the 2.8 million Asian Americans and Pacific Islanders.

I know that my dissent may seem overstated to many reasonable people. But consider: As recently as a few weeks ago, opinion polls showed Proposition 187 getting support even among a majority of Latino voters. That's because, as I have written often on these pages, Latinos are not all that different from voters of any other ethnic group. They worry about the economy and crime and other issues. And they will tell pollsters that they, too, wish that someone would "do something" about the problem of illegal immigration.

But that apparent consensus breaks down when you get to specifics, like asking Latinos whether distant relatives back home should be able to come to this country, legally or not. That's why, with the election season in the home stretch and Latinos starting to realize just how Proposition 187 would hurt their families, friends and neighbors, opinion has swung dramatically against the initiative. A Times poll published last week showed that support had dropped to only 22% among Latino registered voters — a number that does not take into account the sentiment of all the Latinos who cannot vote because they are too young or are not citizens. Even right-wing Republicans like Ronald Reagan could count on at least 30% of the Latino vote. So it is clear that Latinos have turned overwhelmingly against 187 and are likely to also turn against Pete Wilson — and not just on Nov. 8.

I have known and liked Wilson since he was mayor of San Diego. I don't think he's a bigot. But he made a terrible mistake in this campaign. By aligning himself with the immigration issue in its most nativist form, he has given legitimacy to an ugly streak of bigotry in California. And Latinos everywhere will never forgive him for that.

We can no more forget what Wilson has done in the 1994 campaign than African Americans can forget how segregationist governors like Arkansas' Orval Faubus tried to keep black children from getting a decent education in public schools, or than Jews can forget the Rev. Jesse Jackson's "Hymietown" remark in the 1984 presidential campaign. And whatever else can be said about Jackson, he made the remark in public only once and has been trying to bury it ever since. Wilson, on the other hand, has been campaigning against illegal immigrants from Mexico for the better part of a year. Just imagine how Jews would feel if "Hymietown" had been the keystone of a yearlong campaign.

Those are harsh comparisons, but they are not entirely mine. I know that many thousands, if not millions, of Mexican Americans and Mexican citizens feel the same way. Wilson's pro-187 campaign will stick in our craws for generations, the way "Hymietown" will probably always haunt Jackson.

That is why The Times' endorsement of Wilson is not just another endorsement, and why I must register my dissent so publicly. I want people out there to know — especially the young Latinos and Asian Americans who will be the leaders of this state in the future, and, I hope, readers of this newspaper as well — that not all of us here at The Times feel good about Pete Wilson. Many of us share your anger.

DECEMBER 21, 1994

# A Cautionary Lesson for Our Governor

I
T WAS IRONIC and even poetic that former Arkansas Gov. Orval Faubus died last week on the same day a federal judge in Los Angeles dealt a major legal setback to Proposition 187, the mean-spirited initiative California voters approved last month in an attempt — born of frustration and most likely futile — to stop illegal immigration.

To those of us who consider a decent public-school education to be a fundamental right for all children in this country, those seemingly separate events fit together quite nicely. In the 1950s, Faubus defied federal orders to admit black children to white-only public schools and became a lightning rod in the fight against racial segregation throughout the South. In the 1990s, California Gov. Pete Wilson, the chief proponent of Proposition 187, has become a similar symbol by trying to use the controversial initiative to keep illegal immigrant children from attending public schools in this state. But Wilson's status as a Faubus for the '90s is not unalterable. He can be forced to change.

During the highly charged campaign leading up to the November election, Wilson often portrayed himself as the victim of unfair attacks by opponents of Proposition 187. To hear him talk, he was just a well-meaning chief executive who on his watch happened to discover all the economic damage illegal immigrants allegedly do to this once-Golden State. So he sadly took on the distasteful task of bringing the troubling problem to the attention of the federal government and, not coincidentally, California voters. It was not his fault that this had to be done in the same political year that sloppily written and constitutionally dubious Proposition 187 was put on the ballot by grass-roots immigration restrictionists.

The initiative aims to halt illegal immigration not by drying up the jobs

FRANK DEL OLMO

that lure immigrants to California but by barring illegal immigrants from government-paid social services. That includes, most significantly, access to public schools — even if an illegal immigrants' children were born in this country. That runs directly counter to U.S. Supreme Court decisions, one of the main reasons U.S. District Judge Mariana R. Pfaelzer issued a restraining order last Wednesday barring implementation of most of Proposition 187 until legal challenges to it run their course, a process that could take years.

But back to the way Pete Wilson sees things: For just discussing the illegal immigration issue on the campaign stump, he wound up being vilified, especially by angry Latino activists who attacked him as the reincarnation of every historic villain from Cortez to Hitler.

Some of the anti-Wilson rhetoric was overblown. But Latinos did have good cause to be angry with the governor. He blatantly used the anti-immigrant initiative to help revive his reelection campaign, which had once been considered moribund. Wilson may not be a racist villain, but he is clearly an ambitious politician who found a hot-button issue and exploited it — much as Orval Faubus did 40 years ago in Arkansas with school desegregation.

Because Faubus became such a symbol of bigotry in the early civil rights era, it is often forgotten that he was first elected governor in 1954 as a liberal populist who was a moderate on racial issues. But Faubus' biographers agree that in 1957 he took a segregationist stance because he feared being defeated for reelection by right-wing rivals.

So, when it became time for Arkansas to implement the Supreme Court's Brown vs. Board of Education decision by allowing nine black students to integrate Little Rock's Central High School, Faubus played the race card. He threatened to use the Arkansas National Guard to turn black students away, but he was trumped by President Eisenhower, who ordered troops from the 101st Airborne Division to escort the children to class.

"[Faubus'] hubris, his romping ambition, got in the way of his doing what I suspect he knew was right," said Robert Savage, chairman of the University of Arkansas' political science department, in discussing Faubus' career last week. But Faubus' segregationist strategy worked. He won reelection and went on to serve as Arkansas' governor for four more terms. And, as Faubus' obituaries noted, he never did apologize for his actions in 1957.

That final point is what sets Faubus apart from another, better-known politician who came to be closely identified with racial segregation, Alabama Gov. George Wallace. Wallace did apologize for his actions in trying to prevent the desegregation of the University of Alabama in 1963. He did so when he again ran for governor in 1982 — after the 1965 Voting Rights Act gave black voters in Alabama political clout they had not had before. It is not insignificant, I think, that Faubus retired from office in 1967 rather than run before an Arkansas electorate that included newly empowered black voters.

The lesson here for the many Latinos in California and elsewhere who universally detest Pete Wilson is obvious. He can either remain an Orval Faubus of the '90s or become this generation's George Wallace. It all depends on Latinos' willingness to start voting in large numbers, as African Americans did in the segregationist South after 1965.

MAY 11, 1995

# Here's Wilson's Chance to Come Clean

SO IT TURNS OUT that Gov. Pete Wilson once employed an illegal immigrant as a maid. So much for the Scourge of Illegal Aliens, who was counting on that reputation to boost his presidential ambitions, just as it helped him win reelection last year.

I'll be the first to admit there is no great sin in the fact that, while serving as mayor in San Diego in 1978, Wilson and his wife at the time employed a Mexican woman, who was apparently an illegal immigrant, as a housemaid for $25 a day. Employing illegal immigrants was against California law at the time, but that law was never aggressively enforced. And while the Wilsons also violated federal laws by not withholding the housekeeper's Social Security taxes, Wilson's former wife has taken the blame for that oversight, and Wilson has agreed to pay any back taxes and penalties he owes.

But similar excuses have been offered by other candidates for high public office who got hoisted on the immigration petard. Two capable women

FRANK DEL OLMO

President Clinton nominated for attorney general, Zoe Baird and Kimba Wood, had to withdraw when it was learned they had employed illegal immigrants. And what's sauce for Democratic geese is sauce for Republican ganders, as former GOP Rep. Michael Huffington found out in last year's U.S. Senate race against Dianne Feinstein. Revelations that his wife had hired an illegal immigrant nanny may have cost Huffington a close election.

Wilson is trying hard to defuse "Maidgate," as San Diego Chicano activist Herman Baca, a longtime Wilson critic, dubbed this flap (with more relish than imagination). The governor's spinmeisters are claiming the story was leaked by Wilson's GOP rivals to undermine his soon-to-be-announced presidential campaign. And Wilson himself insists he will continue to pound away on the immigration issue. But such bravado rings hollow, for Wilson's political integrity has been badly undermined.

It's not just because having hired an illegal immigrant proves the hypocrisy of Wilson's hard-line stance. Most voters probably assume a certain hypocrisy in the positions taken by most politicians. Wilson's problem is more complicated. Now, from New Hampshire to Iowa, he will have to explain, ad nauseam, how he came to hire an illegal immigrant. And in the process he will have to acknowledge, however indirectly, that there is nuance to this country's immigration problems — shades of gray that Wilson has not discussed much for fear of weakening the gut-level appeal of his "hot button" issue.

Illegal immigrants are so fundamental to California's economy, working everywhere from farms to restaurants to car washes, that it's highly unlikely anyone in this state has not benefited from their labor at one time or another. Certainly, some of Wilson's biggest backers in, say, California agribusiness or San Diego's tourism industry, profit from cheap immigrant labor. Wilson knows this and, not surprisingly, he can discuss the complexities of the immigration issue quite knowledgeably. But why bother when you can get more mileage out of scary commercials that show illegals running across the border? Or when you can win easy votes by lending the legitimacy of your high office to misguided efforts like Proposition 187, the ballot initiative that purported to solve California's immigration problems by depriving illegal immigrants of education and health care — as if social services rather than jobs lure them here.

Large numbers of illegal immigrants in California pose a real challenge for this state. And until recently, we got precious little help from Washington in dealing with the challenge. But all those hard-working immigrants are nowhere near the threat that the overblown rhetoric of Proposition 187's backers and ambitious pols like Wilson makes them out to be.

Maidgate just might push Wilson out of the simplistic and hypocritical stance he has taken on immigration by forcing him to explain the seeming contradiction in his public and private approaches to the issue. And we may not have heard all there is to Maidgate. There are reports in Spanish-language newspapers that Wilson employed at least two other Mexicans whose immigration status was questionable.

As long as there might be another illegal immigrant out there who remembers working for "Señor Wilson," the governor had best shelve the myths he and other restrictionists have tried to sell to the American public and discuss this "hot button" issue in all its daunting complexity. That would be quite a change for the political leader who has done as much as anyone to demonize illegal immigrants in the public mind.

JULY 16, 1995

# Break Apart a Problem Agency

PITY THE U.S. Immigration and Naturalization Service. Once the poorest and most demoralized agency in the federal government, INS is finally getting some respect — and money — from Congress. But it's also getting criticized as much as ever for the things it can't get quite right.

That's because its 20,000 employees, especially the 4,700 agents of the U.S. Border Patrol, are literally on the front lines dealing with illegal immigration, a hot-button issue that every politician from Washington to San Diego wants to look tough about. And when they can't look tough bashing immigrants, they try to look tough by bashing INS for not being tough enough.

Last week, for example, some members of Congress demanded a Justice Department probe of charges by the INS employees union that agency officials in Miami "purposely and actively" deceived members of Congress on an inspection tour by ordering agents to work overtime during the visit and clearing cells of immigrant detainees so the facilities would not look overcrowded. Revealingly, the visitors were not from a committee on immi-

FRANK DEL OLMO

gration but a special "task force" on immigration, no doubt looking for some easy publicity.

Having reported on INS for 23 years, I've lost count of how often agency employees said they longed for more attention from Congress and the public. Well, now that a border incident in South Texas can wind up on front pages from Los Angeles to New York, I can't help but recall the old saying about being careful about what you wish for.

But the INS of today is a better agency than the one I first encountered in 1972, when reporting on an FBI probe of INS corruption. It has more people, better equipment, higher morale and much better leaders.

Doris Meissner may be the smartest and best-prepared INS commissioner ever. By selecting an expert on immigration — Meissner had held immigration posts in both Republican and Democratic administrations and was long affiliated with the Carnegie Endowment for International Peace — President Clinton made a great improvement over the political hacks and retread military officers that previous presidents picked to run INS.

And Meissner has some smart local INS officials, like Silvestre Reyes, Border Patrol chief in El Paso, working for her. A native of Texas, Reyes proved that even the notoriously porous border around El Paso could be controlled, if not completely sealed. He did it by putting his full complement of agents right on the line, pulling them out of so-called area control operations in El Paso's barrios, where they were a constant irritant to U.S.-born Latinos. It was a controversial and costly move.

But it was also creative in a way like nothing else the INS has ever done. And that's what INS is going to need to get a better handle on immigration in the years to come: not tough new laws or tough new agents, but creativity.

Here's my modest but creative proposal: Break up the INS. Not dismantle it completely, of course. But at least break it down into its two main components, immigration and naturalization.

The Border Patrol is one of several agencies, like the Customs Service and Coast Guard, charged with keeping our borders secure. For years, the General Accounting Office, and more recently Vice President Al Gore's Commission on Reinventing Government, have urged their consolidation into a single border-management agency. Resistance to that idea has come from Congress and INS employee unions, proving that they can be as much a part of the problem as INS management.

But beyond better border control, we need to put more thought into regulating the legal entry of foreigners into this country, whether as workers or investors, and promoting the acculturation of those foreigners who stay as immigrants. This responsibility also falls to INS — remember what the N stands for. But naturalization has received even less attention and financial support than the agency's police functions. It would be handled better by a new Bureau of Immigration in the Labor or State Department.

This would not be another redundant bureaucracy, for in the future our problem may not be too many immigrants but not enough — or at least not enough of certain types of immigrants. As our native-born population ages and lives longer, it will need young workers and entrepreneurs to help support it.

In the not too distant future the migration of workers and business people from country to country, especially historically linked neighbors like the United States and Mexico, will be as routine as the flow of goods and capital is today. That means that the INS in its present form and function is a dinosaur — even under the capable leadership of people like Doris Meissner and Silvestre Reyes.

OCTOBER 20, 1996

# Latinos Can Look to an Italian Legacy

PEPPERDINE UNIVERSITY researcher Gregory Rodriguez is getting a lot of well-deserved attention for his recent study titled "The Emerging Latino Middle Class," which uses 1990 census data to counter many of the myths that have come to surround Southern California's largest ethnic group. Like me, Rodriguez thinks Los Angeles has a lot less to worry about in its fast-growing Latino population than political Cassandras on both the rabid right and the radical left would have us believe.

Among other things, Rodriguez found that nearly half of the households headed by U.S.-born Latinos in the five-county Los Angeles area are solidly middle class, with annual incomes above the regional median of $35,000. More than half of these same Latino families also own their own homes, long the quintessential symbol of American middle-class stability.

But I won't rehash Rodriguez's work. It should be studied firsthand by everyone who cares about the long-term future of California and other states with large Latino populations. I'd rather focus on an intriguing parallel that Rodriguez had in mind while doing his research.

As we discussed his findings before publication, at one point we got to talking about New York City's history as the United States' chief port of entry for immigrants in the late 19th century and how Los Angeles is in the same position today.

I remarked that if Los Angeles really is the Ellis Island of the 20th century, as one cliché puts it, then there is one ethnic group whose progress in America offers a hopeful scenario for today's Latino immigrants. But even before I got the words out of my mouth, Rodriguez had already uttered them:

"The Italians," he said with a broad smile as I nodded my assent.

Indeed, there are many similarities between today's Latino newcomers and the Italians who stepped ashore in New York around the turn of the century.

Both are from deeply religious, principally Roman Catholic cultures.

Both tend to have very strong family ties and very large extended families that provide a network of personal support.

Both cultures tend to be highly patriarchal and male-dominated. But women who choose to break out of the macho culture have their own special form of social mobility. They are considered attractive wives and thus widely marry outside the culture, speeding the process of assimilation and acceptance.

Both groups first came to the United States as rural peasants and maintained strong ties to their home areas. Mexicans from Jalisco or Zacatecas remain loyal to their home states, much as Italians from Sicily or Calabria once did.

Both groups experienced a steady return migration. Scholars estimate that fully half of the 4 million Italians who migrated to the United States between 1880 and 1920 eventually returned to Italy, using their American earnings to live more comfortable lives in their homeland. Many Latin Americans have done the same, a point often overlooked in our overheated political debates about immigration.

Despite being of largely peasant stock, both communities became more economically sophisticated in this country, either by finding jobs as skilled blue-collar workers or by building up small retail businesses like restaurants, bakeries and, yes, in a few cases, organized crime.

Finally, like today's Latinos, the Italian immigrants of the late 19th century faced virulent prejudice from native-born Americans who feared that the newcomers were not the same "quality" as previous immigrants and would have preferred to see most of them deported.

In fact, just as a derogatory term applied to Latinos (the hateful term "wetback") can be traced to their immigrant history, so can a common derogatory term applied to Italian Americans. The awful word "wop" originated as an abbreviation used by immigration inspectors at Ellis Island, who applied it to anyone who arrived "without papers."

The most hopeful part of this scenario, of course, is that in spite of the prejudice and other problems Italian immigrants faced, the great majority became upstanding citizens. They not only built solid middle-class communities in and around New York, but also have given that city two mayors, Fiorello La Guardia and Rudolph Giuliani. They also have given us a respected governor in Mario Cuomo, a Supreme Court justice in Antonin Scalia, a legendary business tycoon in Lee Iacocca, great athletes like Joe DiMaggio and countless artists, from Frank Sinatra to Martin Scorsese.

Who is to say that, a hundred years from now, Latinos in Los Angeles and other cities won't be able to look back on a similarly proud history of progress? It's at least as likely as the nightmare scenarios that anti-immigration extremists use to whip up hysteria over the Latinization of the United States.

MAY 18, 2003

# Slow-Motion Carnage at the Border

IF A BOEING 747 with more than 300 passengers plunged into the desert between Los Angeles and Phoenix, it would be big news. And if, a year later, a jumbo jet filled to capacity crashed en route from El Paso to Dallas, that would get our attention too.

Imagine the reaction if the two tragedies were linked: that

a technical problem in the air traffic control system was to blame or that terrorists had brought down both aircraft. Is there any doubt the federal government would move fast to prevent another catastrophe?

It is not that much of an exaggeration to suggest that a human tragedy on the scale of a jumbo jet crash is taking place in the Southwest every year. But hardly anyone notices because the carnage is in slow motion — one or two deaths a day. And the victims are largely anonymous — illegal migrants trying to sneak across isolated parts of the Mexican border.

About once a year we are briefly jolted by appalling incidents like what unfolded last week at a truck stop in Victoria, Texas, about 100 miles southwest of Houston. Police found that as many as 100 people had been jammed into a truck trailer in stifling heat. They had been trapped inside for hours, abandoned by a would-be smuggler. Eighteen died, including a 5-year-old boy in his father's arms.

That figure matched the record-high toll of a similar incident involving undocumented immigrants: Eighteen people died in 1987 after being locked in a stifling railroad boxcar in West Texas. Then there was the incident two years ago outside Yuma, Ariz., in which 14 people died while trying to hike across the desert.

Like so many facets of illegal immigration, precise statistics on just how many people die each year trying to sneak across the Mexican border are hard to come by, much less agree upon. In 2002, for instance, the U.S. Border Patrol counted 371 deaths along the southern border, while the Mexican government's count was slightly higher.

For a few hopeful months after the Arizona tragedy of May 2001, it looked as if the U.S. and Mexican governments had finally been prodded into action. Both nations had newly inaugurated presidents, George W. Bush and Vicente Fox. The two straight-talking ranchers agreed that the immigration control system along their shared border needed fixing and even appointed a team of Cabinet officers to start finding solutions.

Then came Sept. 11, and whatever progress had been made toward a U.S.-Mexico migration accord came to a dead halt as Bush's priorities shifted from Latin America to the Middle East, and from opening the border to closing it down.

Amid the paranoid fears of nativists who would put the Army and Marines on the border, the U.S. government has done an effective job of slowing the movement of people into the U.S. from Mexico. That is why so many would-be migrants are trying ever more dangerous ploys to sneak into this country to fill the menial jobs U.S. citizens won't accept.

Before 9/11, as a step toward making sense out of our broken immigration system, Fox proposed an ambitious scheme to legalize all 3 million to 5 million Mexicans living illegally in the United States. It was clearly too ambitious, given the politics of immigration reform.

But why not start talking with the Mexicans again, this time about something more modest? Say a plan to cooperate with a campaign launched by the Fox government to provide every Mexican citizen living illegally in this country with a secure identity card. These so-called *matriculas* are already issued by Mexican consulates to any Mexican citizen who requests them. Last year 1 million were handed out, 165,000 in Los Angeles alone, according to consular officials — and we should make sure they're easily available to all.

Many banks and even police departments accept *matriculas* as identification cards. Would it be that hard for the U.S. government to do the same? If a *matricula* agreement included a U.S. government pledge that otherwise law-abiding workers would not be deported, the Justice Department could get access to the names and addresses of up to 5 million foreigners living in this country in the shadows. That would only enhance homeland security.

If Mexican migrant workers in the U.S. could live in the open, rather than in a netherworld where they must rely on smugglers to get across the border, there might be less incentive for desperate people to risk their lives, day after scorching day, in the deserts and scrublands of the Southwest.

# CHAPTER NINE

# Law Enforcement and the Military

## *The humanity behind the uniform*

FRANK DEL OLMO SAW similarities in the qualities that attract many Latinos to military service or a law enforcement career: their sense of tradition, pride, patriotism and an appreciation for order. He also saw darker aspects: a disproportionate number of Latinos who had lost their lives in U.S. wars or who had been victims of brutal police conduct.

Del Olmo's columns were woven with personal recollections that had shaped his viewpoints. Readers, for example, learn about his personal military hero: his fiercely patriotic Uncle Frank, who was left paralyzed by a wound suffered in World War II.

And, at the height of Los Angeles' struggles to reform its police force, Frank told of a warning that had a lasting effect. His mother, Margaret, cautioned Frank to always be careful around police because of their mistreatment of Latinos in the working-poor neighborhoods of Pacoima, where he grew up. Del Olmo recalled that conversation after the Rodney King beating took place near his old neighborhood.

# Sgt. Jimmy Lopez May Be the Only Real Live Hero Among the Freed

I DON'T WANT TO ADMIRE Sgt. Jimmy Lopez as much as I do. But, after all, Lopez, a 22-year-old Marine from Globe, Ariz., is an honest-to-goodness military hero. He may be the only genuine hero among the 52 Americans released by the Iranians last week after 444 days as hostages.

My only qualm is that the Latino community has already contributed more than its share of military heroes and martyrs to this country. So many young Latinos get mishandled by this country's educational system that I sometimes wonder if they are taught to believe that they are capable of only one thing — waging war.

Some of us have certainly done that magnificently, and Sgt. Jimmy Lopez fits right into that tradition.

The American GI Forum, a Latino veterans' organization, claims that Mexican Americans have won more Medals of Honor than any other ethnic group. I have never seen the figures to substantiate that claim, but I will take their word for it.

The names of Chicanos who won this country's highest award for military valor dot the local landscape. Many parks, especially in Chicano barrios, are named after them. There's Villegas Park in Riverside's Casa Blanca district and Obregon Park in East Los Angeles. I grew up in Pacoima, where the city's Recreation Center is dedicated to the memory of David Gonzalez, a Pacoima boy who won his Medal of Honor fighting in the Philippines during World War II, and never came back.

Maybe a park will be named after Lopez someday. That is the least that he deserves. Outside Arizona, Lopez and his family did not receive as much attention as some of the other hostages. The only thing about him that caught the national media's fancy was a letter that he wrote to his mother telling her of his craving for her homemade beef tamales.

Life magazine did publish a touching article, however, about his parents, Jesse and Mary, and their four children. But even Life did not reveal a secret that the Lopez family had kept proudly but fearfully for most of the time that Jimmy, as they call him, was held hostage. Their secret was that, on the day of the embassy seizure, he acted with extraordinary courage and engineered the escape of the handful of Americans who managed to get away.

Now the story is coming out, told not only by Lopez's parents but also by several of the Americans who were caught with the Marine sergeant inside the embassy's consulate building on the morning of Nov. 4, 1979.

According to their accounts, about 70 people were in the consulate when Iranian militants stormed and overran the embassy compound. Fifteen were Americans, including several Foreign Service officers much older than Lopez. When the violence outside began, Lopez took control inside. Barking orders like a drill instructor, he barricaded doors and windows, at one point driving back the militants with tear-gas grenades, witnesses said. He also herded people onto the building's second floor, where they would be safer. He held off the militants, single-handedly, for three hours.

"He deserves a large part of the credit for keeping things calm and for keeping the consulate secure for the time that he did," said consular officer Mark Lijek, one of those who escaped with Lopez's help. "He was the youngest American in the consulate, but he took command as though he were a general."

As the situation deteriorated, Lopez began destroying visa stamps and classified documents. He also divided the people with him into small groups and let them out a side door so that they might escape amid the confusion outside. Some of the Americans were later captured. But five got away. They made it to the Canadian embassy and were able to leave Iran a few months later using false Canadian passports.

Lopez did not leave the consulate building until the last of his colleagues were ready to go. His group, which included Consul-General Richard Morefield and Richard Queen, was captured a few blocks from the embassy.

Queen, later freed by the Iranians when he fell ill, knew of Lopez's bravery but could not talk of it publicly because of fears for his safety if the Iranians found out about his actions. Several of the diplomats whom Lopez helped save did tell his family, however. "We were very proud of him when we heard about it," Mary Lopez says now, "but I worried that the Iranians would be rougher on Jimmy because he helped."

Talking with his family by telephone after being freed, Lopez told them that he had, indeed, been put in "some really bad-hole places." But, he added, "at least I got some of the others out, right?"

There had been moments, Mrs. Lopez said, when she had been tempted to reveal her son's actions, particularly when she saw a letter to the editor in an Arizona newspaper suggesting that all Sgt. Lopez was missing while being held by the Iranians was "his tamales."

A friend of the Lopez family told me the other day that Latinos all over the country now are offering to make him tamales. But Lopez deserves more than that as his reward, and will probably get it. Which will make his family and other Latinos very proud. Even me, although I hope a day will come when our young men can be heroic at something other than military exploits.

Amid the national euphoria that has followed the hostages' release, some valid questions have been raised as to whether the 52 Americans are victims rather than heroes. But there were real heroes in the long hostage crisis. Jimmy Lopez was one. So was Warren Christopher, the Los Angeles attorney who, as deputy secretary of state, patiently and stoically negotiated the hostage settlement.

I will be glad when Latino heroes can be lawyer-diplomats like Christopher. In the meantime, of course, I am glad we have Jimmy Lopez.

MAY 26, 1983

# In Appreciation of the GI Generation of Latinos

ALEX SARAGOZA, a historian at UC Berkeley, has something specific in mind when he calls the children of Mexicans who immigrated to the United States in the early part of this century the "GI generation."

"They experienced the New Deal and World War II," the young Chicano scholar says. "They grew up in a time when there was great emphasis on assimilation. When the ideal was being a good American."

Saragoza believes that third-generation Mexican Americans, especially the young activists who led the Chicano civil rights movement during the 1960s, often overlook, or fail to appreciate, the contributions of the "GI generation." Assimilationist views seem quaint when compared to the ardent Chicano pride of the '60s.

Saragoza's words took on a special poignancy for me last week, when I was a pallbearer at the funeral of my uncle, Frank Zavala Rojas.

My uncle had died a week before at the Veterans Administration Medical Center in Sepulveda after spending the last 38 years of his life in a wheelchair. He had been paralyzed from the waist down by a spinal injury inflicted by a German sniper in World War II. Complications from the injury took his life at age 65.

Uncle Frank was born in the Mexican state of Chihuahua. A month later his family settled in Utah. He worked as a ranch hand and field hand in that state and in California before enlisting in the Army shortly after the attack on Pearl Harbor.

Although he was a skilled handyman, my uncle was never able to work again after he returned from the service. Sadly, he spent the rest of his life checking in and out of veterans' hospitals.

I grew up in a fatherless home, so Uncle Frank, who was married to my mother's sister and lived near our home in Pacoima, was one of the two or three men who filled an important gap during my youth. He was an ideal choice for a role model for reasons that had nothing to do with family ties or proximity.

To begin with, he was a big man and yet so quiet, gentle and soft-spoken that I cannot remember his ever raising his voice to me, even when I probably deserved it. It was hard not to respect him and feel affection for him.

He was also a genuine American war hero. Before he was wounded, my uncle had fought in North Africa and France as a sergeant in the 1st Infantry Division. He had landed at Omaha Beach on D-day, and later won a Silver Star for single-handedly turning back a tank attack during the Battle of the Bulge. Among his many other commendations were a Bronze Star and a Purple Heart with three oak leaf clusters.

I remember how proud I felt the first time his wife, Ramona, showed me his medals and the letters of commendation that came with them. I worried that those faded papers might someday fall apart and was glad when my aunt had them framed a few years ago. They hang in a prominent spot in their home, next to a large American flag.

That same flag was draped over Uncle Frank's casket when we carried it from the church last week; it reminded me of how my uncle epitomized the "GI generation."

He was bilingual and bicultural — proud of his Mexican ancestry, yet as patriotic an American as I have ever known. His loyalty to this country was all the more moving because he expressed it so quietly. Though he never objected to my calling myself a Chicano, he once told me that he considered himself "just an American." And when he talked of his military exploits it was matter-of-factly, with no bravado.

After we buried my uncle, I found my thoughts returning to him, and his generation, while I pondered some of the week's news events.

The U.S. Senate had passed the 1983 version of the Simpson-Mazzoli bill, whose main purpose is to restrict future immigration to this country, particularly from Mexico and the rest of Latin America. There is a need for immigration reform, to be sure, but it angers me that some are pushing for it because they fear that Latinos are somehow not quite capable of becoming good American citizens. These restrictionists could have learned a few things from my uncle.

President Reagan was preparing to visit Miami, where he was to appear before a sympathetic audience of Cuban Americans to defend his dubious Central American policies. The violence and bloodshed are no less real in El Salvador and Nicaragua than on Omaha Beach. But the issues are nowhere as clear-cut — something that I know my uncle understood but that Reagan seems unable to grasp.

And that week in Denver a Mexican American, former Colorado state legislator Federico Peña, was the top vote-getter in the mayoral primary. With a little luck, Peña might become the third Latino to be elected mayor of a major U.S. city, with all the opportunities and problems that the job entails.

The issues before young Chicanos like Pena, 36, are more subtle and complicated than the challenges — Depression and war — that faced the "GI generation." But that does not detract from what these older Mexican Americans accomplished.

I will always be proud to look back at one of their best, my Uncle Frank, for reassurance that we are equal to the task.

# The Hush at the Vietnam Memorial

WASHINGTON — If his name had not been at eye level I might never have seen it.

I was visiting the Vietnam Veterans Memorial for the first time, not having been to the nation's capital since the memorial was dedicated last year. The monument is not impressive at first glance — a simple chevron of polished black granite set into a low sloping hillside on the western end of the Washington Mall. But, when I was close enough to see the names of the Americans who died in that war carved into its shiny flat surface, my reaction changed.

The effect of those 57,939 names was sobering. The feelings that they stirred were intensified by the touching scenes that I saw taking place around me. An elderly man tentatively stretched out his hand and slowly passed his fingers across one of the names. A family gazed at another name with a mixture of pride and sadness, while the father focused a camera on it to take a photograph. Here and there flowers were wedged into the crevices between the wall's long granite panels.

Farther away, on a park bench, a husky young man was sitting motionless and silent, his head buried in his hands. A young blond woman, seated next to him, gently stroked his hair, trying to comfort him, or maybe just trying to understand.

Despite the sunshine and blue skies of Washington's springtime and the traffic on nearby Constitution Avenue, and even amid the 100 or so people visiting the memorial that afternoon, the area was hushed, as if we were all in a cathedral. I was walking along the wall, from east to south, when a name in the second line of Panel 44 caught my eye.

Isaac Ramirez Garcia Jr.

My stepcousin Isaac. The dark-skinned, quiet boy with whom I got into so many boyish pranks as a child — whenever my family visited our stepfather's relatives in San Fernando. Isaac, with whom I had lost touch after entering a Catholic high school instead of the local public school. Isaac, whose death I learned about from my mother one afternoon in 1967, when I arrived home from a day of classes at UCLA.

I had not gone to the Vietnam memorial looking for his name, nor for the names of the other young men whom I knew who died in Vietnam — Richard Paco, my cousin Mary Helen's husband of only a few weeks, or Arnold Ramirez, who had been the most handsome and popular guy in the Pacoima neighborhood where I grew up. I wanted to see the monument commemorating their sacrifice. But I would have felt uncomfortable looking for the names of other Latinos of my generation who had gone off to fight a dubious war while I was lucky enough to be in college on a scholarship.

That was why I was so taken aback at seeing Isaac's name, and why I walked quickly to the directory that stands at the entrance to the memorial to be certain that it was indeed his name that had leaped out at me. I leafed through the thick alphabetical listing of the war dead until I found him again: Pfc. Isaac Ramirez Garcia Jr., San Fernando, California.

So I slowly went back down the walk and looked again at the stark letters neatly carved on the shiny black stone. And I started to cry.

Not loudly or openly. But the heavy feeling in my chest and the misting of my eyes was undeniable. I felt suddenly embarrassed, as though everyone nearby must at that moment be staring at me. I walked hurriedly away, stopping at a park bench near the young couple whose quiet, painful vigil I had noticed earlier.

I let the tears flow freely for a minute or so before even trying to compose myself. It was not as easy as I thought it would be, and I began wondering why I was reacting this way. Certainly there was some grief for a lost friend — even if I had known him long ago, almost in another life. And there had to be sadness for the many other men whose names covered that wall — not just the countless Garcias, Chavezes and Ruizes, but the Smiths and Jeffersons as well. There probably was some guilt too, for not having joined them in those faraway jungles.

But positive feelings also helped bring those tears. A sense of awe and wonder that I was able to turn away from the wall where Isaac's name is carved and see the Lincoln Memorial only yards away. And a feeling of pride that, years from now, when future generations of Americans visit that monument to gaze on the stern countenance and ponder the eloquent words of Abraham Lincoln they will be able to walk a few yards down a grassy slope and also see the name of a young Mexican kid from San Fernando who, in

Lincoln's words, gave his last full measure of devotion to his country.

It took me a half-hour to calm down. The young couple had left, walking slowly past me, arm in arm. The man's head still hung low, his eyes focused on the gravel walk as his friend guided him along.

I hurried back toward Constitution Avenue, headed for the State Department Building, a looming presence clearly visible a couple of blocks away. I was going to be late for an appointment, a background briefing on Reagan administration policies in Central America at the Bureau of Inter-American Affairs.

Like other administration officials with whom I had spoken during my visit to Washington, the man who saw me that afternoon would be upbeat about the future in El Salvador, Nicaragua and Honduras. He would be full of assurances that the region's problems could be handled without an escalation of the U.S. military presence there. I half-expected to hear him say that there was light at the end of the tunnel, but he didn't.

And, despite the official confidence expressed about our latest military involvements in remote regions, I am still skeptical. Why is it that all those names carved in black granite don't seem to be as sobering to the decision-makers in Washington as they are to out-of-towners?

AUGUST 6, 1995

# 'To Protect and to Serve' — and Fear

L IKE MANY BOYS who grew up in Southern California, I once considered becoming a Los Angeles Police Department officer. But my mother talked me out of it and in the process taught me a sad lesson that haunts me — and all of Los Angeles — to this day.

When I became an adolescent, after a childhood of playing with every "Dragnet" toy I could get my hands on, she took me aside and told me how the young Anglo policemen who patrolled our neighborhood in Pacoima often harassed her as she walked home at night from her job as a waitress in a Mexican restaurant. Sometimes their crudely stated speculations that this devout Catholic woman was a prostitute or drug addict reduced her to tears.

Then she added a frightened warning I have never forgotten:

"And don't you ever say anything to them, talk back or anything," she said. "They'll beat you within an inch of your life."

I never forgot Mom's warning. And her chilling words came back with special poignancy after the Rodney G. King beating, which took place near my old neighborhood. What a sad commentary they were on an LAPD that "Dragnet" never showed us. A God-fearing mother who raised six children to be hard-working citizens felt she had to prepare her son for life in Los Angeles not only by warning him away from gangs — which she did, quite often — but also by warning him about the LAPD. For in the city's Latino barrios, the LAPD was not to be respected — much less aspired to — but feared.

And now comes last weekend's fatal shooting of 14-year-old Jose Antonio Gutierrez by an LAPD cop, Michael Falvo. Police say the boy was brandishing a semiautomatic weapon on a residential street in Lincoln Heights. Such a weapon was found near his body — but inside a fence and without his fingerprints — after he died. Witnesses, including Gutierrez's mother, say the boy had a flashlight in his hand.

Hearing all of this, I get the sick feeling I have whenever I am reminded of my mother's warning and the fearful look in her eyes.

After the King beating, which was videotaped for all the world to be appalled at, efforts began to reform the LAPD. Starting with the Christopher Commission report and continuing through the selection of a new, non-LAPD chief — Philadelphia's Willie Williams — LAPD's arrogant, macho culture seemed to be changing. Or so I thought.

Yet much about the Gutierrez shooting stands as a stark reminder of how much still needs to be done to reform LAPD. It is one of those violent urban tragedies with no heroes or villains, only victims.

Even at his young age, Gutierrez was a tattooed gang wannabe who went by the nickname "Travieso" — Troublemaker.

Falvo, the officer who shot him, was one of 44 singled out by the Christopher Commission as "problem officers" because of a history of complaints of excessive force or improper behavior. Even if he had been rehabilitated, Falvo's presence on the streets posed a potential embarrassment to the city. What kind of bureaucratic mentality assigns a "problem officer" to LAPD's anti-gang detail, among the department's most sensitive and volatile jobs?

Just how volatile became obvious after the Gutierrez shooting. That same night, and the next sultry evening, rock and bottle throwing broke out in Lincoln Heights. LAPD had to call a citywide tactical alert to bring the situation under control, and at least 20 people were arrested. But the anger remains and the simmering tensions have aroused concern in City Hall, where Mayor Richard Riordan and the City Council urgently want to avoid a replay of the 1992 riots that broke out after the cops who beat Rodney King were acquitted by a jury.

They have reason to be worried. This summer marks the 25th anniversary of serious rioting on the Eastside. Four people died and millions of dollars in damage was done in 1970 during a series of often pitched battles between police and angry Latinos, mostly young gang members. Demonstrations are planned for later this month to commemorate the 1970 riots, and the Gutierrez shooting has handed the organizers a perfect issue with which to stir up old resentments and anger.

Luckily for Los Angeles, Chicano activists aren't the only ones reacting. City Council members Mike Hernandez and Richard Alatorre, who represent the Eastside, are prodding the LAPD to investigate the killing quickly and show some responsiveness to the community. Among others demanding an accounting from LAPD is the United Neighborhoods Organization, which unites most of the area's Roman Catholic churches. UNO represents the kind of solid citizens who usually rally around law enforcement. That they are not is a damning comment on how poorly LAPD's new philosophy of community-based policing is being implemented.

It is plain to see that new damage has been done to LAPD's image in the past few days. I wonder how many more kids are being warned by decent, caring mothers to be afraid of the LAPD.

# It's Baca Against Back Room

*"But this race isn't just about saying yes to Sherman Block. It's about saying no to Lee Baca."* — John Shallman, Block's campaign manager

I HAD NOT DECIDED TO VOTE for Lee Baca until I read that tactless quote from a spokesman for his opponent's campaign in Wednesday's edition of The Times. And despite Sherman Block's untimely death the very next day, I have not changed my mind.

For Block's passing, while tragic, was not unexpected. In fact, it has thrown into stark relief the rank hypocrisy of this year's campaign for Los Angeles County sheriff. And if we voters want to send the county's political establishment a message that such gamesmanship is unacceptable, the way to do it is to vote for Baca.

Block's death was no surprise because for the last several weeks of the campaign virtually the only issue being talked about was the incumbent's failing health, after two bouts with cancer and kidney failure. It was painfully clear that the 74-year-old Block could not serve another four-year term, even if he won reelection.

Then last week Block suffered a serious head injury after falling in his home and was forced to undergo surgery to remove a blood clot from his brain. Even if the sheriff had lived, medical sources told The Times, he faced permanent impairment.

What a tragic denouement to a long and honorable career in public service.

When the county Board of Supervisors selected Block as sheriff in 1972, he brought a breath of fresh air to law enforcement in Los Angeles. His thoughtful, soft-spoken style was a refreshing contrast not only to his imperious predecessor, Peter Pitchess, but also a hopeful counterpoint to the insular and arrogant culture of the Los Angeles Police Department. Even then, the LAPD was showing the first signs of the internal rot that would lead to the Rodney King incident, its terrible aftermath and the Christopher Commission's call for police reform.

But after a solid decade on the job, Block's tenure was marred by a numbing series of scandals in the Sheriff's Department: the theft of drug money by detectives in an elite anti-narcotics unit, several cases of more mundane financial mismanagement and the inappropriate use of force by deputies on the streets and in the county's jails.

The Sheriff's Department problems became so numerous that Block had to face a citizens' reform panel of his own, the Kolts Commission. And anyone with an open mind concluded long ago that the biggest Sheriff's Department in the country needed some fresh leadership.

Which brings us back to Lee Baca, the well-meaning 32-year veteran of the Sheriff's Department who had the temerity to challenge Block in last June's primary election and then surprised everyone by forcing the incumbent into a runoff.

For all his effort, the challenger now is being bad-mouthed by everybody who's anybody in the Los Angeles political establishment.

That is why Block's campaign manager felt free to say what he did about Baca last Wednesday. And it is why I now feel some sympathy for Baca even while I still harbor serious doubts that any insider can fix what's broken in the Sheriff's Department.

If Block's supporters, like Los Angeles Mayor Richard Riordan, really had any courage, they would have forgotten about Baca and bluntly told Block that it was time for him to groom a successor and step gracefully aside.

The biggest hypocrites are the five current county supervisors. They could have mustered the clout to simply force Block out, if they had put their egos and rivalries aside long enough to work together. Instead, they are now working together in an unseemly campaign to urge voters to reelect a dead man.

For if Block wins, the supervisors get to exercise the worst form of political leadership. They can meet in a back room somewhere to handpick his successor. And that is the real reason they are now all ganging up on Baca in a semipanic.

A former regional chief in the Sheriff's Department and professor of police science, Baca has for years tried to cultivate support to run for sheriff, both among law enforcement professionals and local political activists, especially in the Latino community.

And while relatively few of Baca's fellow cops stepped forward to support him, he did succeed in becoming well-known among Latinos.

If Baca wins, which is still a possibility despite all the verbal hits he is taking from the power brokers, it will be because Latinos support him in big numbers. And if that happens, it will serve Los Angeles' political establishment right.

Not because they underestimated the Latino vote, but because they ganged up on a fundamentally decent man whose only sin was challenging an incumbent that nobody else had the guts to take on.

SEPTEMBER 22, 1996

# A Veteran's Cause Paved the Way

D R. HECTOR GARCIA, a family physician in Corpus Christi, Texas, died July 26 after a long illness. He was 82, and his death was hardly noted outside his home state.

But major Texas newspapers put his obituary on the front page. Journalists in the Lone Star State, to their credit, remembered better than their colleagues elsewhere the important role Garcia once played in American history.

In 1948 he founded one of the country's first Mexican American civil rights groups, the American GI Forum. A couple of Latino activist groups had been established before then, and probably hundreds have been founded since. But with an estimated 160,000 members in 24 states, the GI Forum remains among the biggest and most influential.

Some proud GI Forum members say it is also the most important, and it's hard to dispute them. When the GI Forum speaks out on behalf of Latino rights, it has a moral authority other activist groups can't match and that even virulent anti-Latino bigots must respect.

As its name suggests, the GI Forum represents the thousands of Mexican Americans and other Latinos who have served in the nation's armed forces, many in armed conflicts from World War II to the Persian Gulf. At a time when the political rhetoric about this country's illegal immigration problems has a distinct anti-Latino tone, the history of the GI Forum is worth remembering.

Garcia came to the United States in 1918, at the age of 4. His family fled the chaos of the Mexican Revolution like millions of other refugees who wound up in California, Texas and the other Southwestern states. Not long after graduating from the University of Texas Medical School in 1940, he volunteered for the U.S. Army. He served in North Africa and Italy as an infantryman, combat engineer and medical corps officer, earning a Bronze Star.

When the war ended, Garcia opened his Corpus Christi medical practice, where he "delivered thousands of babies," according to a relative, and helped many a returning GI as a contract physician for the Veterans Administration. His experience with the VA bureaucracy convinced Garcia to organize other Latino veterans to fight for the benefits due them. But before long, an incident occurred that catapulted this small-town doctor to national notoriety.

In 1949, a funeral home in Three Rivers, Texas, refused to allow its chapel to be used for the reburial of Army Pvt. Felix Longoria, a local Mexican American who had died fighting in the Philippines. The funeral home director told Longoria's widow that the local Anglo community "would not stand for it," Garcia would later recall.

Garcia and the new GI Forum took up Longoria's cause, raising a fuss that eventually came to the attention of Lyndon B. Johnson, then a U.S. senator from Texas. Johnson intervened and Longoria was reburied, with full military honors, at Arlington National Cemetery.

Longoria's plight convinced Garcia that the GI Forum needed to fight for more than VA benefits. The group had to struggle against discrimination in housing, jobs, education and voting rights. And it did, helping desegregate everything from schools and hospitals to theaters and swimming pools throughout Texas. By the 1950s, Garcia was the first nationally recognized Latino civil rights leader, widely enough known that novelist Edna Ferber used him as a model for a character in her bestselling novel about Texas, "Giant."

But Garcia won far greater honors than that. In 1968, Johnson, by then president, made him the first Mexican American to serve on the U.S. Commission on Civil Rights. In 1984 he became the first Mexican American awarded the Medal of Freedom.

It is partly the fault of those of us in the news media who focus more on the big news of the day rather than on the historic context of that news. But it was also a result of Garcia's own decision to fade into the background in recent years as a younger generation of Latino leaders came to the fore.

The leadership of the GI Forum has begun to shift from veterans of World War II and Korea to Latinos who served in Vietnam and the Persian Gulf. But they're still fighting the good fight that Garcia began.

Just last week, leaders of the local GI Forum announced that they will help organize a Latino consumer boycott of any business whose political action committee donates money to members of Congress who vote for the so-called Gallegly Amendment. This is a provision in a pending immigration reform bill that would allow states to exclude the children of illegal immigrants from public schools.

"If young Latinos are good enough to fight for this country, they are good enough to get an education," said Ruben Treviso, a Vietnam veteran who is a leader of the GI Forum in Southern California.

Dr. Hector, as GI Forum members respectfully called him, couldn't have put it any better.

MAY 11, 2003

# In War, Diversity Can Be a Lifesaver

**L**AST WEEK THEY BURIED the latest — and, one fervently hopes, the last — Latino casualty from the Iraq war.

The death of Army 1st Lt. Osbaldo Orozco of Earlimart, Calif., was not as widely noted as that of other Latino soldiers and Marines who died in Iraq, but his all-too-short life offers a lesson worth pondering by some conservatives in the Bush administration.

I am not referring to the neocon foreign-policy wonks who pushed to use U.S. military power to impose a Pax Americana in the Middle East. Their dubious strategic vision is finally being debated as widely and energetically as it should have been before they ordered young men like Orozco into harm's way.

No, I mean those right-wingers who focus on domestic issues, some of whom helped convince the U.S. Justice Department to oppose collegiate affirmative action programs in two cases now before the U.S. Supreme Court. The court is expected to rule in the cases — filed by white students passed over in favor of minority applicants to the University of Michigan and its law school — later this year.

Conservatives are hoping that a high court dominated by Republican appointees will use the cases to outlaw affirmative action in college admissions once and for all.

That could happen, but the odds became a little less likely when a distinguished cadre of retired U.S. military leaders, including Gen. Norman Schwarzkopf, the commander of U.S. forces in the Gulf War, filed a legal brief with the high court supporting the university's position.

The brief points out that the military "cannot achieve an officer corps that is both highly qualified and racially diverse" unless the service academies (among the most selective schools in the nation) and college ROTC programs have aggressive affirmative action programs. Such programs are needed because racial integration in the armed forces is "a prerequisite to a cohesive, and therefore effective, fighting force."

"People's lives depend on it," the brief concludes.

Which brings me back to 26-year-old Orozco. Like many other Latino casualties in Iraq, he was the son of immigrants — Mexican farmworkers who settled in the southern San Joaquin Valley. But unlike other young Latinos who signed up with the military in hopes of getting an education, Orozco was a gifted athlete who had a scholarship to Cal Poly San Luis Obispo. There he was captain of the football team, was recruited into ROTC and got his commission the day he graduated in June 2001.

Orozco commanded a team of four Bradley fighting vehicles with the 22nd Infantry Regiment. He was killed April 25 when his vehicle rolled over on rough terrain as his unit hurried to support soldiers under enemy fire near Tikrit.

At Orozco's funeral Wednesday, his friends eulogized a courageous young officer. Lt. George Miranda, a pallbearer, recalled his final conversation with Orozco: "He told me to take care of myself and my soldiers."

Clearly, leadership was a lesson Orozco absorbed. People's lives depended on it.

A study in March by the Pew Hispanic Center found that although Latinos and blacks made up 32% of all active-duty military personnel, they represented only 12% of the officer corps. The retired generals and admirals who filed the Supreme Court brief see the need to close that gap. Too bad the Justice Department doesn't.

Every war has unintended consequences. One result of the latest one that supporters of the Bush administration did not anticipate was the degree to which soldiers who were immigrants, or the children of immigrants, would sacrifice for a nation that had not fully accepted them. Even some conservatives in Congress are rethinking their party's anti-immigrant stance and pushing for laws making it easier for "green-card soldiers" and their families to become citizens.

Maybe a few conservatives will reassess their knee-jerk opposition to affirmative action programs that recruit natural leaders like Orozco to be military officers and, eventually, leaders of American society as a whole.

MARCH 30, 2003

# Three for the List of U.S. Heroes

YEARS FROM NOW, three young Marines from the Los Angeles area will be remembered, and honored, for being among the first casualties of the second Persian Gulf war, and not because of their ethnicity.

But for now, the sad deaths of Lance Cpl. Jose Gutierrez, 22, Cpl. Jose Angel Garibay, 21, and Cpl. Jorge A. Gonzalez, 20, are noteworthy not just because they shared roots in the Southland but because they also shared immigrant backgrounds. One wonders what will be made of that by the American xenophobes whose anti-immigrant paranoia has been in full fury since 9/11. Many of them dishonestly lump Latinos and other hard-working immigrants in with the foreign terrorists who threaten the nation's security. Perhaps the loss of such fine young men will undermine that cynical canard once and for all.

Gutierrez was the first of the three to fall in combat, and his immigrant experience was the most dramatic. Orphaned in Guatemala, Gutierrez followed a route taken by other desperate children from Central America, a region still not fully recovered from wars fought there in the 1980s. At 14, he made the risky journey across Mexico, entered this country illegally and made his way to Los Angeles. Here, he was taken in by a foster family, fin-

FRANK DEL OLMO

ished high school and went to community college with dreams of becoming an architect.

Garibay's story is more prosaic but no less touching. He came to this country as an infant from Mexico. His mother settled in Orange County, one of thousands of Mexicans who over two decades have changed the face and the politics of what was once the quintessential white Republican suburb. He wanted to be a police officer.

Gonzalez wanted to be a cop too, and planned to apply for a law enforcement job when his hitch in the Marines was up in a few months. He was the second of six sons born to Mexican immigrant parents in the San Gabriel Valley, and he leaves a wife and a son, born March 3, whom he never saw.

Each of the three was unique, but each was also typical of Southern California's large, youthful Latino population. They were comfortably bilingual and bicultural — playing football and *futbol*, listening to rock as well as *ranchera*.

That they all joined the Marines is no surprise. As the most macho of our military services, the Marine Corps has long had a special appeal for young Latinos. Even as other branches of the military saw Latino enlistment drop because some Latino youngsters didn't meet the higher educational requirements of an all-volunteer force, the percentage of Latino Marines has stayed at parity with the percentage of Latinos in the civilian labor force, 13%. (While I'm citing statistics, let it be noted that about 31,000 noncitizens serve in the U.S. military.)

But the most important thing Gutierrez, Garibay and Gonzalez shared is obvious — although it is the quality overlooked by those who would dismiss, or even demonize, Latino immigrants as "wetbacks" or worse. They were all patriotic and loved the adopted homeland of their families.

And they proved it by making the ultimate sacrifice.

They shared that quality with Latin American immigrants who have served in the U.S. military as far back as the Civil War. The number of Latinos who have fought for this nation has grown most dramatically since World War II, when the children of the first great wave of Mexican migration to this country (refugees of the Mexican Revolution of 1910) did their share of the heavy lifting for what we now call the "greatest generation."

Since then, from Korea to Vietnam to the Gulf War, Latino families have proudly given their best and brightest young people to the service of this country.

As American casualties begin to mount, Latinos mourn all the losses but most especially those of a community that so badly needs idealistic young leaders to help guide its future.

FEBRUARY 8, 2004

# Latinos Vote for Patriotism, Not One-Upmanship

S O WHO IS MORE LIKELY to get Latino voter support in November: a former National Guard flyboy from Texas or a former Navy officer from Massachusetts?

Far more important questions about the Latino vote will be asked before election 2004 is over. And they will focus on far more complex issues, like President Bush's recent guest-worker proposal or his administration's effort to reform American schools so there is "no child left behind."

But for now, with the presidential primaries well underway, an interesting trend may have emerged in two states with large Latino populations: Arizona and New Mexico. Last Tuesday, the acknowledged front-runner for the Democratic nomination, Sen. John F. Kerry of Massachusetts, won easily in both states with solid Latino support — 41% in Arizona, according to one exit poll. But what I find intriguing is who came in second in those two states, both in overall voting and among Latinos. It was neither of the two men most pundits see as jockeying for the No. 2 spot, Howard Dean and John Edwards. It was retired Army Gen. Wesley K. Clark.

In Arizona, Clark got 26.8% of the primary ballots. Among Latino voters, he got 29% of the vote, according to an exit poll by Edison Research. In the presidential caucuses in New Mexico, where 30% of voters are Latino, Kerry won with 37.7% support and Clark got 19%.

Obviously, one should not make too much of voting trends so early in an election year. But the Arizona and New Mexico voting results do offer one useful reminder to the Democrats. They provide more evidence that Latinos do not easily fit into the liberal mold, where too many Democrats try to lump them with African Americans.

Though Latinos tend to favor more spending on schools and many of the government programs backed by liberals, they also tend to be conservative on social issues like abortion and support for the military. At least that is one credible explanation why Clark, who was in uniform until recently, got voter support second only to Kerry, a Vietnam War hero. Of course, the fact that Latinos are pro-military comes as no surprise to anyone who knows the pride that Latino families take in relatives who have served in the armed forces. Walk into almost any Latino home and somewhere on a wall or shelf you'll see prominent photos of fathers, uncles, cousins or siblings in uniform. They may be grainy old pictures from World War II or fresh new snapshots of young men or women serving in the Persian Gulf, but they have a place of honor in the family gallery.

And although not as visible an issue as education, or as emotional a topic as immigration, Latino attitudes toward the military could loom in the background as a key factor that determines whether Latinos vote for Bush's reelection or support his Democratic opponent, who it now appears will be Kerry.

Bush's campaign is aiming to increase his Latino voter support from the respectable 35% he got in 2000 to at least 40% in 2004. They are hoping Latino swing voters will push New Mexico, which Bush lost by 600 votes in 2000, over to the GOP.

For their part, Democrats point to Arizona and Nevada, which Bush won in 2000, in the hopes of gaining enough new Latino votes to win those states. But in a Bush-Kerry race, any discussions of military service are muddled by politically inconvenient facts.

Kerry was a wounded war hero, to be sure, but he returned from Vietnam to publicly criticize the war. There are many veterans who consider that a betrayal of his comrades in arms.

"Throwing those medals away, that could stick in a lot of guys' craw," said Dan Ortiz, a Los Angeles veteran of the 1991 Persian Gulf War. Some Latino families might feel the same way.

On the GOP side, there is the question of whether Bush completely fulfilled his commitment to the Texas Air National Guard or was, as some of his more ardent critics claim, AWOL part of the time. "A lot of vets, it doesn't matter so much what you did as long as you served," said George Ramos, a Vietnam veteran from East Los Angeles. "But some may say Kerry was in 'Nam and the president wasn't, and hold that against Bush."

Late in 2002, a few White House operatives briefly tried to bash Democrats in the Congressional Hispanic Caucus — including some military veterans — because they had voted against the resolution giving Bush the authority to use military force in Iraq. Despite the fact that the caucus is notably more liberal than Latinos on many issues, the GOP ploy generated a nasty backlash.

So a useful reminder Republicans can draw from the Arizona and New Mexico voting is that, given Latinos' positive attitudes toward the military, it might not be a good idea to try such a political stunt again. Better to honor all forms of service and patriotism, as Latino families do, than to try to compare old military records in a tacky version of one-upmanship.

This was Frank del Olmo's final column.

# CHAPTER TEN

# Frankie

## *Life lessons learned from a boy of spark and subtlety*

PERHAPS BECAUSE FRANK DEL OLMO was generally so private, his columns on his son Frankie's battle with autism touched readers with a force that was both tender and powerful. Poignantly he shared his emotions: "What makes it difficult [to write about Frankie] is trying to write with a leaden pain in my heart."

That piercing ache gave way to resolve as he and his wife, Magdalena, researched promising therapies and treatments. Frank championed policies, education and research, while rejecting the stigma some associate with autism.

As Frankie improved, readers learned about his toy Elmo and dog Chocolate. In his final column on autism, Frank said he would write less to spend more time with Frankie. That time proved fleeting. However, Frank's hope for his son still lives.

# When the Biggest Gift
# Is a Little Boy's Hug

*"No two people with autism are the same; its precise form or expression is different in every case … . So, while a single glance may suffice for clinical diagnosis, if we hope to understand the autistic individual, nothing less than a total biography will do."* — Oliver Sacks, "An Anthropologist on Mars"

**M**Y SON — or Frankie, as everyone calls him — is 3 years old, so writing his "total biography" shouldn't be as hard for me as it is. What makes it difficult is trying to write with a leaden pain in my heart.

It has been a year since we learned that Frankie has autism. Or, to use the proper terminology that Sacks and the many kind, caring medical specialists I have come to know this year use, he is "challenged by infantile autism."

I have avoided writing about him until now. Not just because it is painful but because I was trying to fully comprehend what autism is, and what challenges it will pose for Frankie and the rest of our family for as long as he lives.

In simplest terms, autism is a neurological condition that makes it difficult to differentiate among the many sensory stimuli, like touch, light and sound — an ability that other people take for granted. For people with autism, exposure to such stimuli can result in "sensory overload," which they respond to by shutting out the world and withdrawing into themselves.

Of course, I'm still working on the intellectual part of understanding autism. I'm good at that. Years of journalistic training and practice have taught me to step back from even the most complex and emotion-laden topics and to analyze them dispassionately. So I've spent a lot of time researching autism — reading everything from clinical tracts to propaganda for purported miracle cures to the wonderfully written and hopeful book quoted above, which was published earlier this year.

I would not have learned nearly as much as I have without the similarly disciplined research skills of my wife, Magdalena, a former reporter at the Orange County Register. But there are times when our disciplined teamwork wavers, and either Magdalena or I cannot be coolly focused. That's when the sorrow rises to the surface. Then all we can do is dwell on our hopes and fears for a little boy with a soft, sweet smile and big brown eyes that normally sparkle with joy but sometimes glaze over in a distant stare as he is momentarily lost to us. When that happens, Frankie is experiencing sensory overload. Then he will hum monotonously and rapidly rub his hands together while pacing back and forth.

Those are among the most common symptoms of infantile autism. They are the behaviors that a year ago led us to consult pediatric specialists to try to determine why after two years of normal development, Frankie had stopped speaking and was slurring the few words he would say.

The initial diagnosis was made in early January by Dr. Nancy Brill, a pediatric behavior specialist at Kaiser Permanente, where Magdalena works as a communications director. For the next three months, Frankie underwent a series of comprehensive medical tests, some long and painful, to rule out other possibilities, including brain tumors or epilepsy. All the tests were negative. We later got a second opinion from Dr. B.J. Freeman, a noted autism researcher at UCLA.

Like Brill, Freeman concluded that Frankie's autism was mild and, with sufficient early intervention therapy, his prognosis was hopeful. He could look forward to an education and productive adulthood — perhaps even a creative one, if the remarkable people Sacks profiles in his book are potential models.

Sometimes, when the insurance paperwork mounts, or we're stuck in traffic while trying to rush Frankie to one of his many therapy appointments, that hopeful prognosis is all we have to keep us going.

It has been especially tough this holiday season — the first in which we have been not just aware that something was troubling Frankie but acutely aware of exactly what it was. It has been such a difficult time that I found myself avoiding holiday parties and decided I was in no mood to send out Christmas cards. I couldn't even bring myself to help Magdalena trim our Christmas tree. I concentrated on Frankie instead, playing with him and trying to keep him focused on Christmas books and songs. He sings a pretty fair "Frosty the Snowman."

That's a good sign, of course. The therapies are helping. Frankie is speaking again, even if many words still are slurred. With encouragement and guidance from a skilled behavior therapist and the caregivers at his preschool, he is beginning to play with other children. That's a breakthrough, since a symptom of classic autism is a tendency to withdraw from contact with people. Some people with autism literally cannot tolerate being touched.

Of all the things I've learned this year, that is the one that both frightens and reassures me. It frightens me to think my son would ever shy away from my touch. And it reassures me because it suggests that Sacks' conclusion is correct and that every individual with autism is unique. Which means that somewhere, somehow, Frankie can find his niche.

Thankfully, Frankie not only allows us to touch him, he enjoys it. Although he is well past the toddler stage, he cuddles like a newborn infant. I now treasure that physical warmth in a way I might never have if he were "normal." I'm counting on it to help me get through the holidays and a new year of new challenges for Frankie.

APRIL 30, 1996

# A Happier Birthday for Frankie at 4

MY SON Frankie turned 4 last week, giving our family a chance to celebrate not just his birthday but also the progress he's made recently overcoming the effects of infantile autism.

I first wrote about him last Christmas, at the end of a difficult year filled with anxiety over the struggles he would face his entire life dealing with a condition I thought was rare and untreatable. That column reflected my anguish at the time.

I still have concerns about Frankie. And unanswered questions about autism — mostly centered on its causes and possible cures. But for now, my hopes, and my spirits, have been lifted. That's because the improvement in Frankie's health has been so encouraging. A careful diet has reduced the number of colds, ear infections and stomach ailments he suffered. That in turn has made him more receptive to learning ways of coping with the most obvious symptoms of his autism — self-stimulatory behavior like hand-wringing, pacing and humming.

Only rarely does Frankie now "self-stim." That's a shorthand term we autism "experts" use. I mean expert in the broadest sense, including not just the researchers and clinicians I've interviewed on the subject but the hundreds of wonderful lay people I have heard from since that first column, who deal with autistic individuals as family, teachers or simply friends. All had valuable insights to offer.

Credit for Frankie's progress starts with the behavior modification therapists who work with him almost every day, either at home, at his preschool or in clinical settings. His favorite is Hank Moore, who studied at UCLA under a pioneer in the treatment of autism, Dr. Ivar Lovaas. Some of Lovaas' theories are controversial, but Frankie loves Hank. And Frankie's mother and I, his teachers and even his little playmates have learned how to better engage Frankie by watching him interact with his favorite "buddy," Hank.

Frankie's also talking a lot more. Not always clearly, and still not at the level of most 4-year-olds. But compared with the long silences of a few months ago, he's a regular chatterbox. Lately he's become fascinated with ocean creatures like whales and dolphins and an octopus he saw at the Monterey Bay Aquarium. Other parents may grow weary of the popular children's song about whales, "Baby Beluga." I can't hear Frankie sing it enough.

But for all the hope I now have for Frankie, I am more deeply troubled than ever by how much must be done to better understand autism and to help individuals afflicted with it.

When I assumed it was rare, for example, I was looking at data that put its prevalence at four in every 10,000 children. But those numbers reflected research done in the 1940s. A conference held last year by the National Institutes of Health concluded that two out of every 1,000 children suffer from autism symptoms, a spectrum that ranges from those so severely disabled that they must be institutionalized to children with problems like attention deficit disorder. NIH concluded that autism now is the third most common childhood developmental disability, after mental retardation and cerebral palsy.

The lack of sufficient biomedical research into autism's possible cures also helps explain why I mistakenly assumed it was not treatable. I've spoken with enough researchers to know that the question of whether autism is curable is still open to debate. But there is no doubt that it is treatable. The challenge for a family with an autistic child is in determining what treatments might work, because each case is unique. Frankie, for example, has benefited from therapies involving physical exercise and the use of music as a learning tool.

Next on the horizon for Frankie are new medical treatments, some still in the experimental stage, to deal with his physical symptoms and maybe, just maybe, help find a cure for autism.

He's fortunate that we live in Southern California, where autism research is being done at UCLA and UC Irvine. And I might never have found out about that research without the help of a Los Angeles-based non-profit group called Cure Autism Now (CAN) and the Frank D. Lanterman Regional Center, a state-funded agency for children with special needs.

Tellingly, CAN was founded not by medical professionals but by parents of autistic children who wanted to keep themselves abreast of research in the field. They found that it is not just woefully underfunded but also subject to widespread misunderstanding even among physicians. That is why CAN has opted to leave parent-support activities to agencies like the Lanterman Center while it focuses on identifying innovative autism research and raising money for it.

As I talk with folks at CAN and the Lanterman Center, I realize that my wife and I are going through a process of consciousness-raising. We are moving beyond anguish and starting to ask hard questions about autism — of doctors, of insurers, of schools and of elected officials responsible for health policy. For example, how much new research money will the NIH be putting into what it now ranks as the third most common childhood developmental disability in this country?

# A Child Untickled
# by the New Elmo

**M**Y WIFE, Magdalena, may be the only Christmas shopper who is not sorry she didn't buy a Tickle Me Elmo when she had the chance. It was weeks ago, before the $25 talking doll based on a Sesame Street character became this year's hot toy, selling (in a few reported instances) for hundreds of dollars.

She was in a toy store with our 4-year-old son, Frankie, when she noticed the doll. Frankie likes Elmo, so she asked if he wanted one.

"No," he replied quietly. "No Elmo."

For Magdalena and me, that brief conversation had all the profundity of a prayer. For, as readers of this column may remember, Frankie has autism. A year ago, we didn't know if a simple exchange of words with our son would ever be possible.

I first wrote about Frankie's autism last Christmas, in an admittedly downbeat column. So I feel obligated — but also very happy — to report that Frankie made great progress in 1996. He is much further along the road to recovery than I had dared hope a year ago, even if many challenges still remain.

Autism is very hard to define, much less treat, because its symptoms cover a wide spectrum. Some people with autism must be in mental institutions all their lives. On the other extreme, researchers theorize that many children with common learning disabilities (like attention deficit disorder) may have mild forms of autism.

Frankie's autism falls somewhere toward the mild end of that spectrum. He is among the 45% of autistic children who may recover and lead fairly independent lives. But to prepare him for "normal" life, especially the start of his formal education in a classroom setting, he needs intensive therapy during the preschool years while his young brain is going through a period of rapid, critical development.

The challenge that Magdalena and I faced this year was identifying the most effective therapies for him, and paying for them once we did. As the family of any autistic child will attest, that's a lot tougher than it sounds.

Once Frankie is in a therapy program, specialists deal with him on a one-to-one basis, often for hours at a time. The cost can be prohibitive, even for a well-to-do family. Many health insurers refuse to pay for such therapies, putting an extra burden on stressed-out families or forcing overburdened school districts and public health departments to foot the bill. My wife and I had to retain an attorney this year to help Frankie get some of the therapies he is legally entitled to.

But it's been worth all the expense and trouble, for we have regained the little boy we had lost.

As recounted last year, we became aware of Frankie's autism at the age of 2, when he stopped speaking and began to ignore toys and playmates. He would pace constantly, rubbing his hands together and humming to himself — symptoms of sensory overload.

Today he rarely lapses into such behavior, unless he is tired or feeling sick. The rest of the time he seems more like any other preschooler, albeit one about 3 years old instead of 4. Dr. Ivar Lovaas, the noted UCLA autism researcher who is overseeing Frankie's treatment, tells us this "developmental delay" is typical of recovery from autism.

"I no longer consider autism a disease or a disability, but a delay," said Lovaas, a psychologist who is somewhat controversial for having challenged the scientific paradigm that defined autism as a mental illness. He and his students treat autism with behavior intervention therapy, one-to-one tutoring that uses rewards (like small treats or effusive praise) to teach autistic children everything from colors to toilet use to social skills.

"We're not trying to cure a disease called autism," Lovaas emphasized. "We're finding ways to teach a different kind of nervous system."

The aim is to have Frankie prepared to enter a mainstream classroom when he starts kindergarten or first grade instead of segregating him in a special-education class.

Frankie was first exposed to behavior intervention therapy at the Center for Autism and Related Disorders, a private agency run by former students of Lovaas. He made such dramatic progress with just a few hours of therapy that we decided to enroll him in the institute run by Lovaas himself.

But while more intensive, the Lovaas program is far more expensive. It costs $60,000 per year to provide the 40 hours per week of therapy Lovaas recommends. But he insists it is cost-effective, saving society from having to support autistic adults on welfare or in mental institutions.

I'll leave the public-policy ramifications of autism for future columns. For now, it's wonderful to be able to talk with Frankie again. Or to watch him play make-believe games with his favorite toys — pretending is one more thing that many children with severe autism cannot do.

One of Frankie's favorite toys is a stuffed Elmo doll his cousin Raquel gave him. This Elmo is worn and faded from many washings and doesn't talk. But Frankie always keeps it close by. Frankie wades in his pool with Elmo, gives Elmo rides in a wagon and often insists that Elmo be buckled into his own car seat in our family van.

Frankie wasn't interested in Tickle Me Elmo, his mother found, because he already had "my Elmo." That's fine with us.

More important, it's fine with Frankie. We know because, thank God, he told us.

<br>

DECEMBER 21, 1997

# To Gift of Hope, Add a Bonus: Love

A COLLEAGUE dropped by my office last week for a sobering conversation — one I've become sadly accustomed to having in the three years since my 5-year-old son, Frankie, was diagnosed as having infantile autism.

My colleague once worked as a correspondent in London and had just heard from friends there who were devastated at having received a similar diagnosis for their 2-year-old boy. Would I be willing to talk with his friends to offer advice from my own experience, he asked. And what, precisely, is autism?

As always, I said yes to the former question and did my best to answer the latter.

I first wrote about Frankie's autism two Christmas seasons ago with the same sense of fear and loss that my colleague's friends in London must feel. A healthy, happy child who had developed normally for two years suddenly stopped speaking, withdrew from social contact and lapsed into increasingly bizarre behaviors.

It took the better part of a year for us to get a definitive diagnosis. And even then we were warned by some of the top specialists in the field that there is no cure for autism and that Frankie would face lifelong challenges.

But in time we also learned from other parents with similar experiences — particularly a wonderful Los Angeles couple named John Shestack and Portia Iverson — that autism is treatable. Just as important, we learned that biomedical research, especially on how the brain can be taught to compensate for damage or slow development, is finding effective new treatments for autism and may eventually discover a cure.

That is why Frankie's mother, Magdalena, and I now wage a two-front war against autism. On the public side we have tried to help the organization that Shestack and Iverson founded, Cure Autism Now, raise awareness of the need for more biomedical research into autism. On the personal side we have explored a variety of treatments that have been shown to help some children with autism, to determine whether they might be useful for Frankie.

He has so far responded well to auditory training, to help him learn to distinguish sounds more clearly; music therapy, which helps him exercise those parts of the brain that control conceptual thinking; and sensory integrated therapy, which has helped him coordinate his physical movements — climbing, jumping and even walking normally.

The core of our son's treatment, a behavior modification program pioneered by Dr. Ivar Lovaas at UCLA, continues to be successful. For the last year and a half, Frankie has spent 40 hours a week being tutored by Lovaas Institute therapists. They've taught him to count, spell, draw and respond appropriately to playmates and teachers.

He's made such rapid progress that in September, the school district in which we live agreed to place him in a mainstream kindergarten classroom with 29 non-disabled children. There he is accompanied by a "shadow" therapist who intervenes when and if Frankie needs help. It's an important experiment, for if children with autism can be mainstreamed, it will eventually reduce the cost of educating them and perhaps even reduce their social isolation by getting them used to interacting with non-disabled peers.

Now we are exploring other treatments to help accelerate Frankie's ability to learn by "rewiring" his young brain. His pediatrician, Ricki Robinson of La Cañada, a CAN board member who specializes in treating children with autism, referred Frankie to a wonderful form of play therapy developed by Stanley Greenspan, a noted child psychiatrist. A therapist engages Frankie in games and other forms of play that help him develop and learn to express emotions like fear and joy.

In the long run, Greenspan's "floor play" therapy may prove as fundamentally important to Frankie's growth and development as the learning skills provided by his Lovaas therapists. One of the criticisms of Lovaas' technique is that it is rote learning, which does not do enough to help an autistic child's emotional development.

I'm not sure how valid that criticism is. Just the other day Frankie surprised us when one of his favorite Lovaas therapists was leaving after a tutoring session.

"Bye, bye, Danny," Frankie said to the young man as he walked to our front door, adding after a brief pause, "I love you."

How and where did Frankie begin to comprehend a concept like love? Did he react naturally to the closeness and affection he has come to feel for several of his Lovaas-trained therapists? Or was it the Greenspan therapy that drew it out? We probably won't know the answer until Frankie, hopefully, can tell us more in his own words.

In the meantime, I'm less concerned about how that small but significant breakthrough occurred than that it did. For while I am more than ever convinced that successful treatment of autism is possible, I have also come to realize that it must be done in incremental steps, and with an open-minded approach to a variety of therapies.

I'm looking forward to the new surprises Frankie will have for me in 1998 — and also to that phone call from London. It's nice to finally offer not just advice but hope.

# Facing Loss but Keeping Hope

FATHERS ALWAYS UNDERESTIMATE how mature their children are. In my case, it took a death in the family to show me how much my "babies" have grown. And for my 6-year-old son, Frankie, in particular, the loss of a beloved great aunt had a significant consolation. His caring reaction to the grief of the adults around him marked the latest step in his fight against autism, a severe neurological disorder.

Frankie's autism was first diagnosed four years ago. I've written about him every holiday season since, not just to share information about autism — the third most common developmental disability among children — but also to offer encouragement to other parents with autistic children. For despite all the challenges Frankie faces, he's made remarkable progress.

The number of children diagnosed with autism and related disorders like Asperger's syndrome and pervasive developmental disorder keeps growing. Cure Autism Now, a national organization of autism researchers and parents whose children suffer from the disability, estimates that one of every 500 children has autism or a related disorder.

But Frankie's experience proves that many of those children can recover if intervention occurs early enough. With the right combination of therapies and educational opportunities, autistic people can become productive members of mainstream society rather than being institutionalized, as sometimes happened in the past.

The foundation of Frankie's treatment remains the intensive behavior modification provided by the Lovaas Institute for Early Intervention, established by a pioneering autism researcher at UCLA, Dr. Ivar Lovaas. But this year Frankie's big breakthrough came through a treatment program called Fast ForWord.

Originally designed to help children with dyslexia, Fast ForWord uses computer games to hone the listening skills of children so that they hear the nuances of speech more clearly. After spending most of the summer in Fast ForWord sessions, Frankie in the fall was able to enter a mainstream first-grade class at a Glendale public school.

Frankie is accompanied in his classroom by a school district aide, Jeff

Decker, whose own background in behavior modification was augmented through training by Lovaas therapists. Frankie's teacher, Kristy Peterson, and his 19 classmates have also been wonderfully supportive.

What made this holiday season particularly nice is the fact that, for the first time since he was diagnosed, Frankie was acutely, excitedly and happily aware of Christmas. Like any normal child, he chatted incessantly about Santa, Rudolph, the Grinch and other seasonal characters. He sang carols and other holiday songs and eagerly helped decorate our Christmas tree.

Last month, as my wife, Magdalena, unpacked some decorations, Frankie found an old Santa Claus costume in the mix. Still in his Halloween mode, he put the oversized outfit on and paraded through the house shouting "Ho ho ho!" Magdalena captured the moment on film, and that photo became the Christmas card we sent to our family this year.

I was addressing those cards two Saturdays ago when I called my uncle, Joseph Torres, to ask about his wife, Esperanza, who has been seriously ill with severe diabetes.

Aunt Hope — as everyone knew her — meant a lot to my family. Ever since my own mother died 15 years ago, we have focused holidays and special family gatherings around her Mission Hills home.

I was pleasantly surprised when Uncle Joe said Aunt Hope was in fine spirits. She had even found the strength to go shopping for a Christmas tree. Without realizing it, I rejoiced that Aunt Hope would be with us for another Christmas. Sadly, I was wrong.

The very next morning, in predawn darkness, Uncle Joe called to tell me Aunt Hope had suffered a diabetic seizure and cardiac arrest during the night. She was dead at 80.

I'd been bracing myself for Aunt Hope's death for months, so despite my distress I was able to make it through the next two days — a rosary service in her memory, the funeral Mass and her burial. But as my grief fades, I will always carry special memories of how my two children conducted themselves during those somber days.

My daughter, Valentina, spoke beautifully at the Mass, delivering a heartfelt eulogy to Aunt Hope. I really shouldn't have been surprised. Although I too often still think of her as an adolescent, she's 23 now and a Stanford graduate.

But Frankie was the biggest surprise.

He was curious, as any small child is when first facing the reality of death. He was full of questions, like where heaven is and whether Aunt Hope would ever return from living there with Jesus. But he was also caring.

His therapists have tried to explore feelings like joy and sadness with him, concepts often difficult for children with autism to grasp. It was clear from his subdued manner after Aunt Hope died that Frankie does understand the concept of sadness, as surely as he comprehends the joy of Christmas.

Frankie still has lots of growing up to do, and difficult challenges ahead. Sometime next year, we will phase out of the Lovaas program and face the prospect of Frankie doing his classroom work alone or with minimal support from an aide.

But even amid the sadness of family tragedy, I became more confident than ever that Frankie will continue to overcome his autism. Not just because he has family, therapists, teachers and classmates who support him, but because he has a special new angel watching over him — an angel named, so very aptly, Hope.

DECEMBER 26, 1999

# A Difficult Year With Progress Hindered, but Not Without Hope

Y 7-YEAR-OLD SON, Frankie, wants a puppy. For most parents that would make the choice of his Christmas gift very easy. But Frankie has autism. And that can complicate even the simplest decisions about our family life.

I have occasionally written about Frankie ever since he was first diagnosed with this mysterious neurological disorder five years ago. I try to offer information, and maybe some hope, to readers who face similar challenges.

Frankie continues to make progress, thankfully, but full recovery eludes him. He can't be cured until a cure for autism is found. And as he grows older, life keeps putting new, more complex, obstacles in his path toward a normal life.

People with autism have their brains wired so that stimuli most of us take for granted — like sound, light and touch — affect them differently. They often have a more difficult time learning academics and engaging in social interaction than nondisabled children. In extreme cases, they withdraw completely from social contact with other people.

One in 500 children is affected, although statistics compiled this year by the California Department of Developmental Services indicate a "dramatic" increase in its incidence here — more than 210% between 1987 and 1998. Yet autism research remains woefully underfunded.

What made 1999 so difficult for Frankie was that his treatment became more complicated in March when we learned that his autism is accompanied by epileptic aphasia — mild seizures in the brain that also affect his ability to communicate. Epileptic aphasia is different from epilepsy and was only recently discovered thanks to research into the biomedical causes of autism.

Frankie's diagnosis came after brain specialists conducted a 24-hour EEG on him at the recommendation of his pediatrican, Dr. Ricki Robinson of La Cañada, an expert on the treatment of autism and other neurological disorders.

The diagnosis was the classic good news/bad news dilemma. The good news is that brain seizures can be treated with medication. The bad news is that it would take lots of experimentation to find the right medication and dosage for Frankie.

That difficult trial-and-error process continued most of the year and is still not finished. Dr. Robinson tells us that Frankie has unusual brain chemistry, so his reaction to medications is often unpredicatable and, at times, frightening. A mild sedative he was given for the EEG left him in a near-comatose state in an emergency room. Other medications have caused hyperactivity, sleeplessness and even auditory hallucinations.

Recently we finally found a medication that seems to have minimal side effects. But we may still have to find another to help reduce the involuntary motor tics — like handwringing and humming — that Frankie can lapse into when having a seizure.

An especially frustrating result of this experimentation is that it has interfered with Frankie's progress in school and complicated his ability to blend into a mainstream classroom.

His teachers and classmates at a public school in Glendale are friendly and caring, but there are times when Frankie's autism and brain seizures leave him in virtual isolation.

Sadly, he is becoming increasingly aware of the fact that he is different from other children. He said recently that he understands how Rudolph the red-nosed reindeer felt when he couldn't join in reindeer games because "sometimes kids don't want to play with me."

Just as troubling is the fact that he has stalled in learning to read. He can sound out words that are spelled phonetically. But he is lost with irregularly spelled words and can't make sense of sentences. We are exploring new therapies and learning methods to help him. Last summer he completed Fast ForWord, a computer-based phonics program for children with auditory processing problems like dyslexia. Next on tap is the Lindamood-Bell reading and speech program.

This year Frankie was phased out of the intensive behavior modification therapy he received at the Lovaas Institute for Early Intervention, a clinic founded by a noted UCLA autism researcher, Dr. Ivar Lovaas. I remain a proponent of Lovaas' once-controversial teaching methods. They gave Frankie a firm foundation for everything he's been able to learn since.

But even with the measurable progress Frankie has made with the help of Lovaas and Robinson and many other specialists, we must find answers to some hard and painful questions in the coming year. What will help him read? What could get him to initiate more play with other children? Will he need new medications, not just to calm motor tics but to better control his severe allergies, which can also set off autistic behavior when they flare up?

Then amid these concerns, just a few weeks ago, came the question of whether we should get Frankie a puppy.

He's always been curious about animals, and we are fortunate to have kind neighbors with friendly and approachable dogs — a golden retreiver named Brandy and a pug named Milo.

If Frankie didn't have autism or severe allergies, he'd have his puppy in a minute. But like so many things other kids take for granted — a slice of pizza (Frankie's allergic to wheat) or an ice cream (and dairy products) — we must be careful and do some research first.

Frankie's allergist has advised against keeping a dog in our house. So the answer may be a pre-trained dog for the backyard, perhaps one that didn't make the cut as a guide dog for the blind. I'm exploring that option now.

But even if everything works out and we find a calm, patient pet dog for Frankie, there will be a lingering sadness in my heart because I couldn't get my son the puppy he wrote to Santa about.

Maybe someday. Yet another hopeful dream to sustain us through another year with Frankie.

DECEMBER 24, 2000

# This Year, Frankie Finally Got His Puppy

FOR ALL the difficulty autism poses for my 8-year-old son, Frankie, this holiday season has helped me realize how much progress he's made fighting the mysterious neurological disorder that afflicts him.

Not everything went smoothly for Frankie in 2000. Indeed, when the year began, my wife, Magdalena, and I were as worried about his future as we'd ever been — perhaps even more frustrated than we were when his autism was diagnosed five years ago.

Because of all the time and effort Magdalena and I have put into learning about autism and its possible treatments since Frankie was diagnosed, we have been able to help him overcome its more obvious symptoms. We worked with our doctors to identify medications to control the allergies that can set off autistic behaviors. And after intensive therapy at UCLA's respected Lovaas Institute for Early Intervention, we were able to enroll Frankie in public school.

Unfortunately, this year we were forced to conclude that our noble experiment at a mainstream education for Frankie was — at least temporarily — a failure. He handled kindergarten and the first grade with the help of a Lovaas aide in the classroom. But he began to fare badly after that support was withdrawn, and his second-grade studies were accelerated, at the behest of our school district.

By last spring, Frankie was so frustrated with trying to learn to read that he was refusing to try. He had fallen behind his classmates in other learning skills, and his public behavior had regressed badly, so that he was often withdrawing into his own private world rather than interacting with peers.

In near-desperation, we began to pull Frankie out of school early, creating an educational program tailored to him that included Lovaas therapists and the innovative Lindamood-Bell reading program, which has proved successful in helping children with dyslexia learn to read. Frankie responded so well to the Lindamood-Bell method that, during the summer, Magdalena and I made what at first seemed like a risky decision: to home-school Frankie in the fall.

It proved to be one of the best things we've done for him. That is largely because of the patience and natural teaching ability of Frankie's favorite aunt. My sister, Elisa Garcia — "Aunt Lisa," as Frankie calls her — ran Head Start programs in the Antelope Valley before I shanghaied her into helping us with our son's home-schooling.

As radical as it may sound, home-schooling is easy to do, especially in the primary grades — at least for those families with adults who are able and willing to guide children through the required state curriculum. There are many reputable and long-established home-schooling associations that provide guidance about the legal requirements and the necessary books and materials at a reasonable cost.

But I must be honest. Even for two professional parents, home-schooling a child with autism would not have been nearly so successful without someone like Frankie's Aunt Lisa to help out. She has always had a special rapport with Frankie.

He is reading now, not just on his own but with genuine enthusiasm. Frankie keeps a daily journal and is full of questions that he asks in an increasingly sophisticated vocabulary.

Just how sophisticated became clear when Frankie wrote a letter to Santa Claus asking — just as he had last year — for a puppy. He didn't get a dog back then because we were still trying to bring Frankie's allergies under control, and his doctor warned us that a new pet could complicate the process.

Frankie's health is better now, and his Christmas wish was more specific. The dog, he wrote Santa, was to be a brown Labrador retriever. And each word — except retriever, which even gives me a little trouble — was spelled correctly.

I knew Aunt Lisa was in the habit of taking Frankie to the public library once a week to pick out new books to read. And that several of those books have lately been about dogs. But Frankie was so knowledgeable and precise as to what kind of pet he wanted that I knew there would be no avoiding the issue this year. So I began perusing the Internet, calling dog breeders and reviewing the many suggestions sent to me by kind readers last Christmas after I wrote about Frankie's unfulfilled wish for a puppy.

This year Frankie got his dog — a few days before Christmas so a vet could make sure the puppy was healthy. And my son knows his mind well enough that he even rejected my simplistic suggestion for a name: Cocoa.

"His name will be Chocolate," Frankie wrote to Santa, spelling that big word right.

DECEMBER 23, 2001

# Daring to Dream of Frankie's Future

THIS YEAR I finally allowed myself to start dreaming about my son's future again.

Although Frankie continues to struggle against the effects of autism, a mysterious neurological disorder, his improvement has been so steady that at times he seems a completely normal 9-year-old, right down to braces for his teeth and a growing interest in video games and the latest cartoon series (his favorite is "SpongeBob SquarePants").

I sometimes find myself musing about Frankie's future not with the concern and fear I often felt when he was first diagnosed with autism six years ago. Now I can envision him achieving things once thought impossible for all but the most exceptional autistic children.

Despite his challenges, Frankie is now reading and doing math at third-grade level, thanks to home schooling by my sister, Lisa Garcia, an experienced Head Start teacher. While Aunt Lisa focuses on the education basics, my wife, Magdalena, and I continue to seek new or innovative therapies that will help Frankie prepare for his eventual return to the classroom.

Recently, Frankie's therapists at the Center for Autism and Related

Disorders in Encino have been trying to teach him to understand another person's perspective, something most children learn naturally but that people with autism must be taught. On the medical side, our pediatrician, autism specialist Dr. Ricki Robinson, has Frankie in two therapies intended to help his brain better process what he hears. She explains that Frankie's problem is not that he can't hear certain things but that he hears everything too well, so he sometimes isn't able to distinguish important sounds from background noise and gets easily distracted.

One therapy Robinson has prescribed for Frankie is Tomatis auditory training, which teaches him to focus on a primary sound, such as a teacher's voice. The other is an experimental therapy called interactive metronome. It requires that Frankie clap his hands or tap his feet in time to a metronome. The exercise trains his brain to ignore distractions. Just as important are classes Frankie takes to strengthen muscles and increase coordination and confidence and to give him positive experiences interacting with other kids. With the help of his gymnastics coach, Rory Baggao, he has become adept at forward rolls. He also enjoys an exercise and movement class taught by former Dodgers pitcher Jim Gott, himself the father of children with autism.

But life is not all work for Frankie. This year he has made great strides in learning how to play. Lots of the fun is provided by Chocolate, the Labrador retriever we got him last Christmas. Chocolate is now much bigger but still playful and eager for his young master's attention.

Frankie takes an art class for children with special needs at Education Spectrum in Altadena. His teacher, Vicki Howard, has nurtured an artistic streak in him. He loves to draw and paint, and does so with a precise style. Could it be that his artistic and visual skills are developing more rapidly to compensate for the difficulty he has processing sound? Only the future will tell.

But at least I now find myself thinking about Frankie's future and feeling hopeful about it.

I'm confident that he will be back in a classroom someday. He may be older than his classmates due to his developmental delays. And his peers may find his behavior eccentric. But with proper support, he'll be able to hold his own academically. College or trade school and a career are not out of the question.

Of course, I am not so naive as to think there are no more struggles ahead. If the last six years have taught Magdalena and me anything, it's that nothing will ever come easily or quickly for Frankie. But good can come, if we are patient and persevere.

DECEMBER 22, 2002

# Powers That Be Should See the Needs of Frankie

THERE IS good news and bad this holiday season regarding my son, Frankie, and other children like him who have autism.

Frankie is 10 now, and the good news involves his personal progress against the neurological disorder that impairs a child's ability to speak, learn and respond to people.

The bad news involves political shenanigans that could deny many autistic children the costly therapies my wife, Magdalena, and I fought so hard to get for Frankie.

I shudder to think how far behind other children Frankie would be today were it not for the difficult odyssey our family began eight years ago, when doctors diagnosed his autism and told us there was no cure.

At the time, we were so desperate to help our son that we didn't dwell on what might have caused brain damage in an otherwise healthy toddler.

Instead we immediately contacted specialists and studied the work done by autism researchers. This convinced us Frankie's situation wasn't hopeless.

The process of rewiring Frankie's brain has taken us from behavioral therapies to specialized treatment for reading and hearing disorders to gymnastics classes to help him become better coordinated.

When we realized Frankie could not function effectively in a regular classroom, we home-schooled him with the help of my sister.

Frankie returned to a classroom last summer, at a private school in Sherman Oaks that specializes in the education and treatment of disabled or emotionally disturbed youngsters.

Frankie can keep up with his classmates with the help of an aide, but he is still easily distracted. But he genuinely likes school and his teacher. He has even accepted the fact that he must finish his homework before he can play video games — although not without the complaints of a typical 10-year-old: "Do I have to?"

In many ways, Frankie is so close to normal that it is sometimes easy to forget how far he's come. But the stories of other autistic children remind me.

Many more are being told, now that researchers have confirmed a suspicion I had, that there are many more kids like Frankie than anyone had realized.

In October, UC Davis reported that the number of California children with diagnosed autism increased nearly 300% between 1987 and 1998, an upsurge that is no statistical quirk.

When we first learned of Frankie's autism, experts said four in 10,000 children had the disorder. Today, the estimate is one in 250.

Some public health officials and politicians are pushing for more research to find a cure, but others have cynically moved to protect legally vulnerable rear ends.

I refer to a recent effort by Eli Lilly & Co., the giant pharmaceutical company, to deflect hundreds of lawsuits by parents of autistic children who suspect a Lilly-manufactured vaccine additive, thimerosal, may be a culprit in the autism epidemic.

Lobbyists for Lilly could not persuade Congress earlier this year to enact legislation that would shift the autism lawsuits to a federal vaccine-injury compensation program.

Then last month, just hours before the final congressional vote on the Homeland Security Act, U.S. Rep. Dick Armey (R-Texas) quietly tacked two paragraphs onto the 247-page bill that gave Lilly what it wanted.

Armey says he acted on his own because protecting vaccine manufacturers from costly lawsuits is a matter of national security. "I did it and I'm proud of it," he said. Maybe he'd feel different if, like U.S. Rep. Dan Burton (R-Ind.), he had a grandchild with autism.

"Millions of children across the country were exposed to this mercury-based preservative at a time when concerns about its health effects were emerging," Burton told Congress in an unsuccessful effort to have the thimerosal provision dropped. (For the record, we are not involved in any lawsuits against Lilly.)

Burton and others in Congress will try to revisit the issue when a new

Congress convenes in January, by which time Armey will have retired. But excising the provision won't be easy, given that Lilly's chief executive, Sidney Taurel, is an advisor to President Bush on domestic security and a former Lilly executive, Mitchell E. Daniels, is the White House budget director. The close ties between Lilly and the White House make this old political reporter wonder if Armey really was the prime mover behind the amendment.

Whatever answer finally emerges, for now I am grateful Frankie is making progress. If only I could share my hope with the many other parents just now embarking on the long journey to help their autistic children. The road has just been made a little rougher.

DECEMBER 21, 2003

# Frankie's Journey Toward Manhood

THE NORMAL RULES of child development have not always applied to my son, Frankie, who was diagnosed with autism almost 10 years ago.

Although he will not turn 12 until next spring, his fast-growing body is already showing signs of puberty. And although he sometimes still acts like a sweet little boy, at other times he displays an independent streak that borders on defiance — like many youngsters his age.

Frankie is a bright boy. He is also extremely verbal, a fact that sets him apart from the autistic children who cannot speak as a result of the mysterious disorder that interferes with their brains' normal development, impairing the ability to communicate and interact socially.

When Frankie was first diagnosed, it was estimated that one in 2,500 children suffered from autism. The number is now closer to one in 250, and the reasons for it are passionately debated by parents and public health specialists.

Are we simply better at diagnosing autism now? Or are environmental factors — something in our food or perhaps in childhood vaccines — triggering the disease more frequently?

Whatever the cause, California is in the forefront of states trying to cope with the effects of the apparent epidemic. A well-documented surge in the number of children diagnosed with autism clearly put an unexpected dent in the state Department of Health and Human Services, which provides services to families under California's groundbreaking Lanterman Act of 1969.

It was a caseworker at the Lanterman Regional Center in Los Angeles who, in 1995, first helped my wife, Magdalena, and me understand how much we could do for Frankie if we were willing to fight for his rights — for educational programs that meet his special needs, for instance — under the Lanterman Act and related federal laws. Those rights and our advocacy skills proved extremely useful over the ensuing years as we identified innovative therapies that might help Frankie.

We were also fortunate to have the resources to pay for those therapies when our school district or insurers would not. Most did benefit Frankie, from the applied behavior analysis first developed by researchers at UCLA to the Tomatis hearing treatment to the Greenspan floor-play method to the Lindamood-Bell reading program. But I can only wonder what it must be like for parents who are just setting out to help a newly diagnosed child. If we are indeed experiencing an autism epidemic, then the financial challenge of helping these children lead normal lives will only grow.

I will always be glad we were able to meet Frankie's needs early on, when his young brain could still be retrained. But I am coming to realize that his progress was a mixed blessing. Even as these therapies have helped Frankie come closer to being like a normally developing child, he is becoming ever more conscious of the fact that he is different.

Like other children with high-functioning autism, a sudden change in routine can throw Frankie completely off kilter. Take school, for instance. This was Frankie's second year back in a classroom setting after two years of home-schooling. It has not always been a smooth transition.

He attends Village Glen, a private school in Sherman Oaks affiliated with the HELP Group, a nonprofit agency that serves children with special needs. His teacher, Stacey Lauderdale, is very smart and patient. But Frankie's anxieties about loud or sudden noises (like the alarm bells that signal school fire drills) can provoke him to angry outbursts that disrupt the class.

Sometimes unexpected noises even make him angry with his Labrador retriever, Chocolate. Normally he's very affectionate with our big, friendly dog. But when Chocolate suddenly bounds into the backyard, loudly chasing a cat or squirrel, Frankie will shout at the top of his lungs, "Make him stop barking!" Somehow, Frankie is going to have to learn that the world won't stop for him.

Pondering the changes Frankie is undergoing, I recalled conversations I had with some of the autism specialists who treated Frankie. As they helped him learn to speak again or to make eye contact with other people, I would celebrate his progress. But they would wisely try to temper my expectations, warning me to be prepared for a difficult adolescence; that the confusion and angst even normal youngsters face at that awkward age would be compounded by Frankie's awareness of his disability.

I have dreaded Frankie's adolescence. But there is no postponing it. My little boy is becoming a young man. He's going to need more of my time, which is one reason I will write less frequently for this page. He's also going to need more privacy than I have allowed him. He'll need it to decide how he prefers to cope with autism.

So the two great gifts I can give Frankie this Christmas, and in years to come, are my presence and his privacy. And he shall have them both.

"My dream is that I can be a
great man like my dad so I can
do good things like he did."

—

*Frankie del Olmo, Age 12*
*Homework Assignment*
*April 27, 2004*

# INDEX